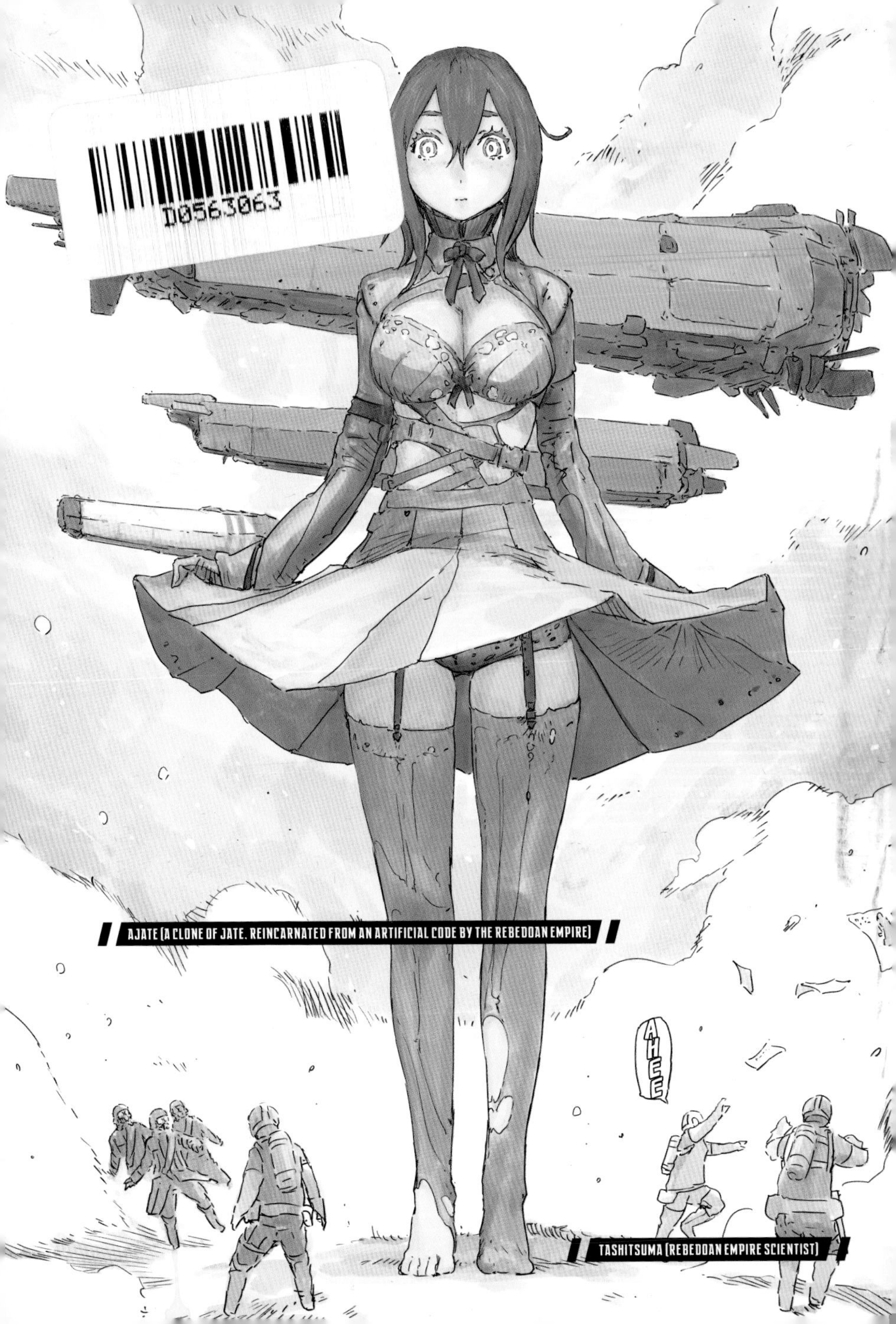
AHEE!
AJATE (A CLONE OF JATE. REINCARNATED FROM AN ARTIFICIAL CODE BY THE REBEDOAN EMPIRE)
TASHITSUMA (REBEDOAN EMPIRE SCIENTIST)

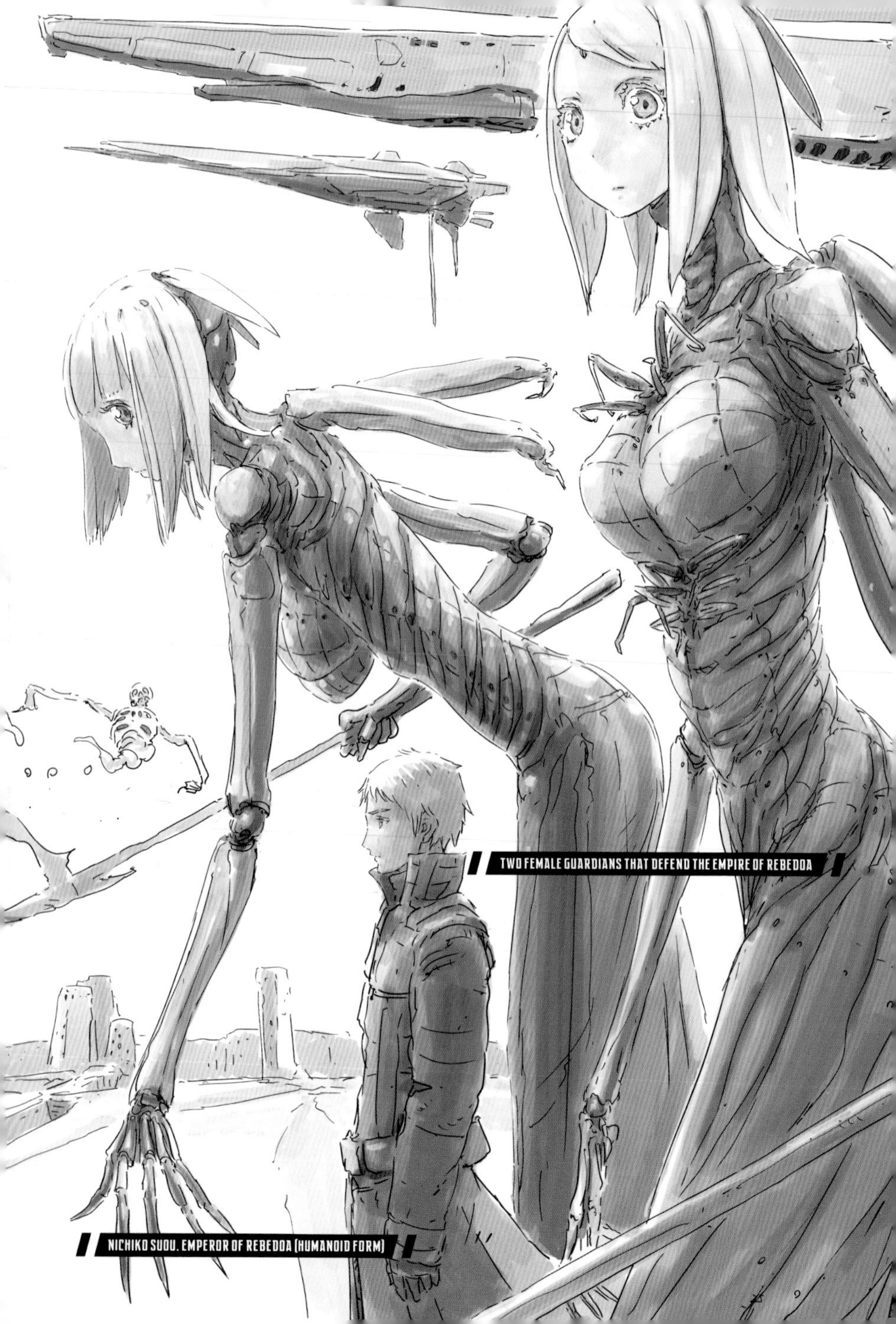
TWO FEMALE GUARDIANS THAT DEFEND THE EMPIRE OF REBEDOA
NICHIKO SUOU, EMPEROR OF REBEDOA (HUMANOID FORM)

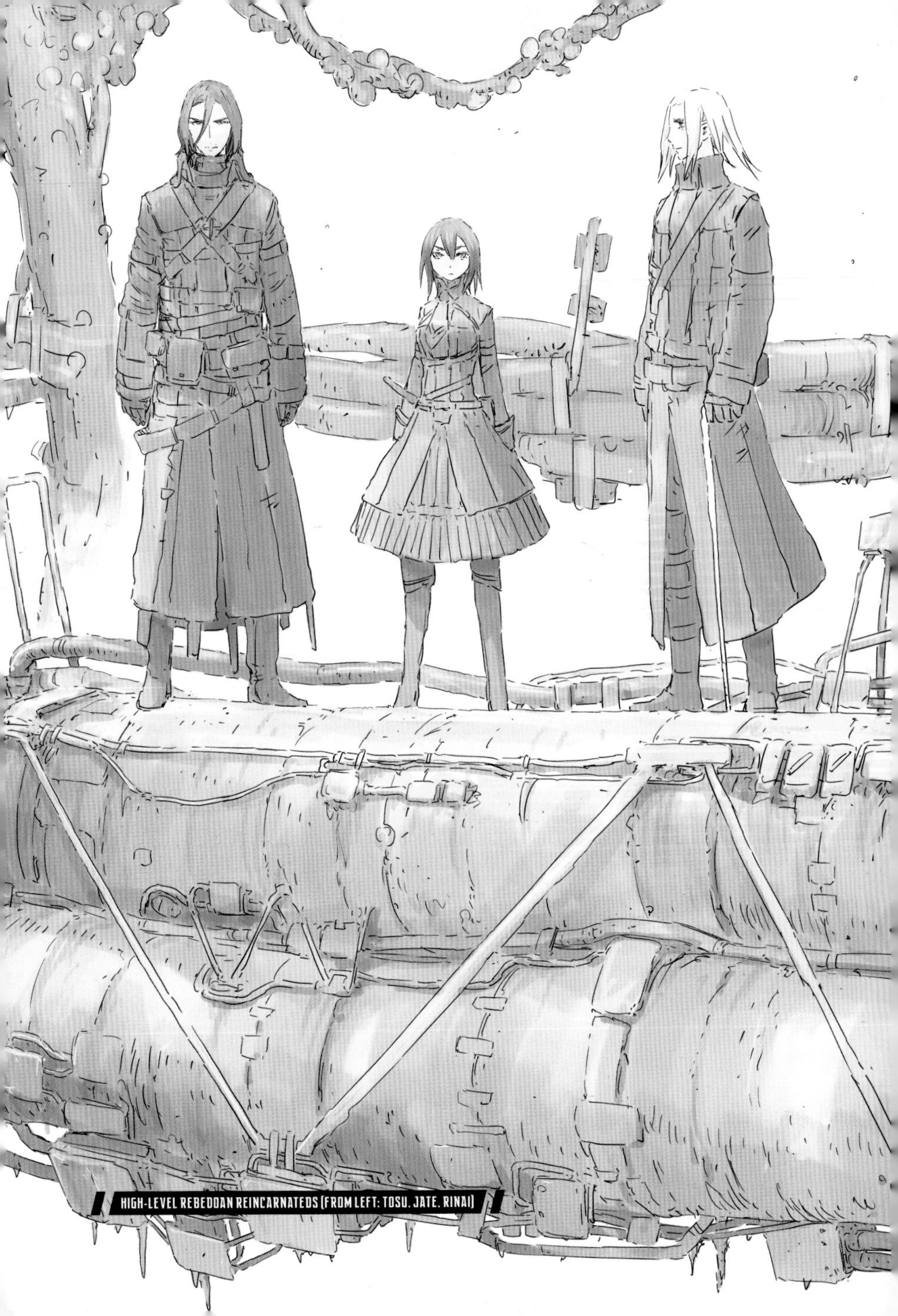

HIGH-LEVEL REBEDDAN REINCARNATEDS (FROM LEFT: TOSU, JATE, RINAI)

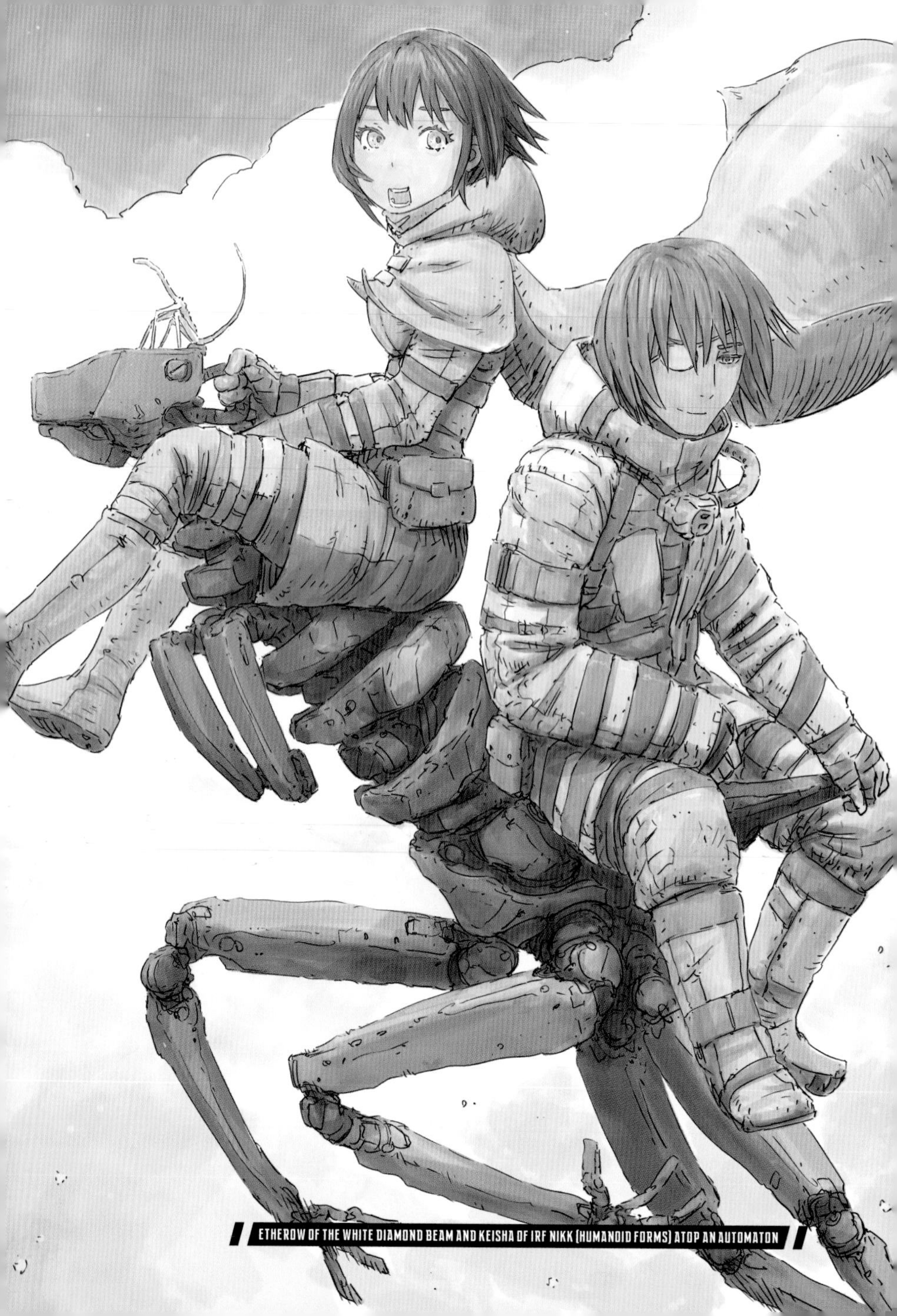

ETHEROW OF THE WHITE DIAMOND BEAM AND KEISHA OF IRF NIKK (HUMANOID FORMS) ATOP AN AUTOMATON

APOSIMZ

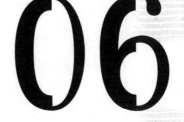

**TSUTOMU
NIHEI**

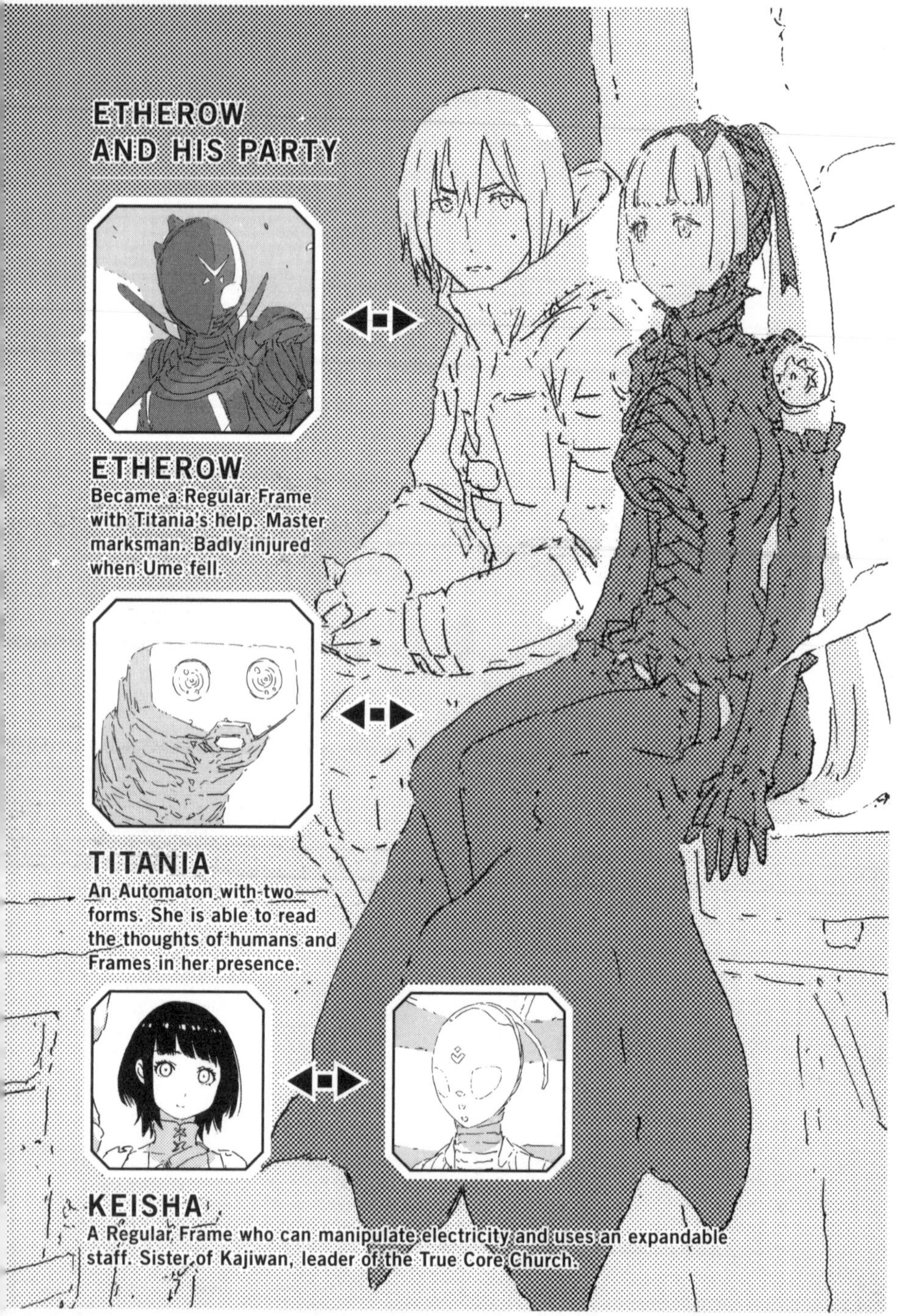

ETHEROW AND HIS PARTY

ETHEROW

Became a Regular Frame with Titania's help. Master marksman. Badly injured when Ume fell.

TITANIA

An Automaton with two forms. She is able to read the thoughts of humans and Frames in her presence.

KEISHA

A Regular Frame who can manipulate electricity and uses an expandable staff. Sister of Kajiwan, leader of the True Core Church.

APOSIMZ

PLOT AND CHARACTER INTRO

REBEDOAN EMPIRE

A militant state with powerful, heavily-armed forces that continues to invade various regions. Has many Regular Frames in its ranks.

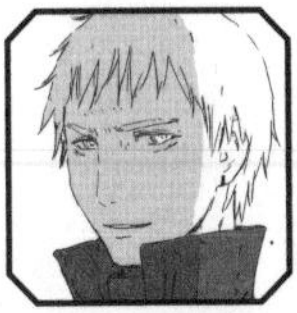

NICHIKO SUOU

The Emperor of Rebedoa. He is currently creating powerful, high-level Regular Frames.

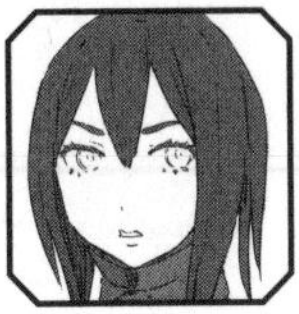

JATE

A high-level Reincarnated of the Rebedoan Empire. Has the ability to manipulate automatons.

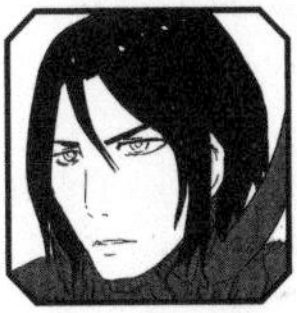

TOSU

Member of the Rebedoan Imperial Forces. Has the ability to manipulate metal.

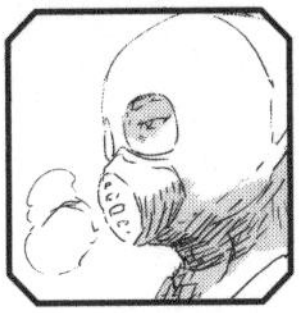

TASHITSUMA

Member of the Imperial Science Division. Successfully created a Regular Frame clone of Jate.

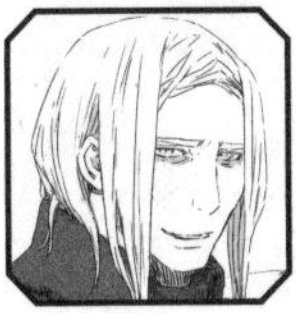

RINAI

Reincarnated.
An old friend of Jate.

TRUE CORE CHURCH

Organization created by Kajiwan to gather those afflicted with Frame disease. Bestows certain sufferers with knowledge and power, turning them into "Regenerateds." Views both the Empire and humans as enemies.

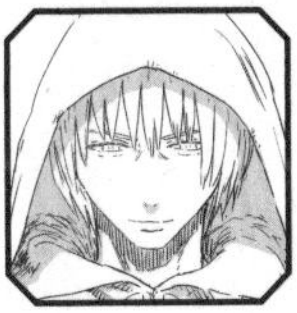

KAJIWAN

The last King of Irf Nikk. Using the powers of the mysterious Frame created from Titania's stolen arm, he became a Regular Frame himself. Has the ability to produce fireballs.

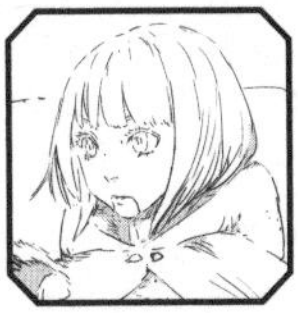

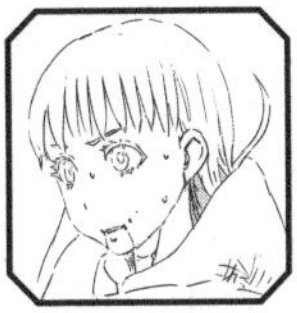

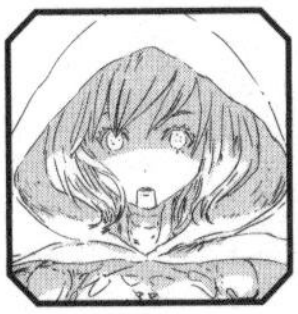

JINATA, TASURI, FIISA

Regular Frames of the Church. Their abilities only allow them to fight against other Regular Frames.

Previously

After much devoted care, Etherow's body recovers by leaps and bounds, giving Keisha hope. The Empire, after suffering guerrilla attacks from the True Core Church and Keisha's party, dispatches the scientist Tashitsuma, and Rinai, a Reincarnated with mysterious powers, to the Northern Composite Slab Region. Tashitsuma uses a newly-developed artificial code to create a giant clone named Ajate. Can he successfully turn her into a Regular Frame...?

CHAPTER 31

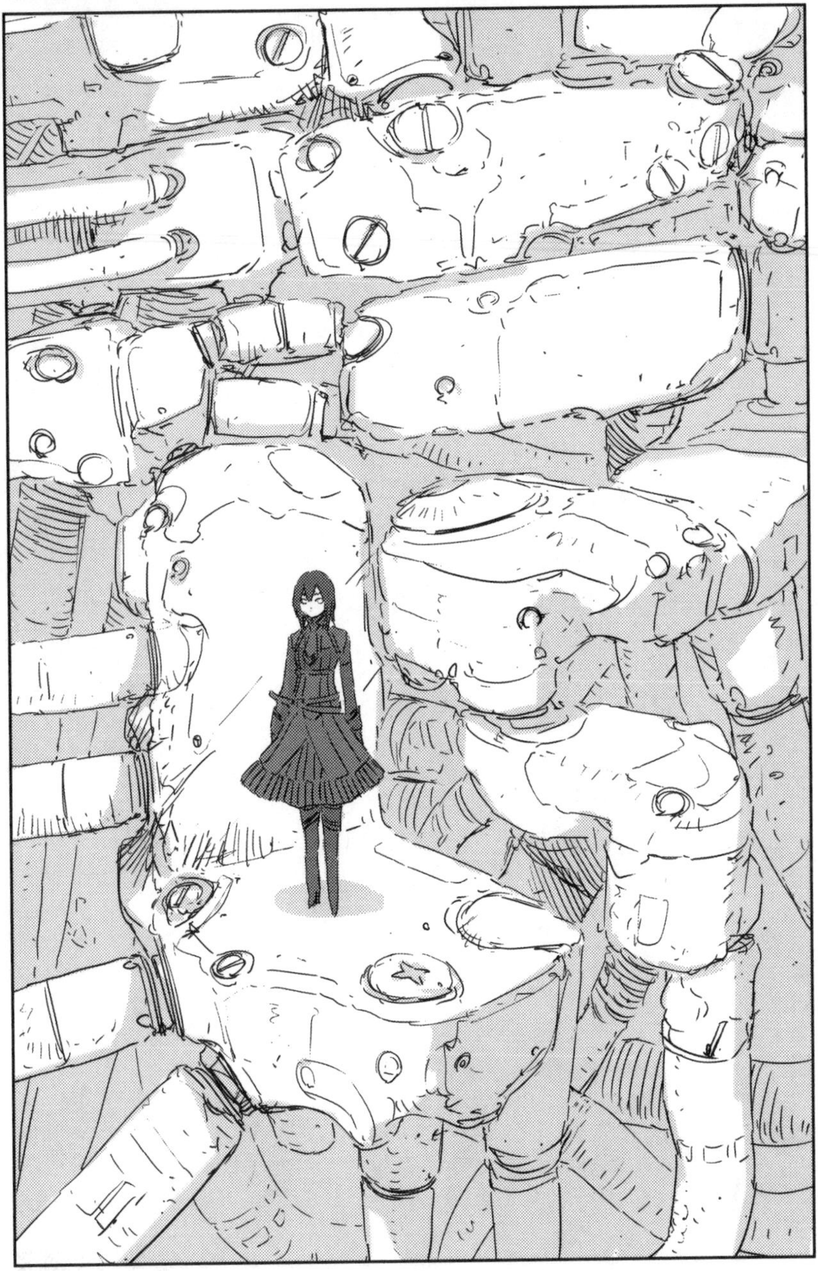

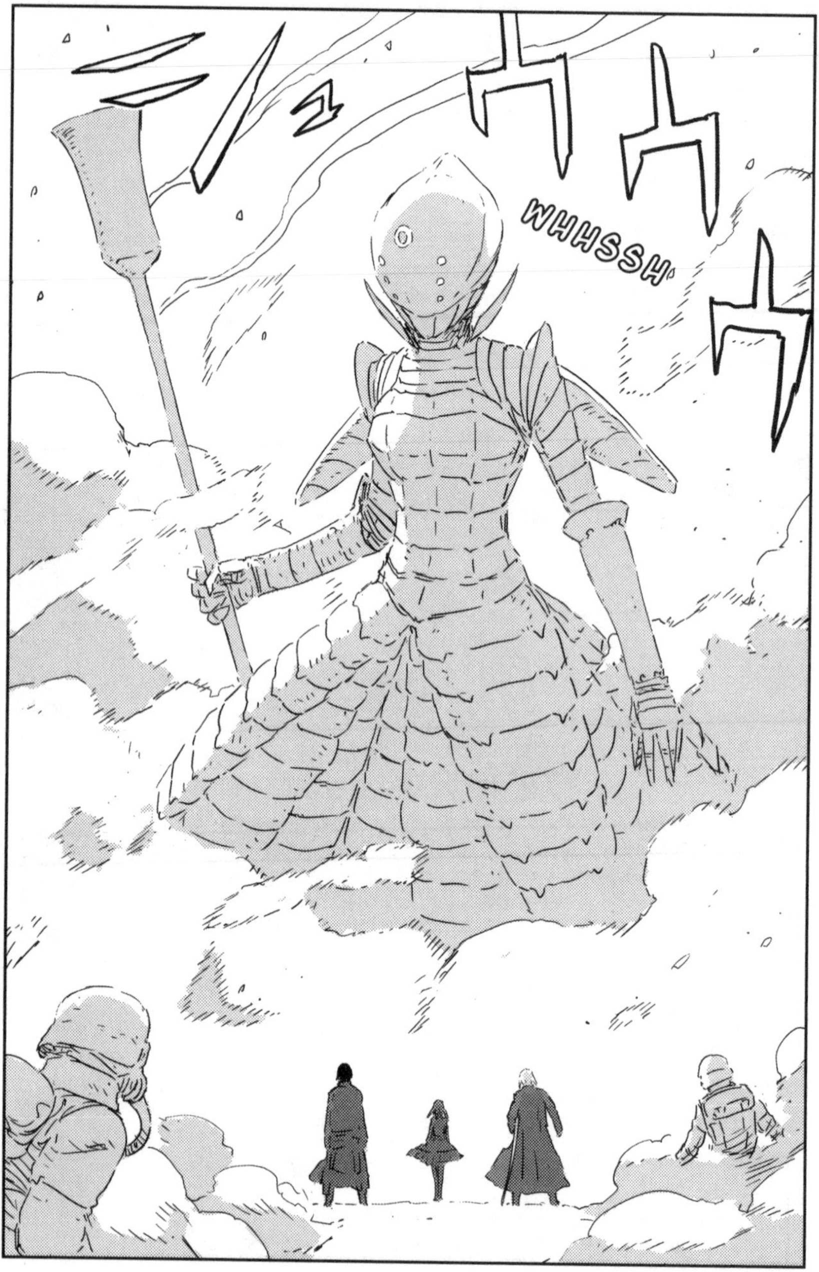
WHHSSSH

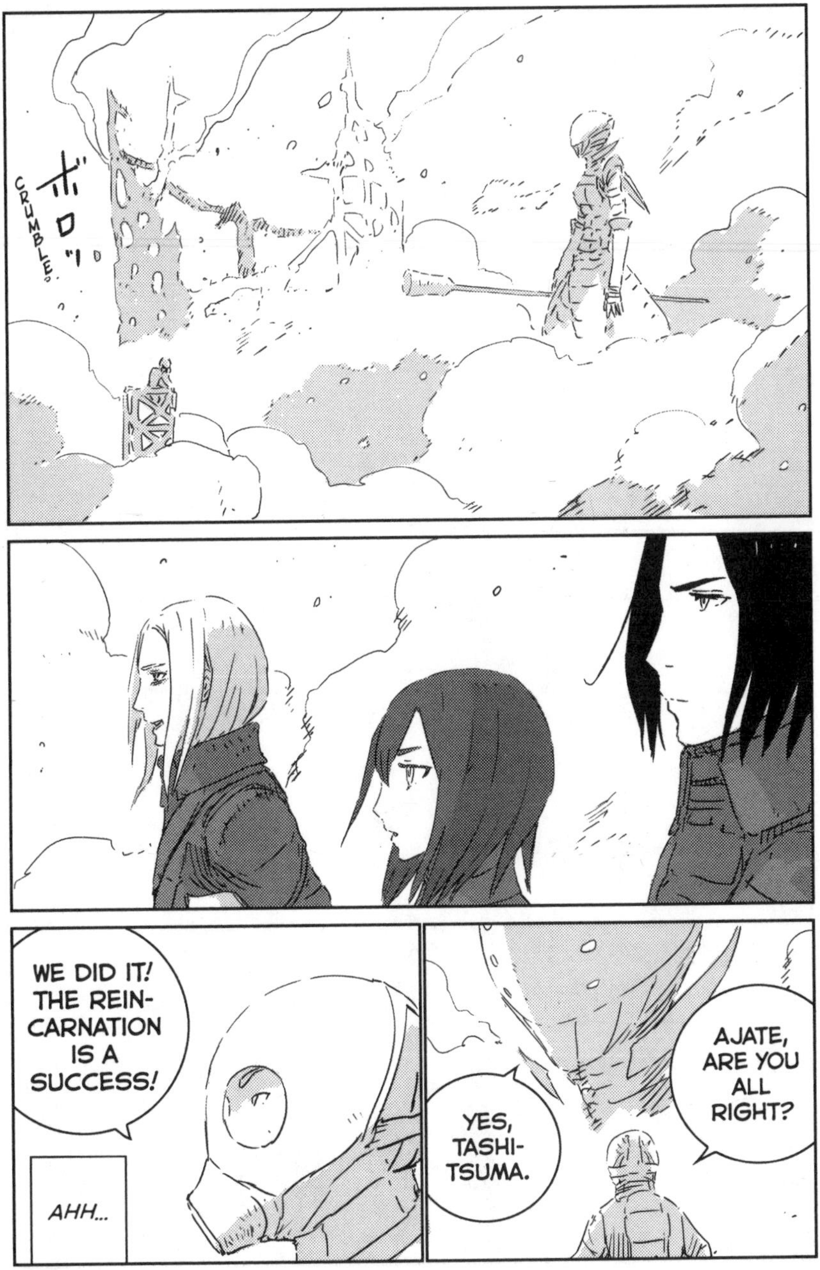
ボロッ
CRUMBLE.
AJATE, ARE YOU ALL RIGHT?
YES, TASHITSUMA.
WE DID IT! THE REINCARNATION IS A SUCCESS!
AHH...

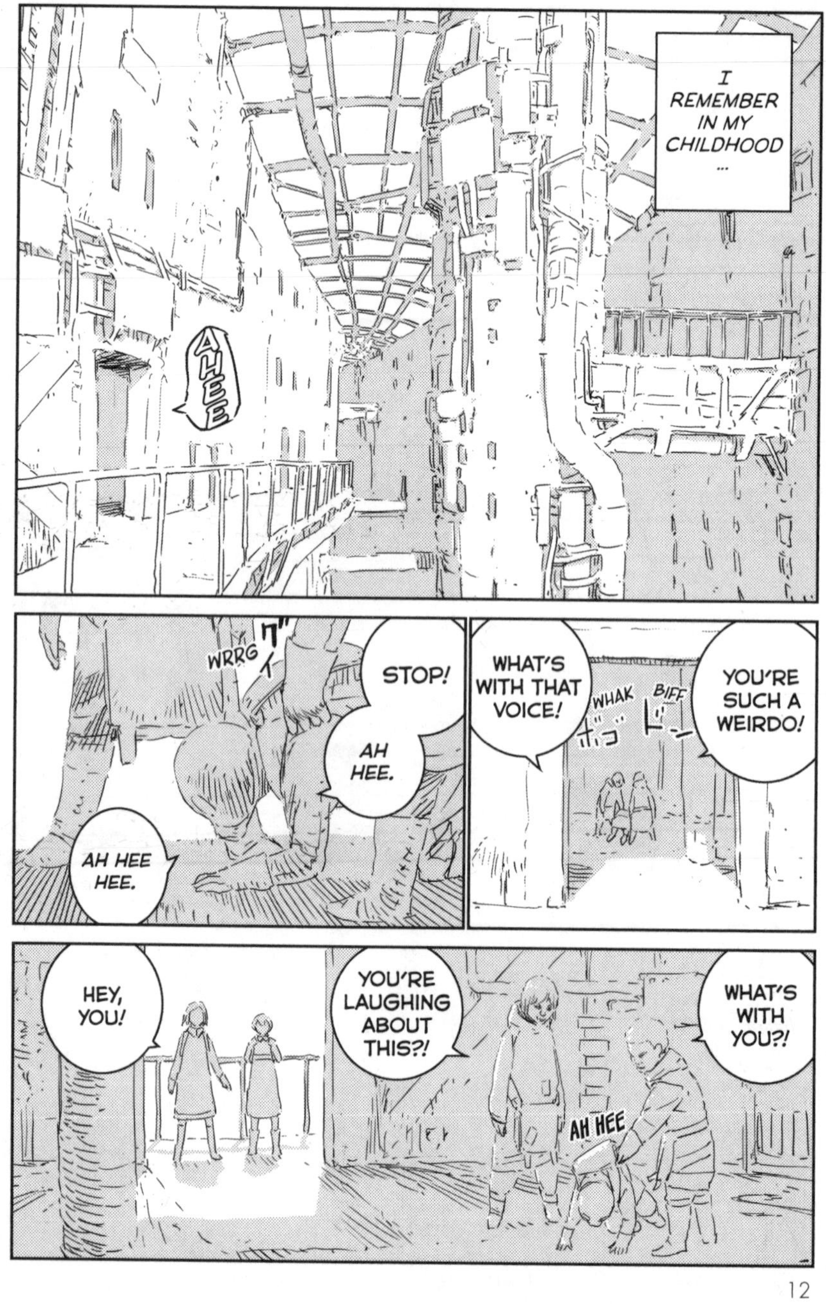

I REMEMBER IN MY CHILDHOOD ...
AHEE
YOU'RE SUCH A WEIRDO!
BIFF
WHAK
WHAT'S WITH THAT VOICE!
STOP!
WRRG
AH HEE.
AH HEE HEE.
WHAT'S WITH YOU?!
AH HEE
YOU'RE LAUGHING ABOUT THIS?!
HEY, YOU!

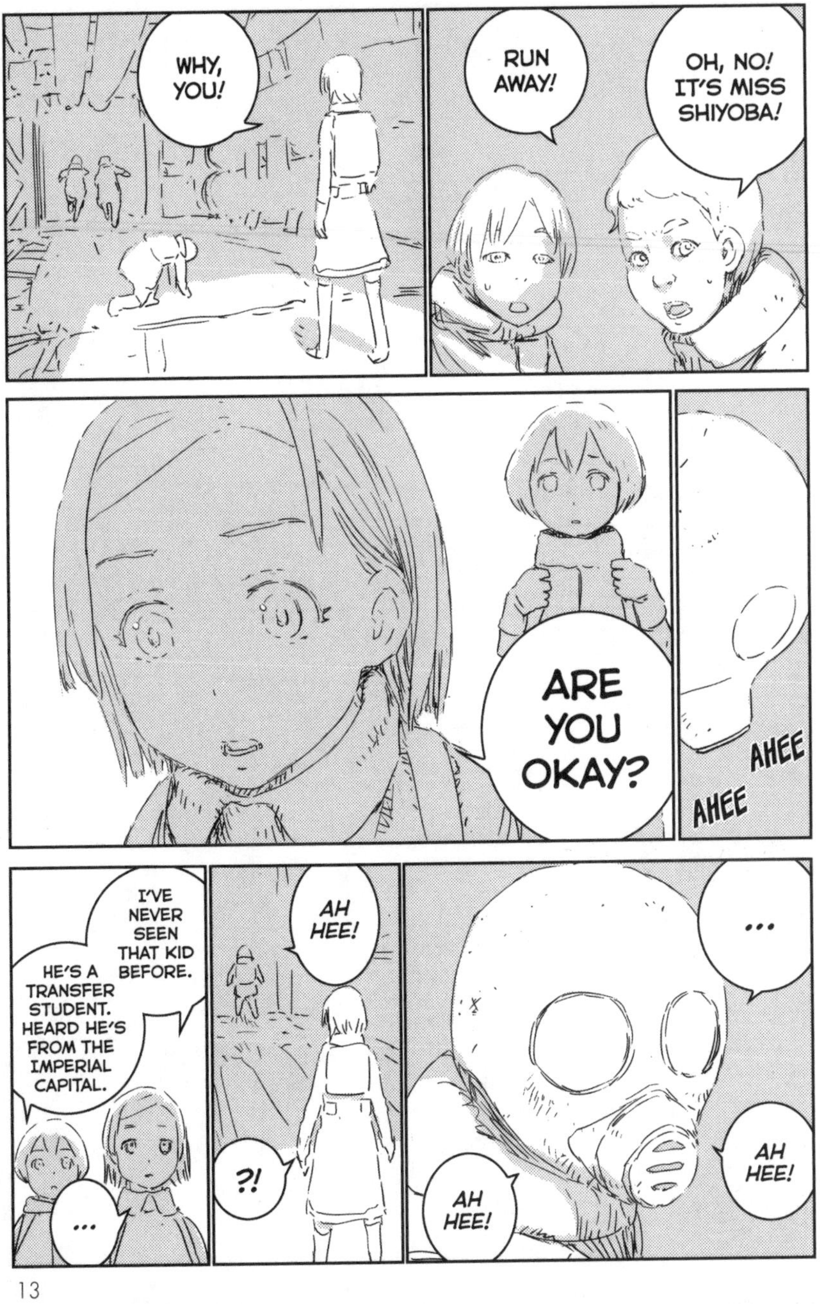
OH, NO! IT'S MISS SHIYOBA!
RUN AWAY!
WHY, YOU!
AHEE
AHEE
ARE YOU OKAY?
...
AH HEE!
AH HEE!
AH HEE!
?!
I'VE NEVER SEEN THAT KID BEFORE.
HE'S A TRANSFER STUDENT. HEARD HE'S FROM THE IMPERIAL CAPITAL.
...

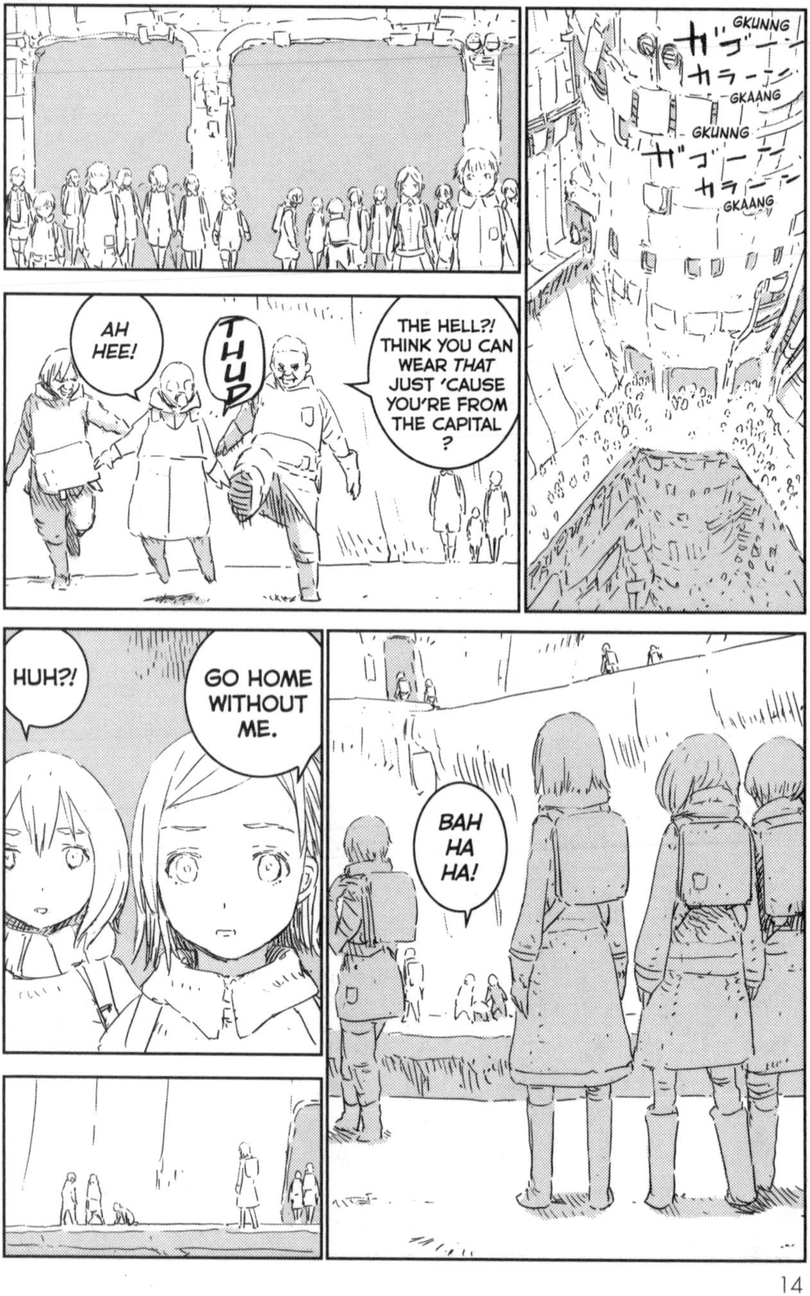
ガゴーン
GKUNNG
カラーン
GKAANG
GKUNNG
ガゴーン
カラーン
GKAANG
THE HELL?! THINK YOU CAN WEAR *THAT* JUST 'CAUSE YOU'RE FROM THE CAPITAL?
THUD
AH HEE!
BAH HA HA!
GO HOME WITHOUT ME.
HUH?!

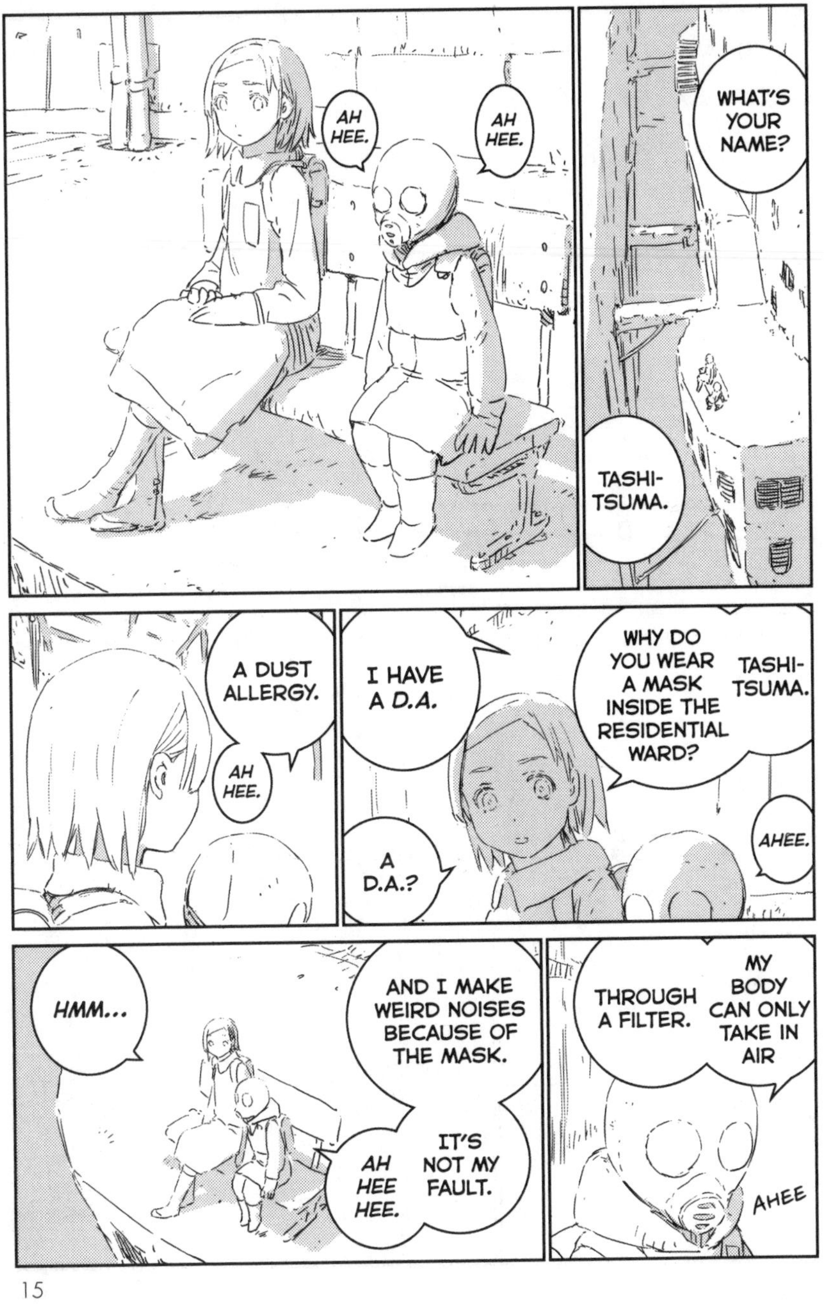
WHAT'S YOUR NAME?
TASHI-TSUMA.
AH HEE.
AH HEE.
TASHI-TSUMA.
WHY DO YOU WEAR A MASK INSIDE THE RESIDENTIAL WARD?
AHEE.
I HAVE A *D.A.*
A D.A.?
A DUST ALLERGY.
AH HEE.
MY BODY CAN ONLY TAKE IN AIR
THROUGH A FILTER.
AHEE
AND I MAKE WEIRD NOISES BECAUSE OF THE MASK.
IT'S NOT MY FAULT.
AH HEE HEE.
HMM...

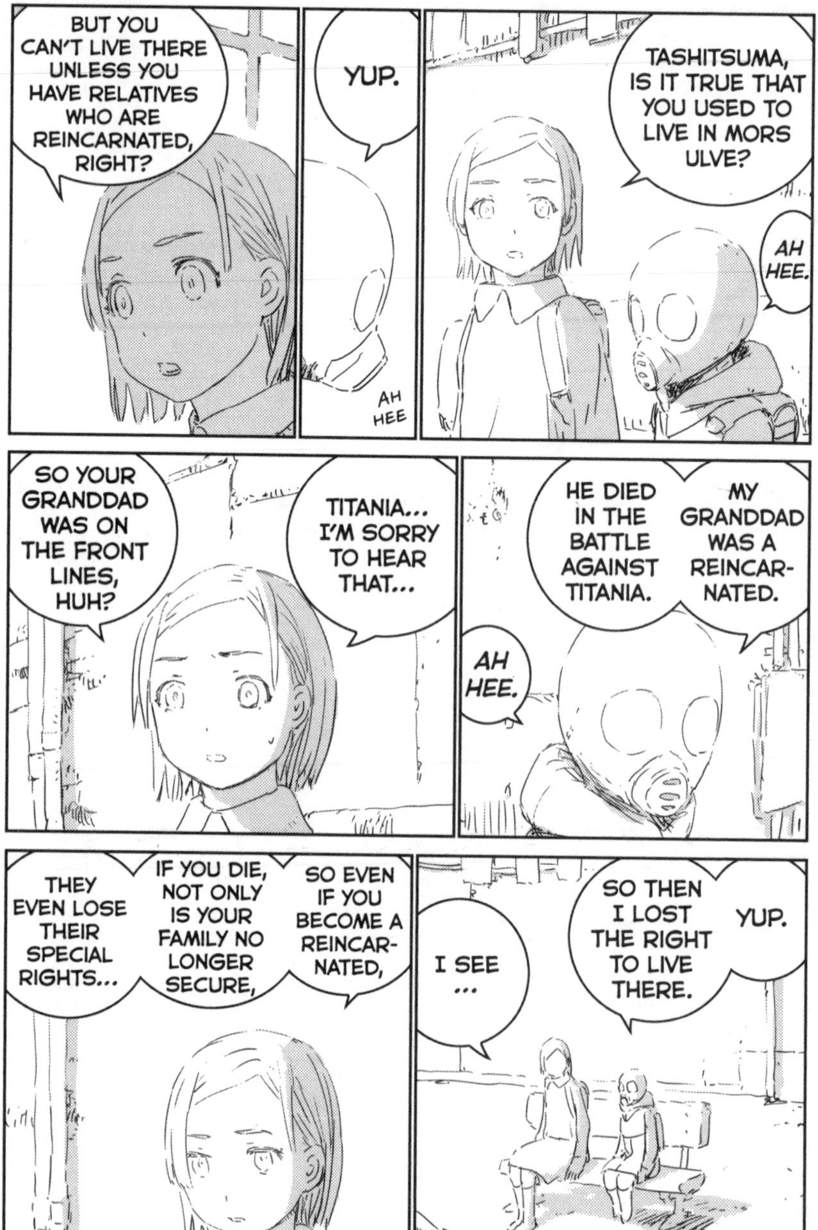
TASHITSUMA, IS IT TRUE THAT YOU USED TO LIVE IN MORS ULVE?
AH HEE.
YUP.
AH HEE
BUT YOU CAN'T LIVE THERE UNLESS YOU HAVE RELATIVES WHO ARE REINCARNATED, RIGHT?
MY GRANDDAD WAS A REINCARNATED.
HE DIED IN THE BATTLE AGAINST TITANIA.
AH HEE.
TITANIA... I'M SORRY TO HEAR THAT...
SO YOUR GRANDDAD WAS ON THE FRONT LINES, HUH?
YUP.
SO THEN I LOST THE RIGHT TO LIVE THERE.
I SEE ...
SO EVEN IF YOU BECOME A REINCARNATED,
IF YOU DIE, NOT ONLY IS YOUR FAMILY NO LONGER SECURE,
THEY EVEN LOSE THEIR SPECIAL RIGHTS...

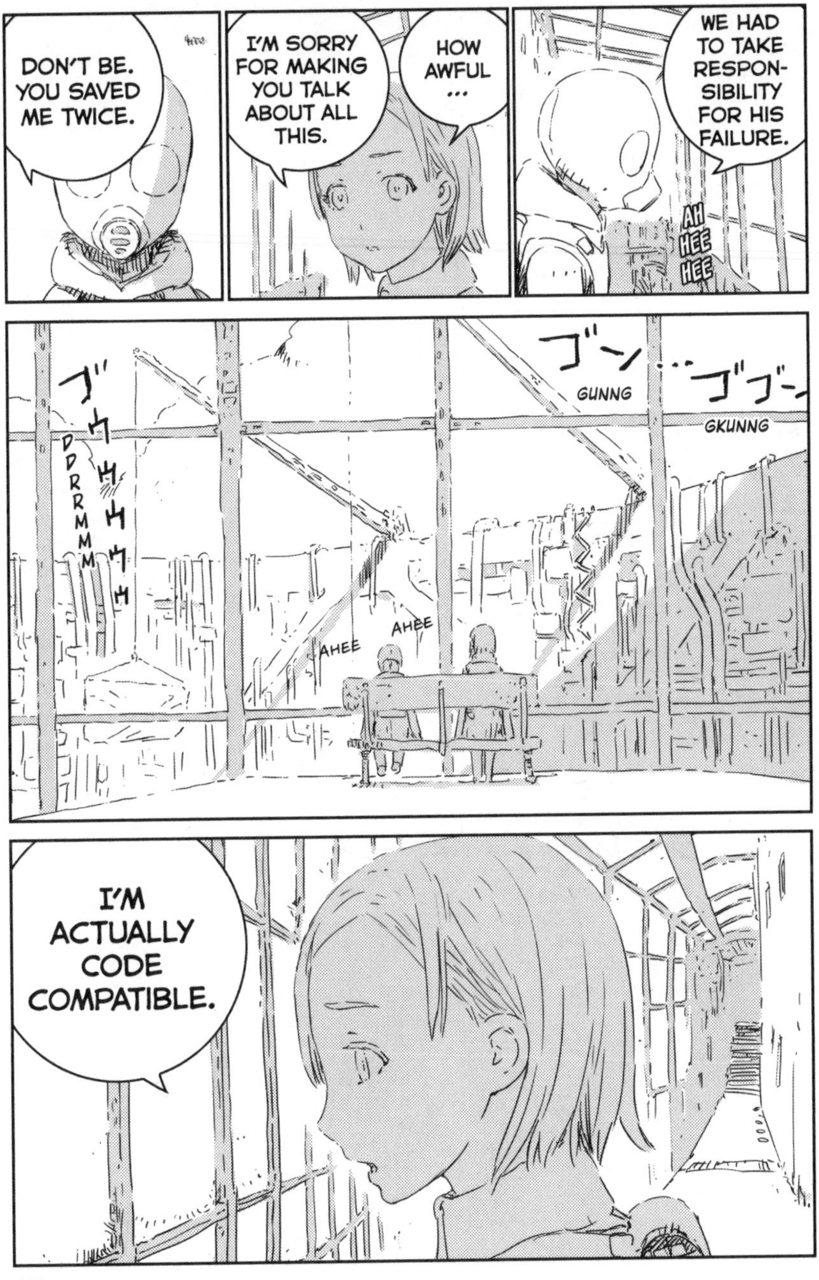
WE HAD TO TAKE RESPON-SIBILITY FOR HIS FAILURE.
AH HEE HEE
HOW AWFUL ...
I'M SORRY FOR MAKING YOU TALK ABOUT ALL THIS.
DON'T BE. YOU SAVED ME TWICE.
GKUNNG
GUNNG
AHEE
AHEE
DDRRMMM
I'M ACTUALLY CODE COMPATIBLE.

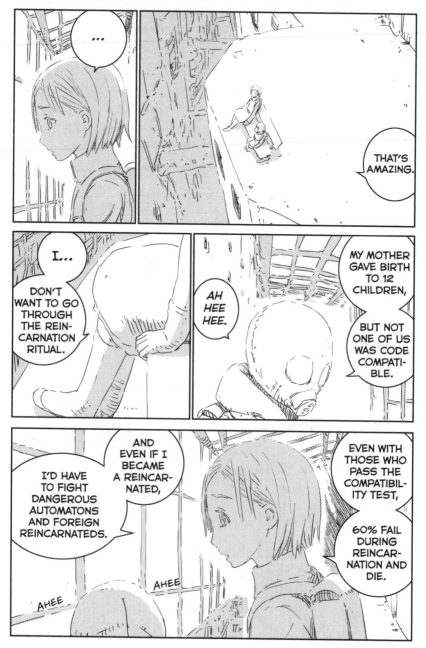

THAT'S AMAZING.
...
MY MOTHER GAVE BIRTH TO 12 CHILDREN,
BUT NOT ONE OF US WAS CODE COMPATIBLE.
AH HEE HEE.
I...
DON'T WANT TO GO THROUGH THE REINCARNATION RITUAL.
EVEN WITH THOSE WHO PASS THE COMPATIBILITY TEST,
60% FAIL DURING REINCARNATION AND DIE.
AND EVEN IF I BECAME A REINCARNATED,
I'D HAVE TO FIGHT DANGEROUS AUTOMATONS AND FOREIGN REINCARNATEDS.
AHEE
AHEE

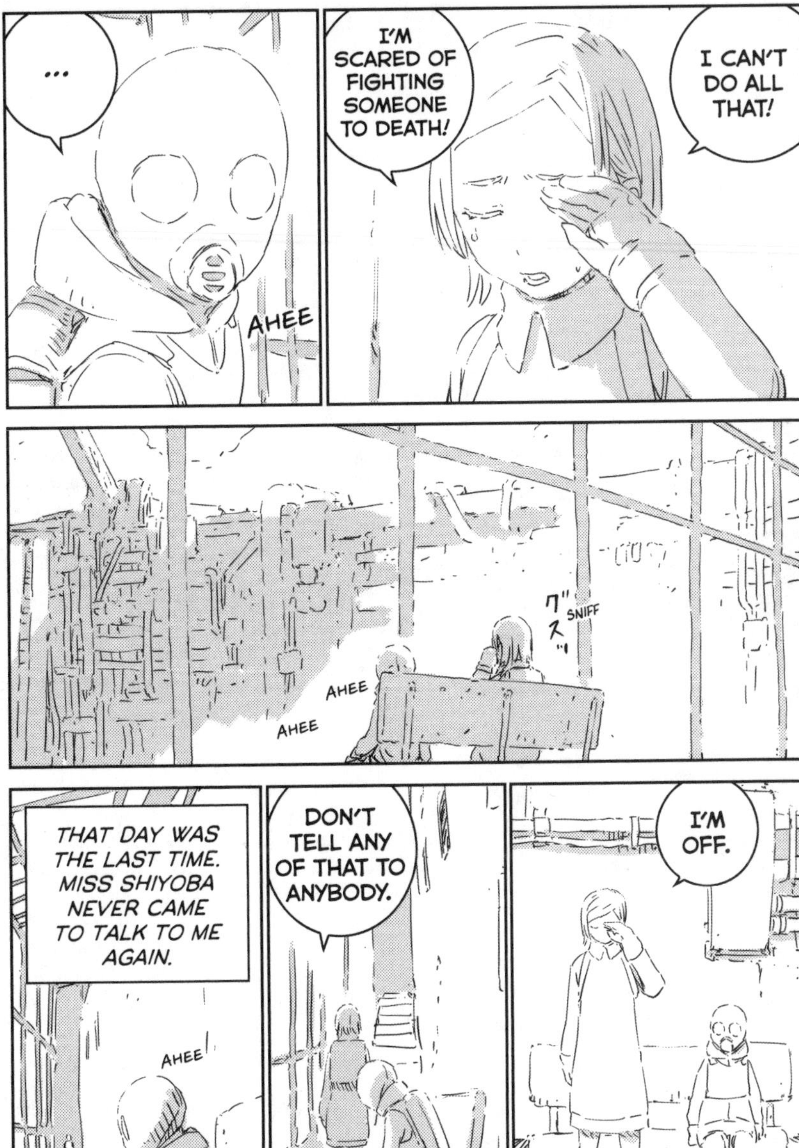
I CAN'T DO ALL THAT!
I'M SCARED OF FIGHTING SOMEONE TO DEATH!
...
AHEE
グスッ
SNIFF
AHEE
AHEE
I'M OFF.
DON'T TELL ANY OF THAT TO ANYBODY.
THAT DAY WAS THE LAST TIME. MISS SHIYOBA NEVER CAME TO TALK TO ME AGAIN.
AHEE

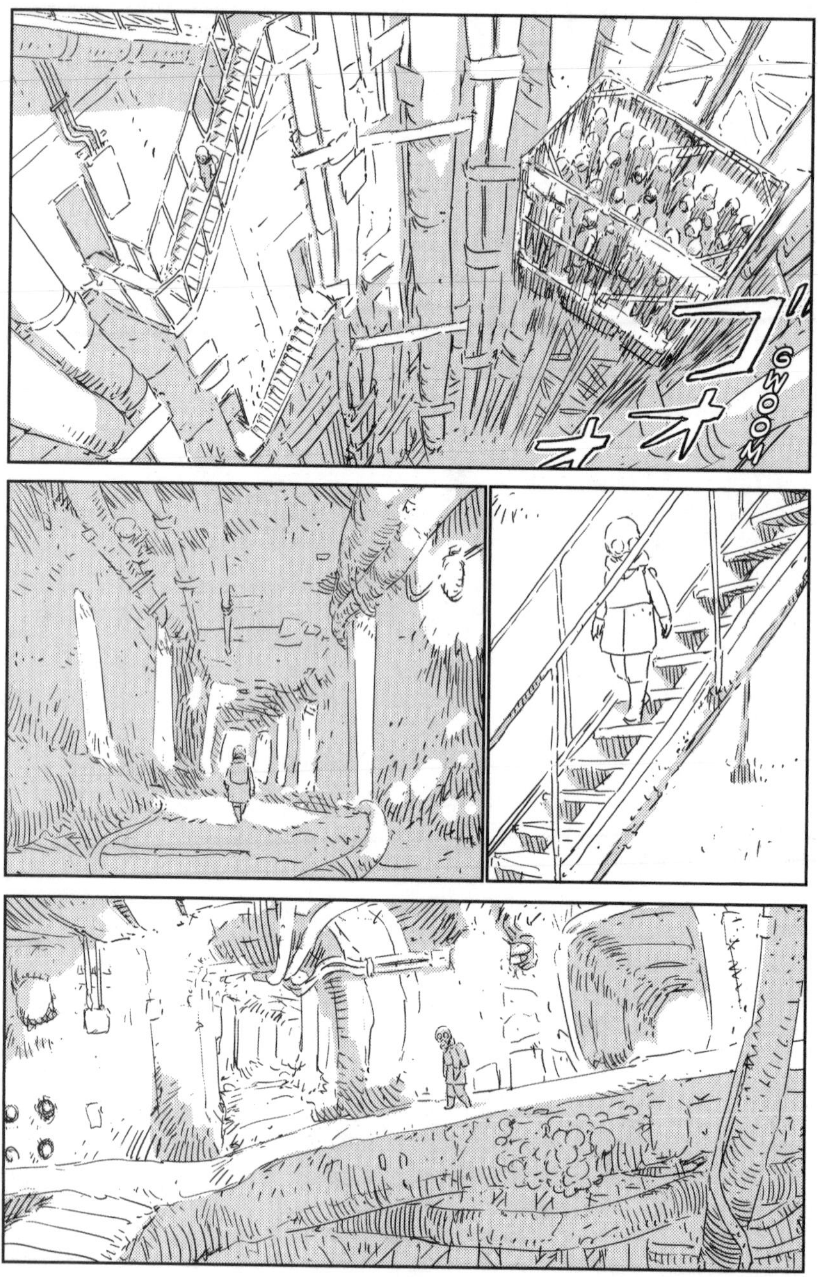
ゴオオ
GWOOM

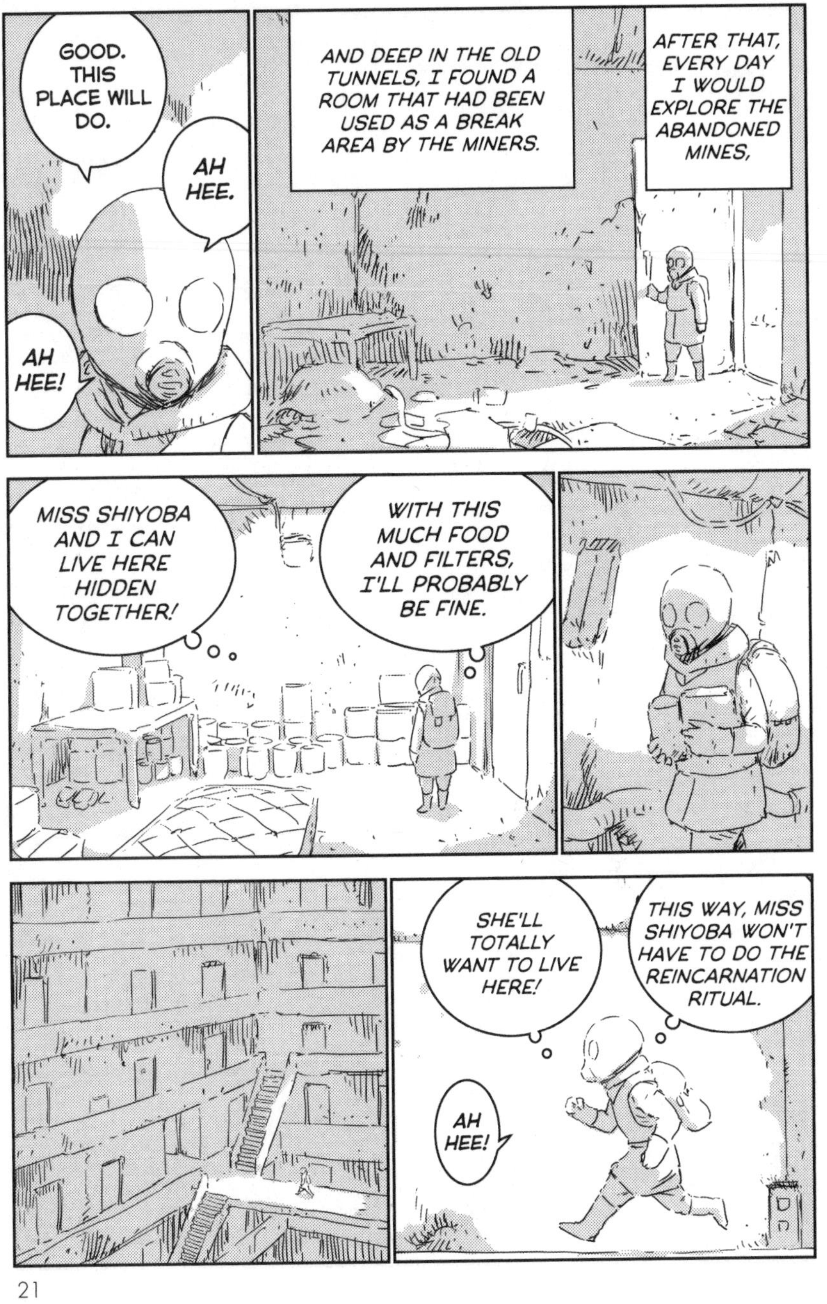
AFTER THAT, EVERY DAY I WOULD EXPLORE THE ABANDONED MINES,
AND DEEP IN THE OLD TUNNELS, I FOUND A ROOM THAT HAD BEEN USED AS A BREAK AREA BY THE MINERS.
GOOD. THIS PLACE WILL DO.
AH HEE.
AH HEE!
WITH THIS MUCH FOOD AND FILTERS, I'LL PROBABLY BE FINE.
MISS SHIYOBA AND I CAN LIVE HERE HIDDEN TOGETHER!
THIS WAY, MISS SHIYOBA WON'T HAVE TO DO THE REINCARNATION RITUAL.
SHE'LL TOTALLY WANT TO LIVE HERE!
AH HEE!

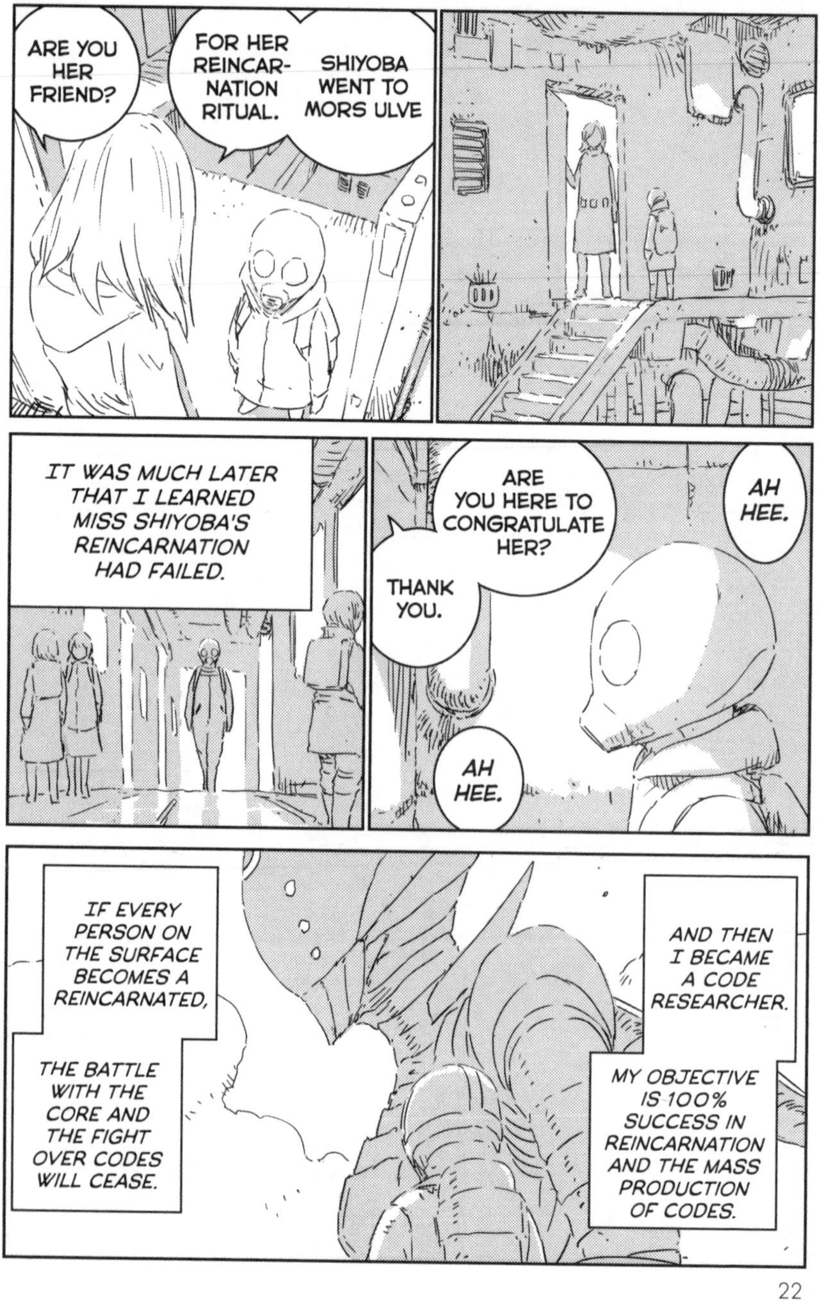
SHIYOBA WENT TO MORS ULVE
FOR HER REINCARNATION RITUAL.
ARE YOU HER FRIEND?
AH HEE.
ARE YOU HERE TO CONGRATULATE HER?
THANK YOU.
AH HEE.
IT WAS MUCH LATER THAT I LEARNED MISS SHIYOBA'S REINCARNATION HAD FAILED.
AND THEN I BECAME A CODE RESEARCHER.
MY OBJECTIVE IS 100% SUCCESS IN REINCARNATION AND THE MASS PRODUCTION OF CODES.
IF EVERY PERSON ON THE SURFACE BECOMES A REINCARNATED,
THE BATTLE WITH THE CORE AND THE FIGHT OVER CODES WILL CEASE.

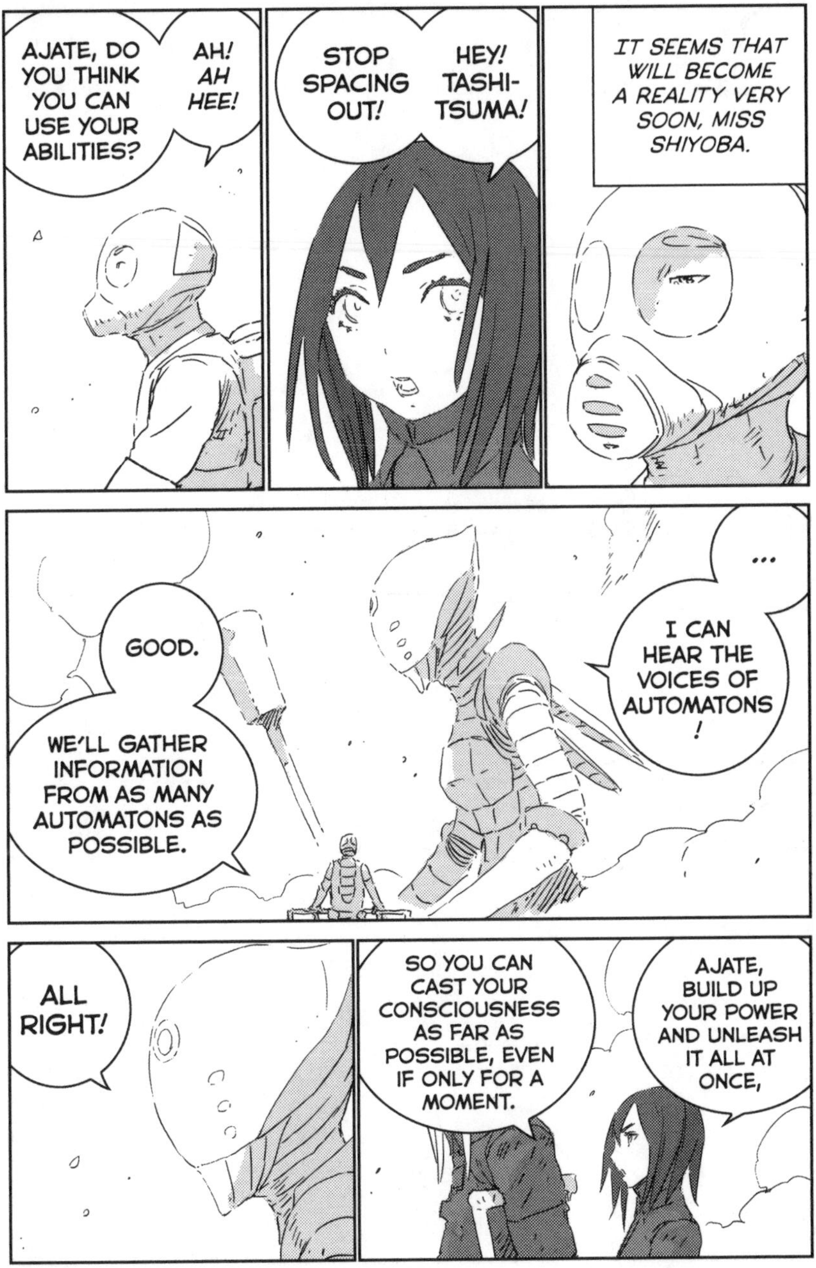
IT SEEMS THAT WILL BECOME A REALITY VERY SOON, MISS SHIYOBA.
HEY! TASHI-TSUMA!
STOP SPACING OUT!
AH! AH HEE!
AJATE, DO YOU THINK YOU CAN USE YOUR ABILITIES?
...
I CAN HEAR THE VOICES OF AUTOMATONS!
GOOD.
WE'LL GATHER INFORMATION FROM AS MANY AUTOMATONS AS POSSIBLE.
AJATE, BUILD UP YOUR POWER AND UNLEASH IT ALL AT ONCE,
SO YOU CAN CAST YOUR CONSCIOUSNESS AS FAR AS POSSIBLE, EVEN IF ONLY FOR A MOMENT.
ALL RIGHT!

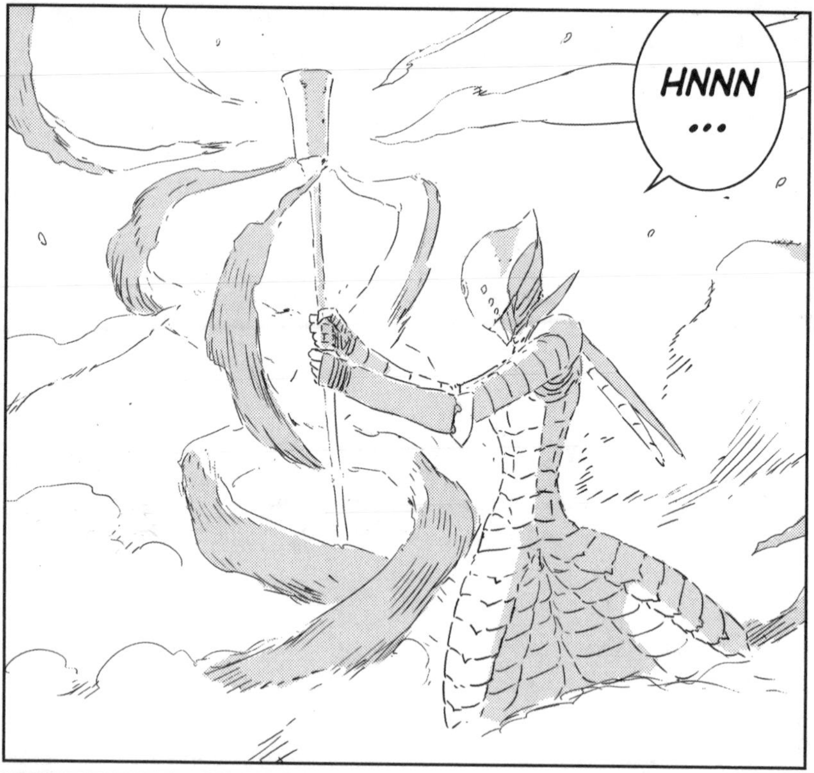
HNNN...

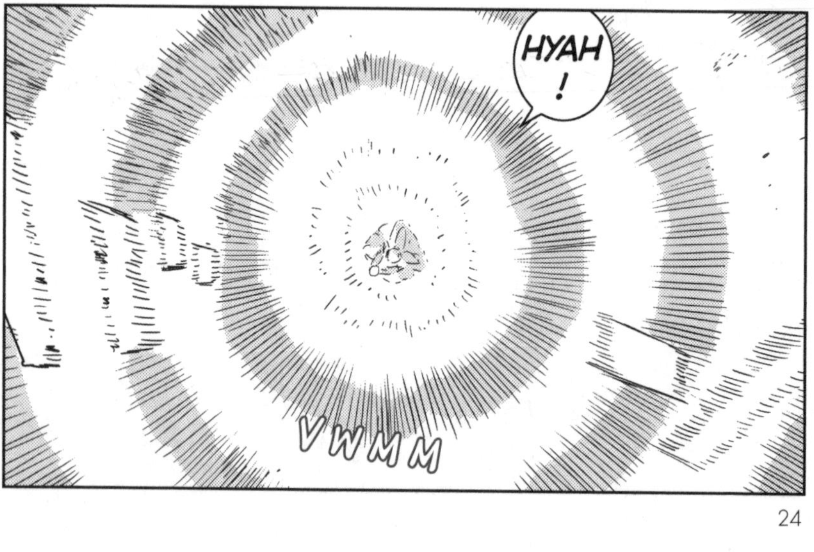
HYAH!
VWMM

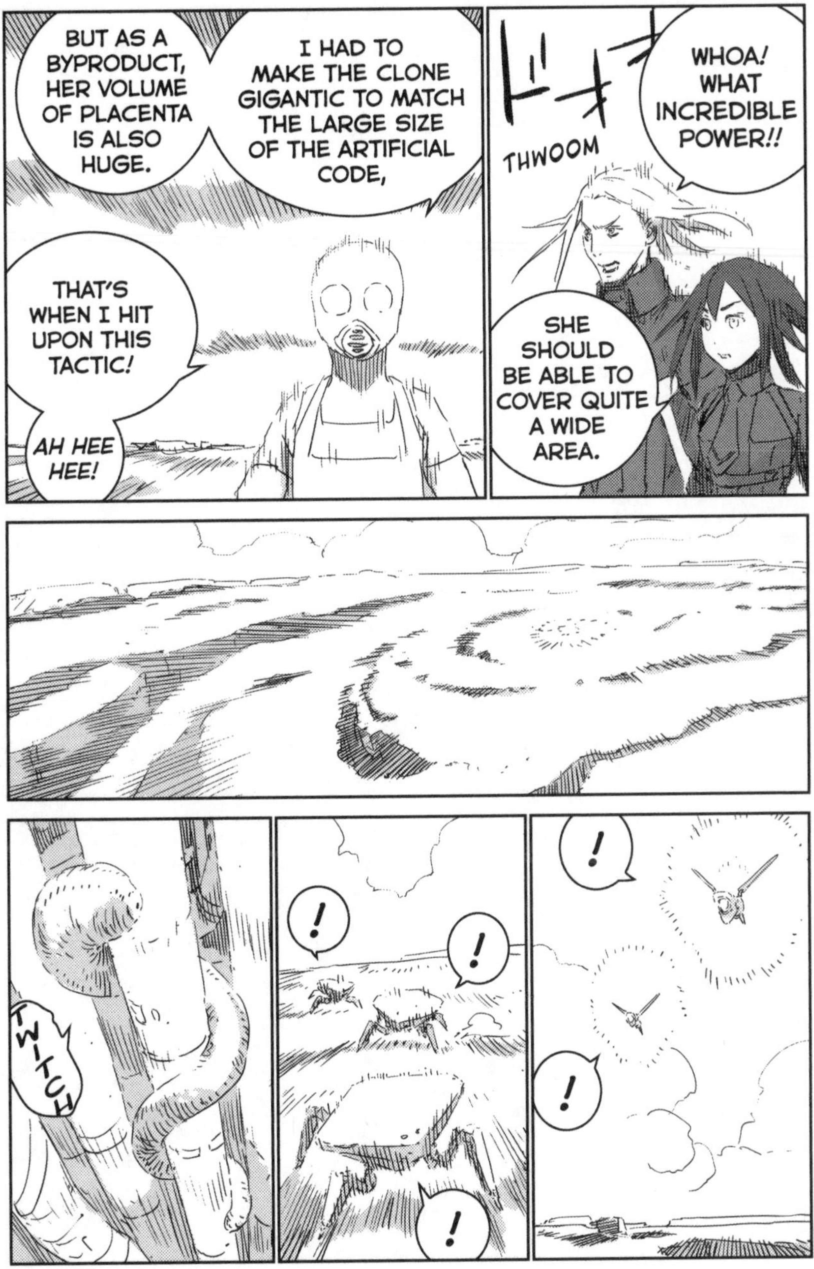
WHOA! WHAT INCREDIBLE POWER!!
THWOOM
SHE SHOULD BE ABLE TO COVER QUITE A WIDE AREA.
I HAD TO MAKE THE CLONE GIGANTIC TO MATCH THE LARGE SIZE OF THE ARTIFICIAL CODE,
BUT AS A BYPRODUCT, HER VOLUME OF PLACENTA IS ALSO HUGE.
THAT'S WHEN I HIT UPON THIS TACTIC!
AH HEE HEE!
!
!
!
!
!
TWITCH

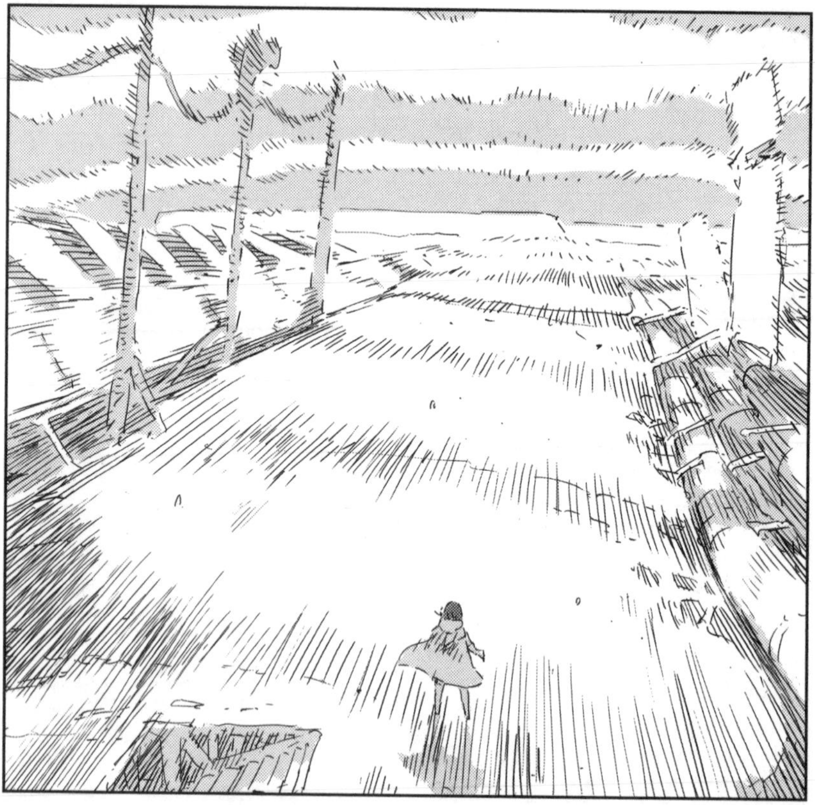

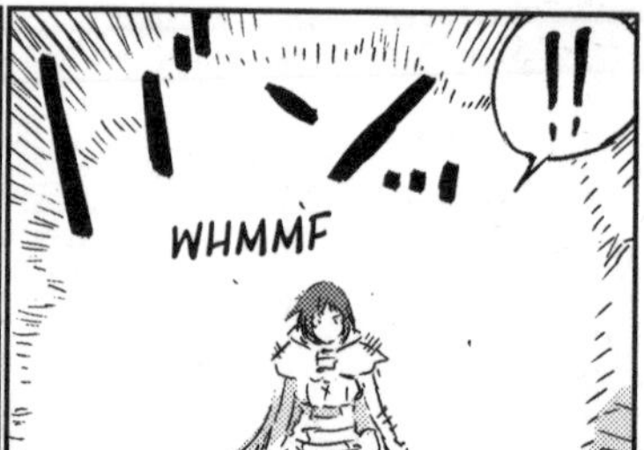
!!
WHMMF

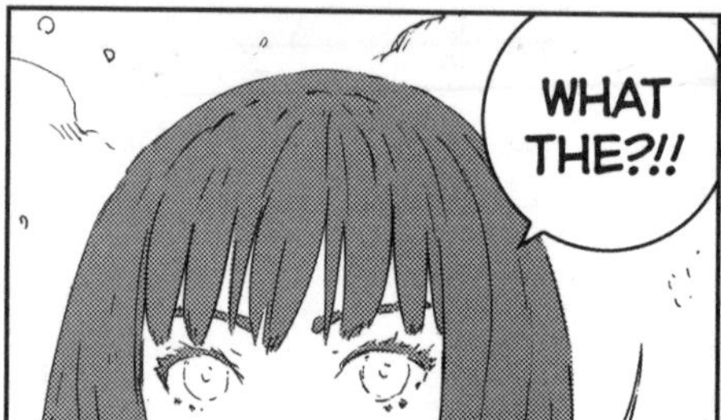
WHAT THE?!!

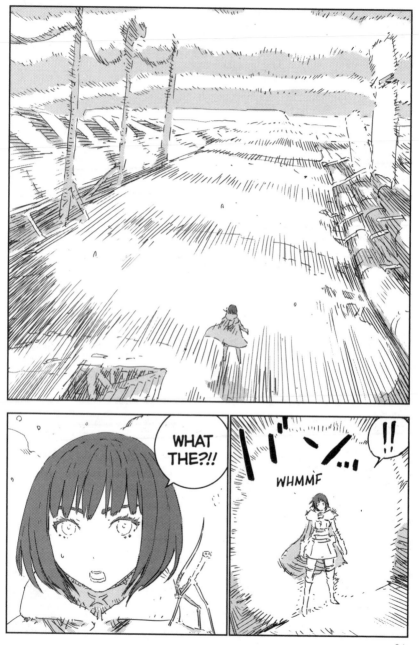

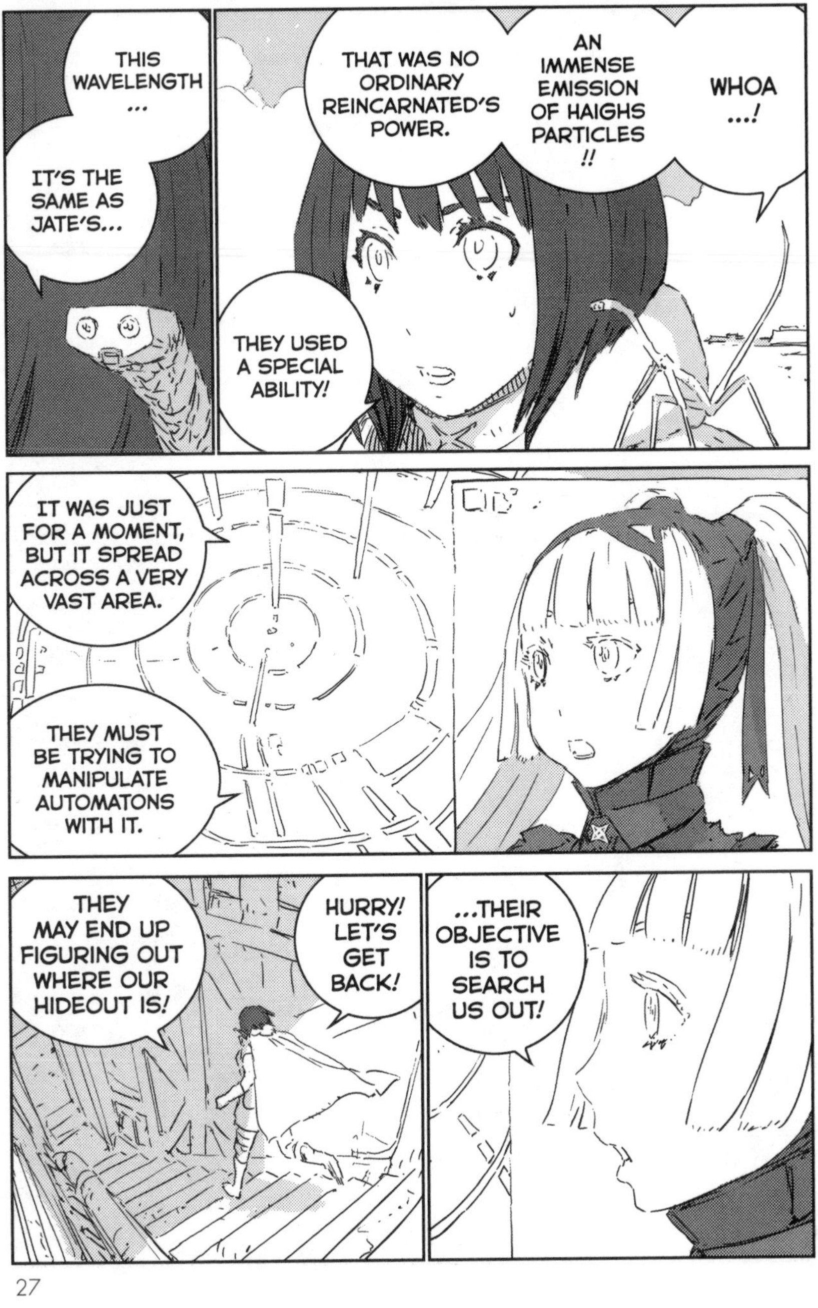
WHOA ...!
AN IMMENSE EMISSION OF HAIGHS PARTICLES !!
THAT WAS NO ORDINARY REINCARNATED'S POWER.
THEY USED A SPECIAL ABILITY!
THIS WAVELENGTH ...
IT'S THE SAME AS JATE'S...
IT WAS JUST FOR A MOMENT, BUT IT SPREAD ACROSS A VERY VAST AREA.
THEY MUST BE TRYING TO MANIPULATE AUTOMATONS WITH IT.
...THEIR OBJECTIVE IS TO SEARCH US OUT!
HURRY! LET'S GET BACK!
THEY MAY END UP FIGURING OUT WHERE OUR HIDEOUT IS!

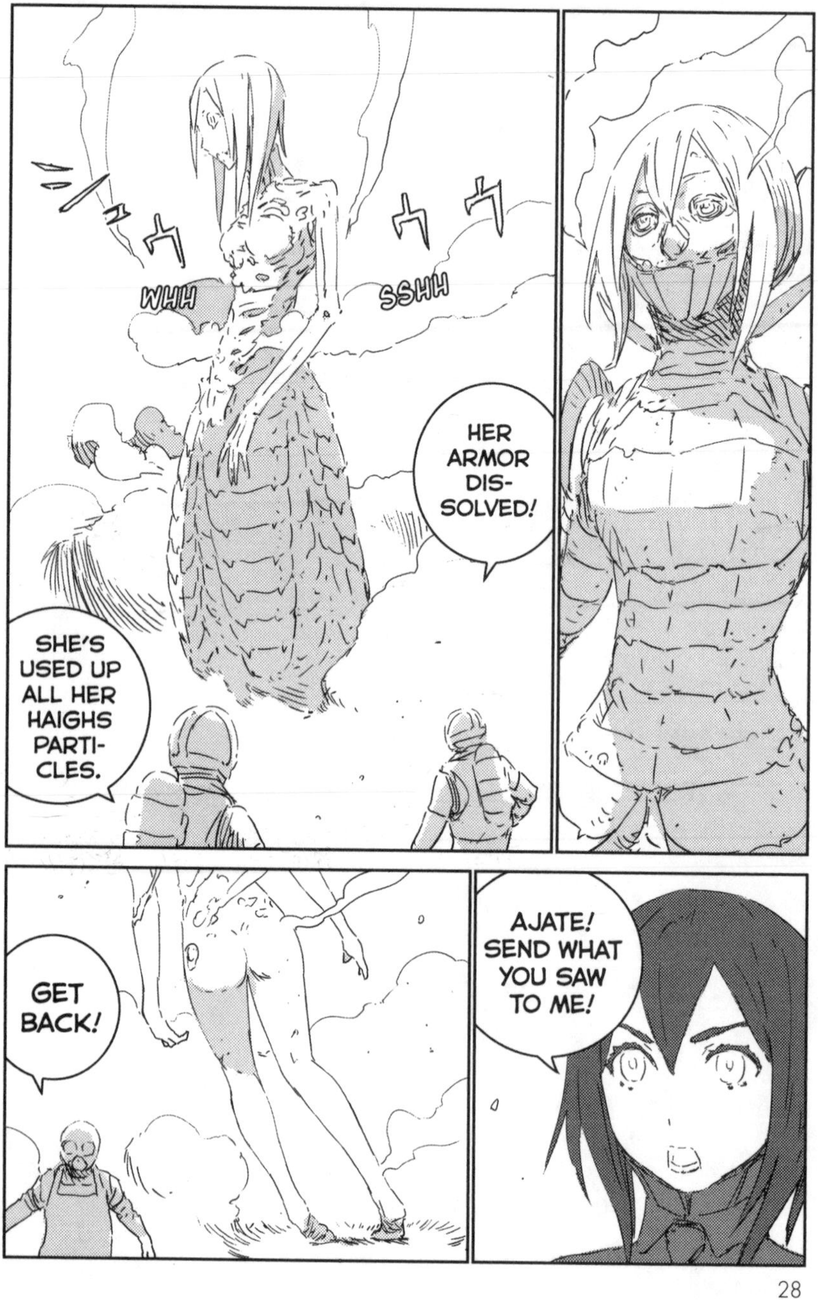
WHH
SSHH
HER ARMOR DIS-SOLVED!
SHE'S USED UP ALL HER HAIGHS PARTICLES.
AJATE! SEND WHAT YOU SAW TO ME!
GET BACK!

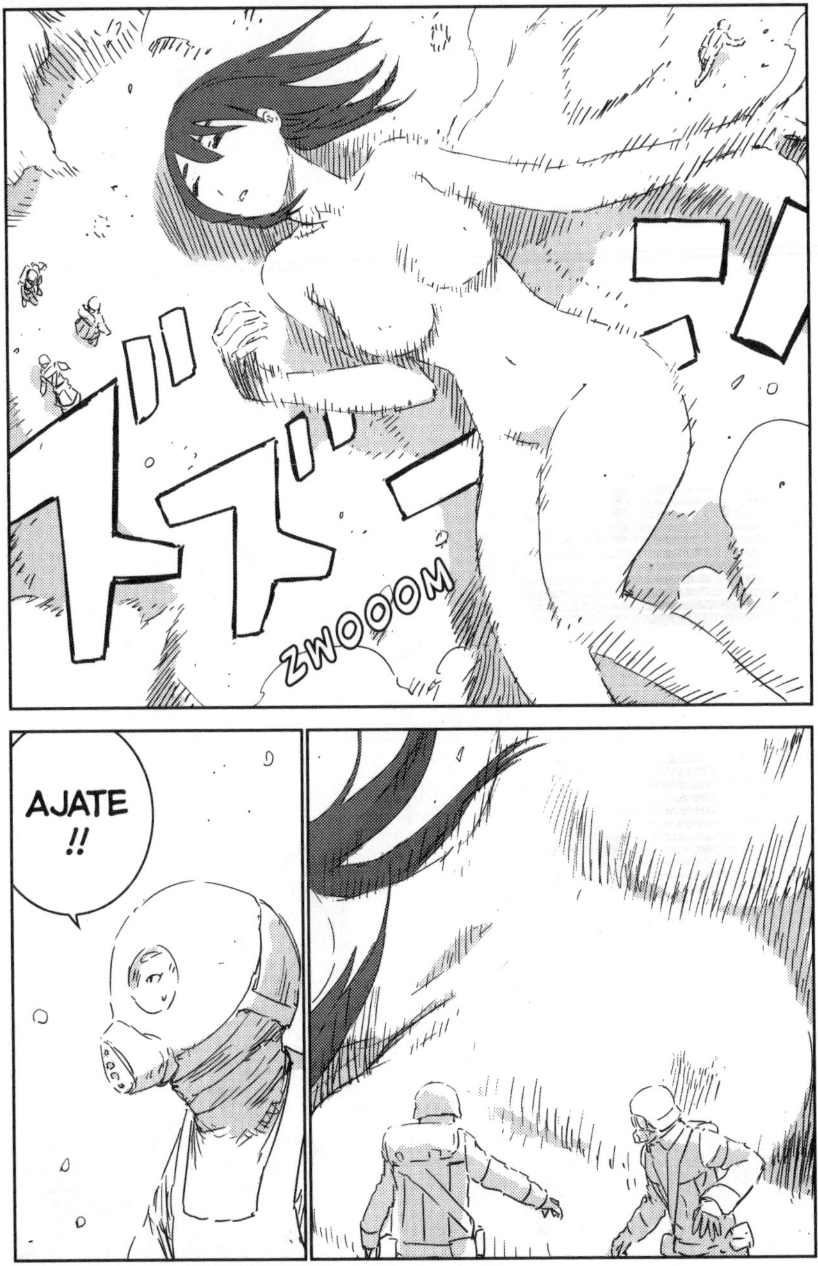
ZWOOOM
AJATE !!

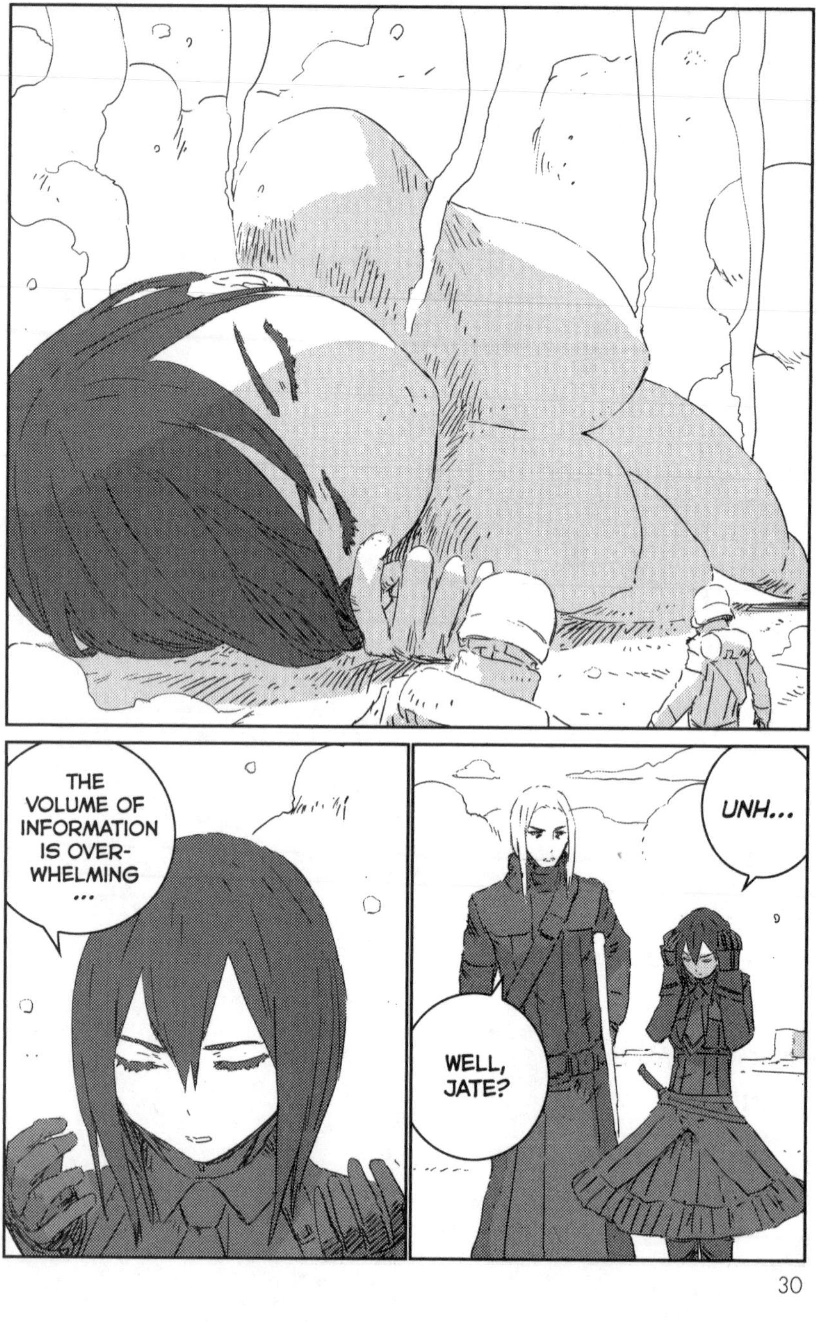
UNH...
WELL, JATE?
THE VOLUME OF INFORMATION IS OVER-WHELMING...

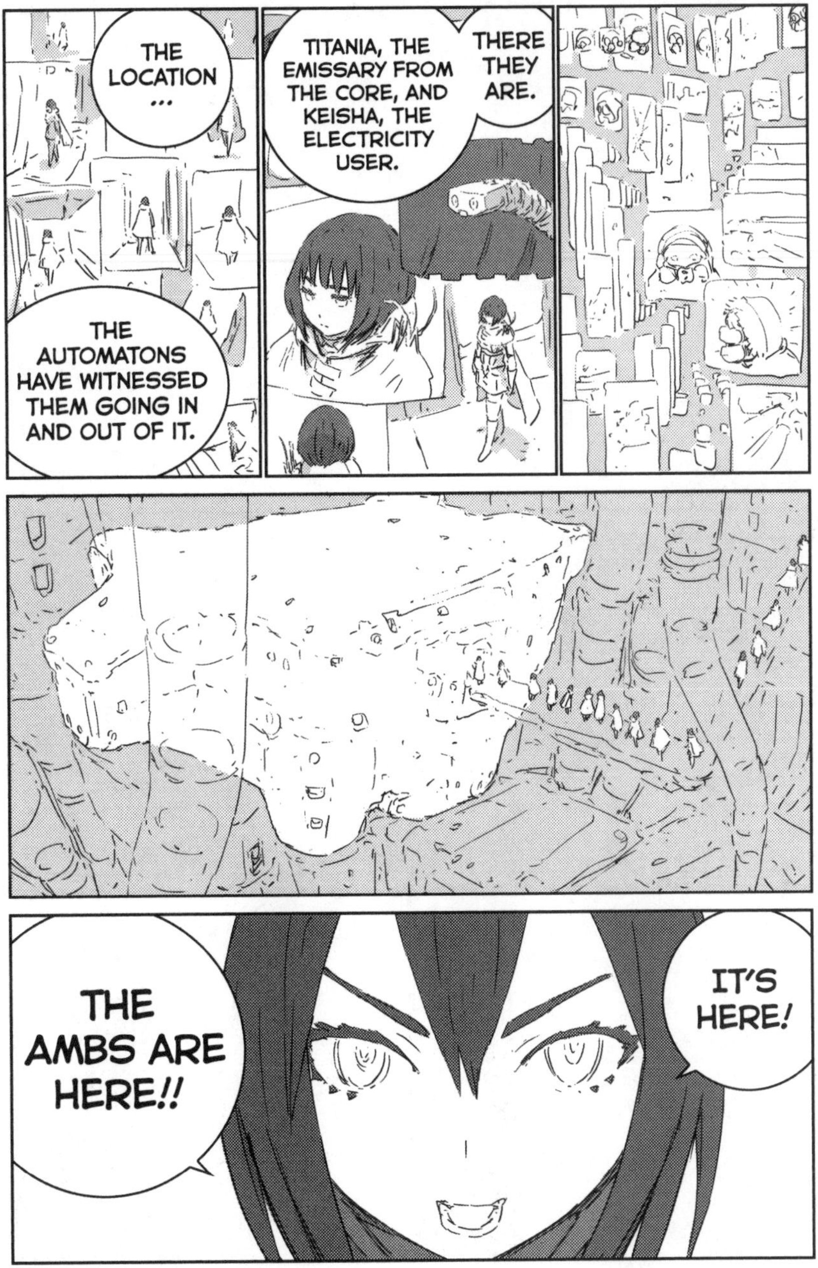
THERE THEY ARE.
TITANIA, THE EMISSARY FROM THE CORE, AND KEISHA, THE ELECTRICITY USER.
THE LOCATION ...
THE AUTOMATONS HAVE WITNESSED THEM GOING IN AND OUT OF IT.
IT'S HERE!
THE AMBS ARE HERE!!

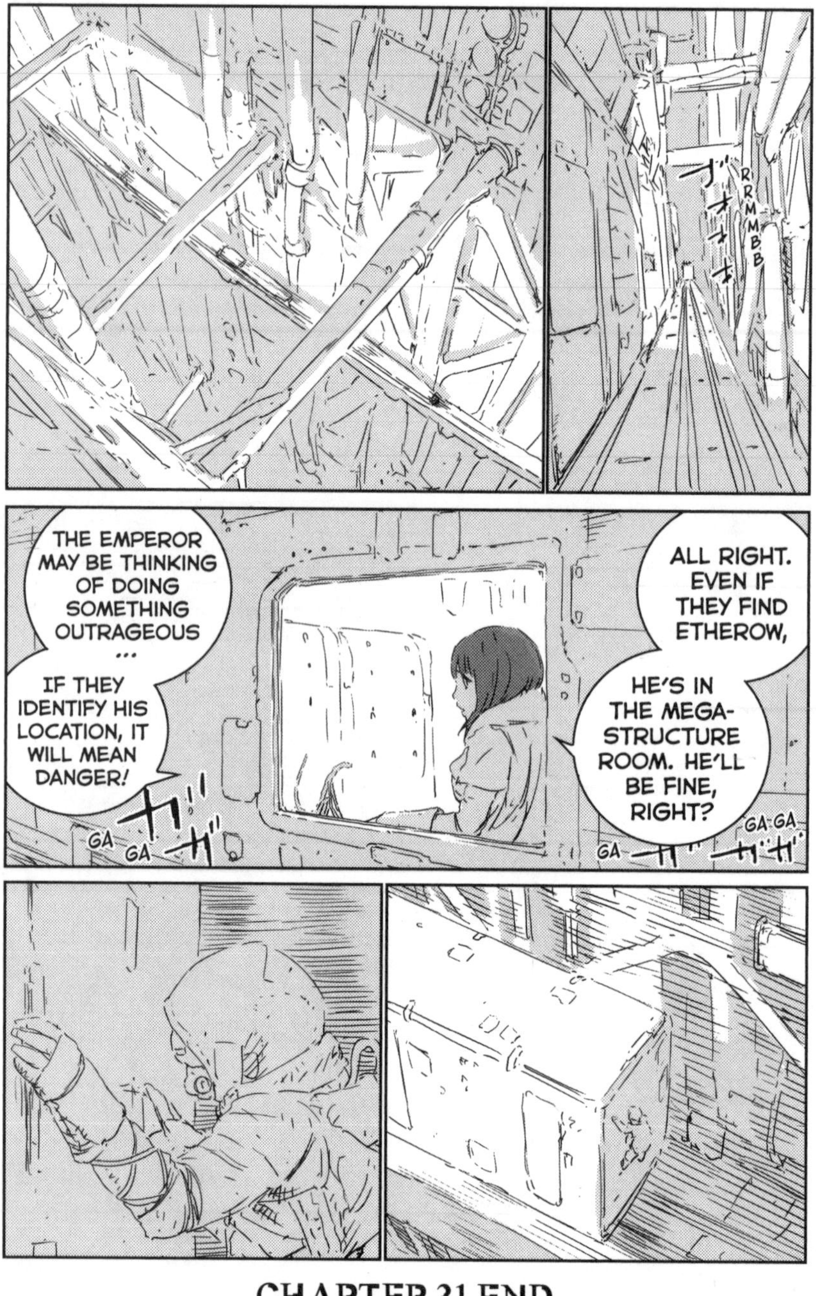
ゴォォォ
RRMMBB
ALL RIGHT. EVEN IF THEY FIND ETHEROW,
HE'S IN THE MEGA-STRUCTURE ROOM. HE'LL BE FINE, RIGHT?
GA GA
GA
THE EMPEROR MAY BE THINKING OF DOING SOMETHING OUTRAGEOUS ...
IF THEY IDENTIFY HIS LOCATION, IT WILL MEAN DANGER!
GA
GA

CHAPTER 31 END

CHAPTER 32

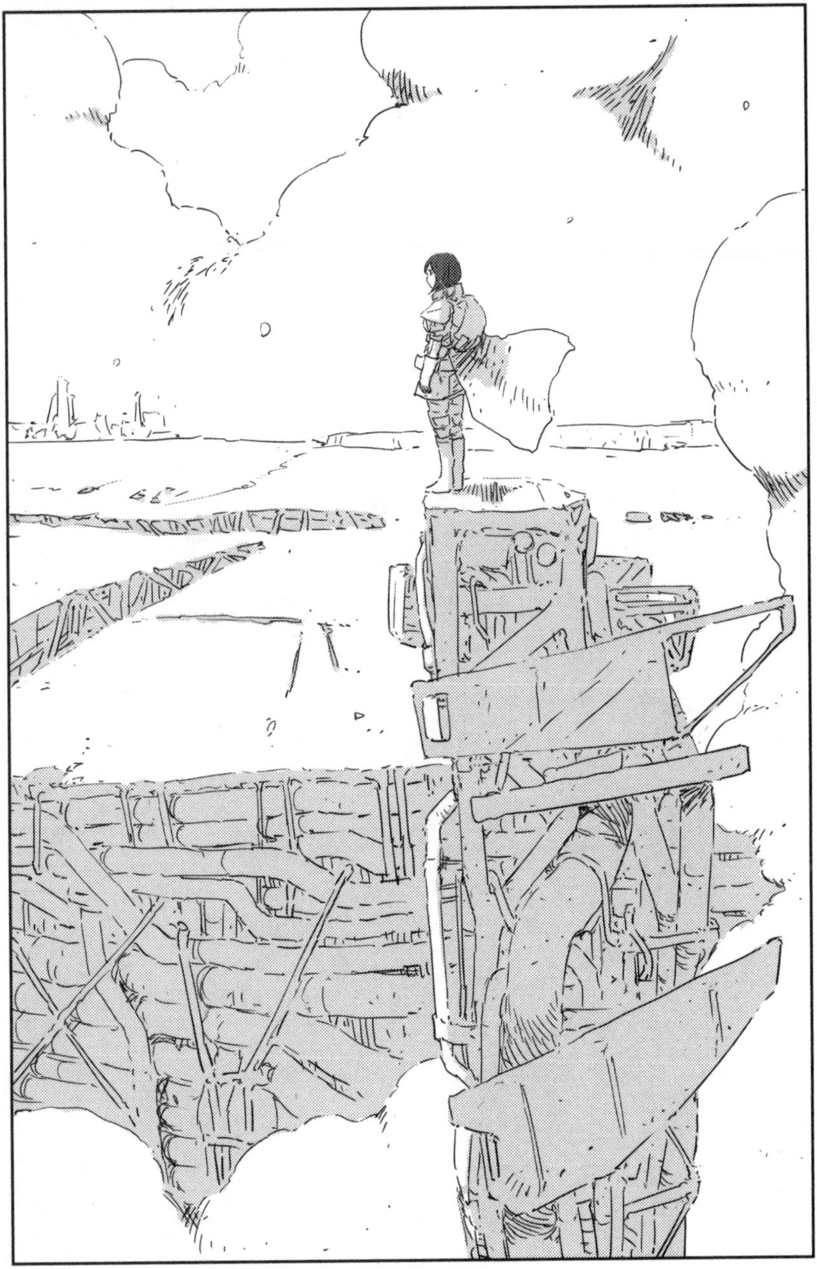

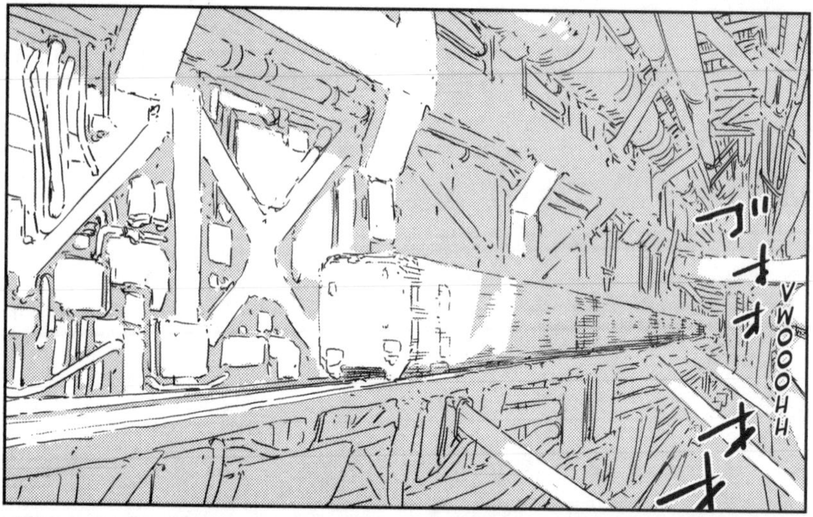
ゴォォォォ
VWOOOHH

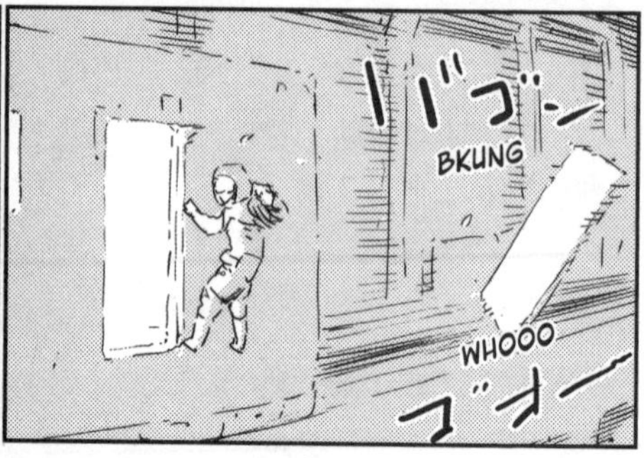
バゴーン
BKUNG
WHOOO
ゴォー

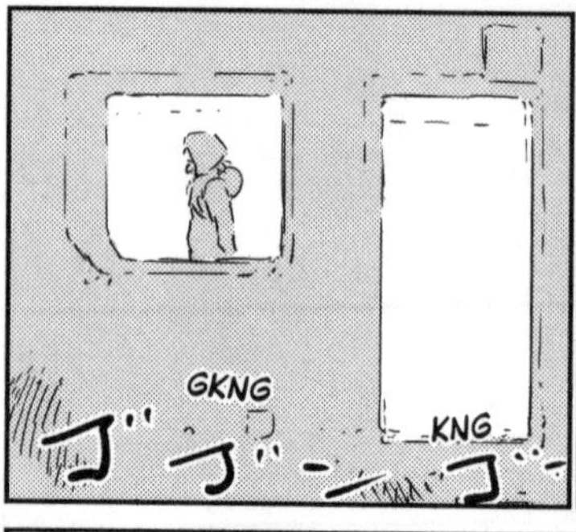
GKNG
KNG
ゴゴーンゴー

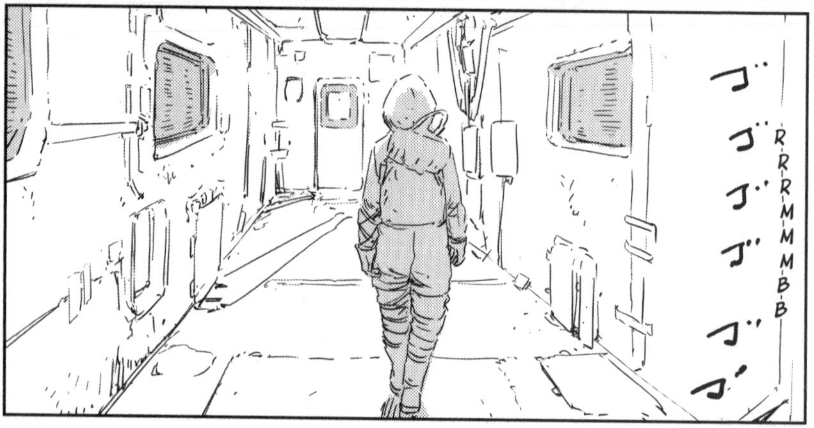
ゴゴゴゴゴゴ
RRRMMMBB

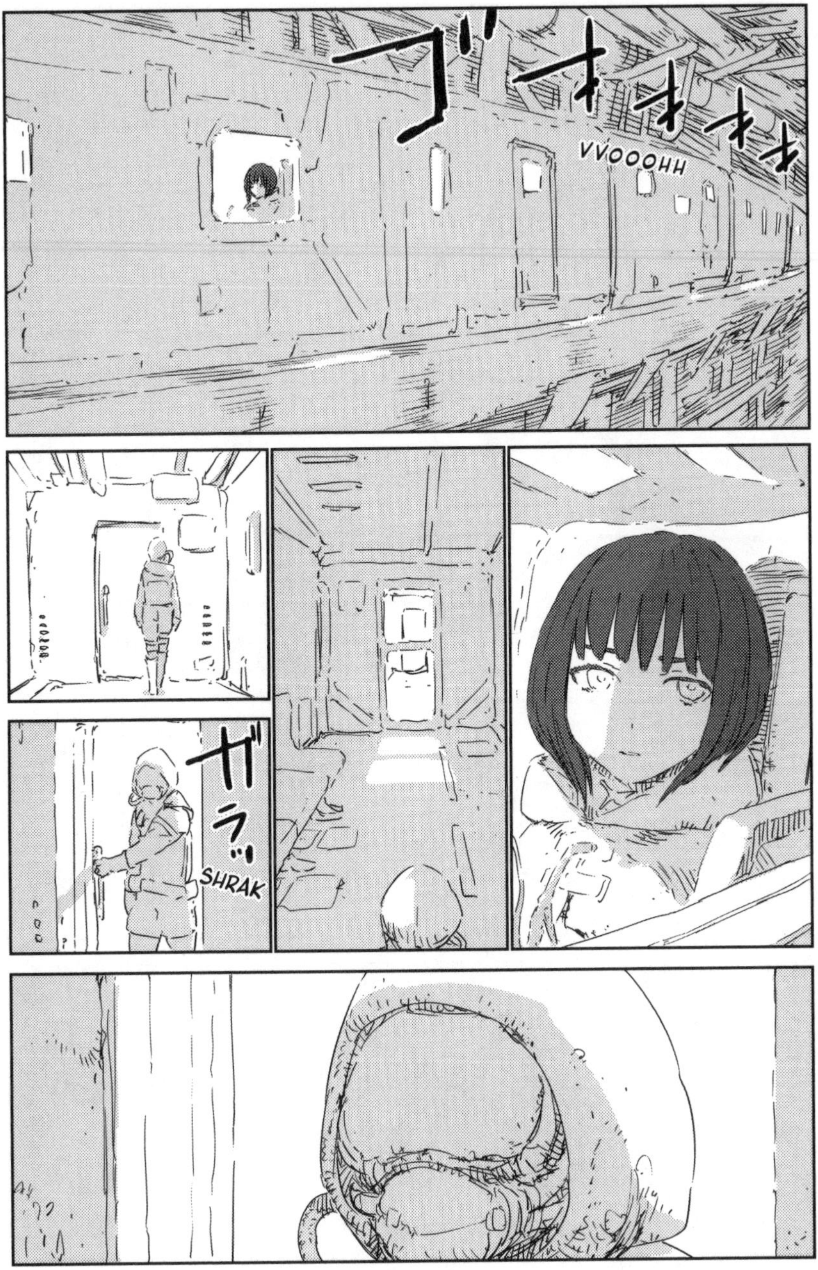
ゴオオオオ
VVOOOHH
ザラッ
SHRAK

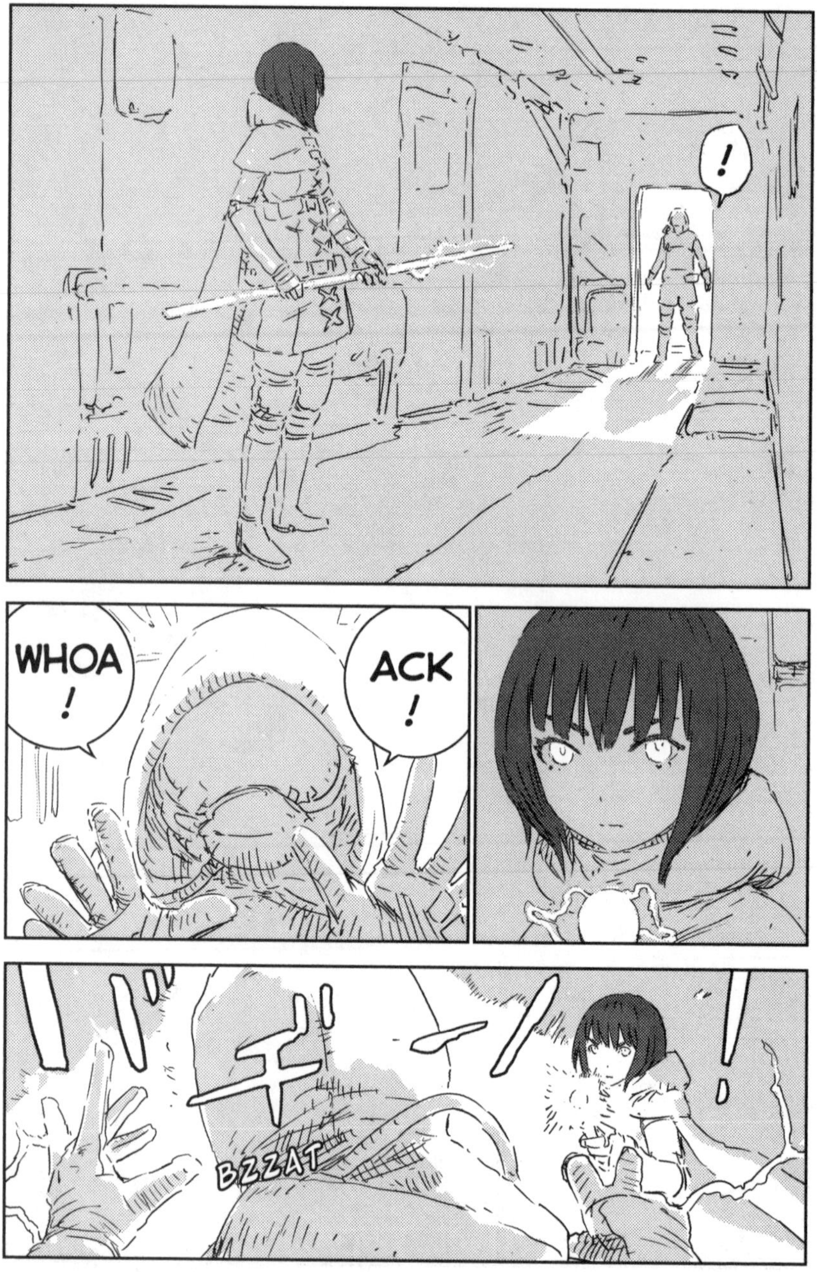
!
ACK!
WHOA!
BZZAT

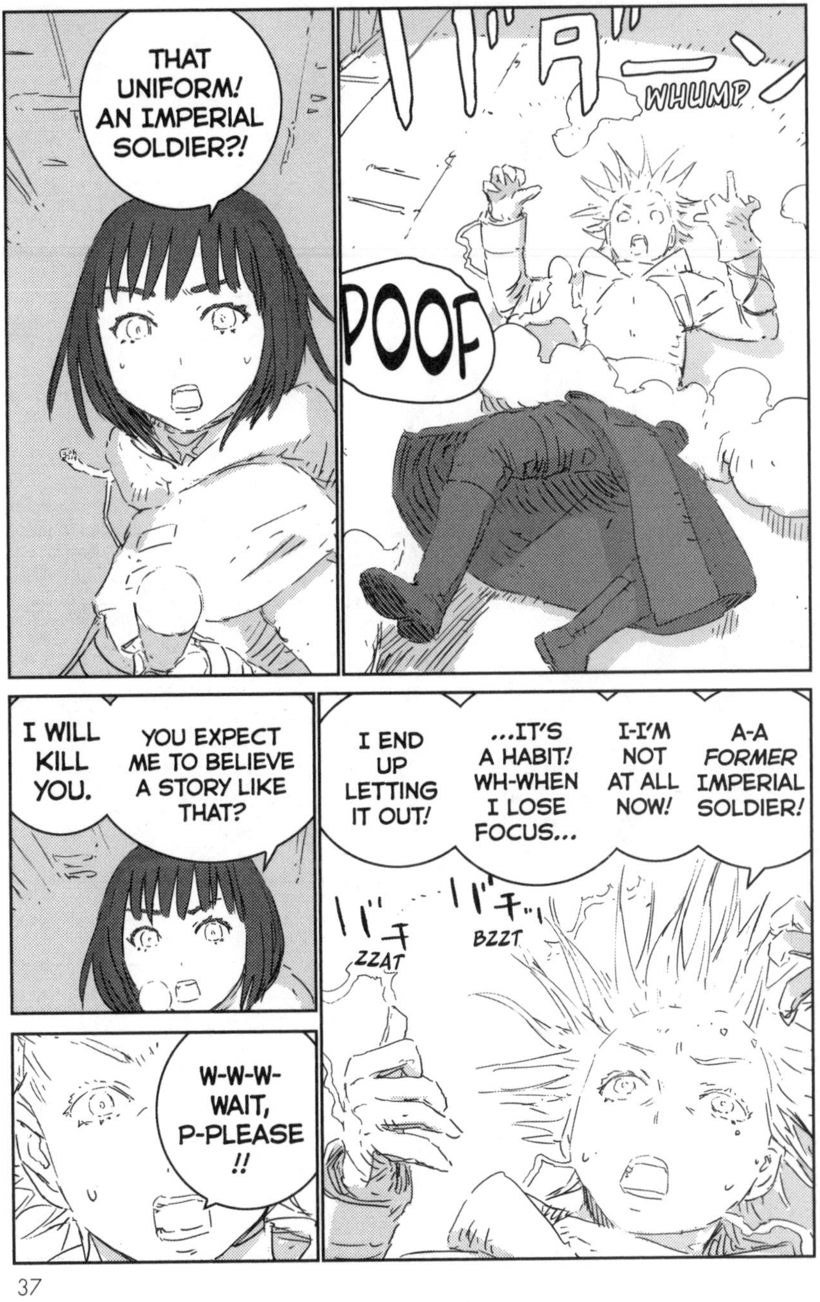
WHUMP
POOF
THAT UNIFORM! AN IMPERIAL SOLDIER?!
A-A FORMER IMPERIAL SOLDIER!
I-I'M NOT AT ALL NOW!
...IT'S A HABIT! WH-WHEN I LOSE FOCUS...
I END UP LETTING IT OUT!
BZZT
ZZAT
YOU EXPECT ME TO BELIEVE A STORY LIKE THAT?
I WILL KILL YOU.
W-W-W-WAIT, P-PLEASE!!

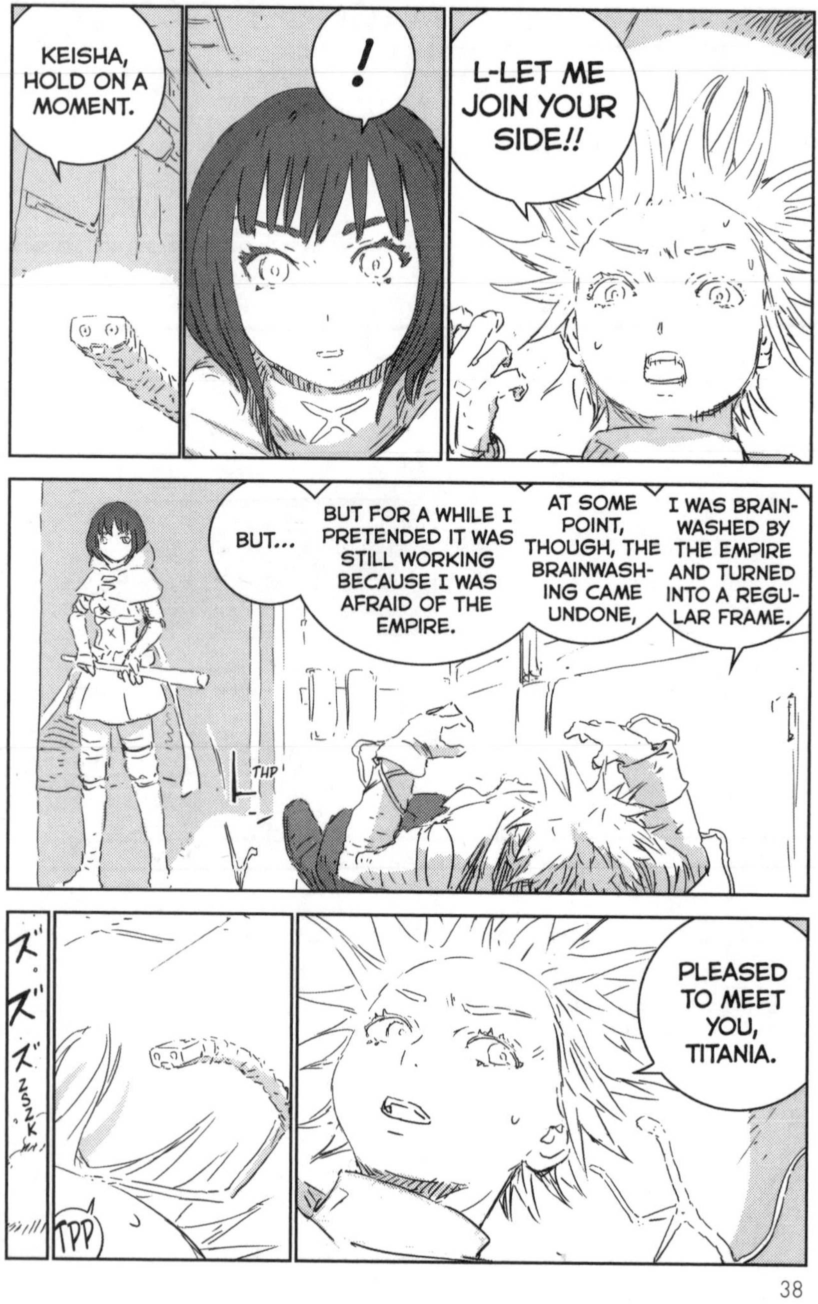
L-LET ME JOIN YOUR SIDE!!
!
KEISHA, HOLD ON A MOMENT.
I WAS BRAIN-WASHED BY THE EMPIRE AND TURNED INTO A REGU-LAR FRAME.
AT SOME POINT, THOUGH, THE BRAINWASH-ING CAME UNDONE,
BUT FOR A WHILE I PRETENDED IT WAS STILL WORKING BECAUSE I WAS AFRAID OF THE EMPIRE.
BUT...
THP
PLEASED TO MEET YOU, TITANIA.
ズズズ
ZSZK
TPP

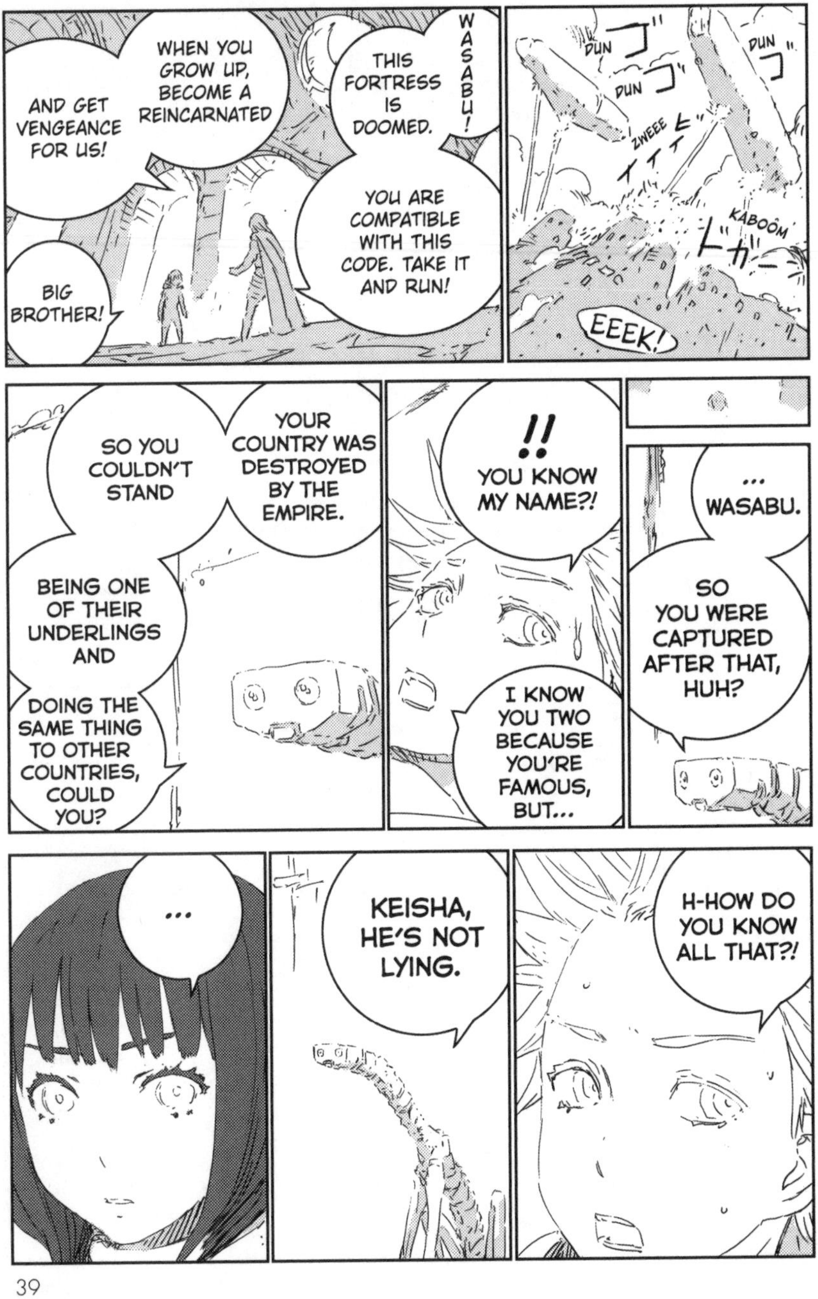
DUN ゴ
DUN ゴ
DUN ゴ
ZWEEE ビイイイ
KABOOM ドガー
EEEK!
WASABU!
THIS FORTRESS IS DOOMED.
YOU ARE COMPATIBLE WITH THIS CODE. TAKE IT AND RUN!
WHEN YOU GROW UP, BECOME A REINCARNATED
AND GET VENGEANCE FOR US!
BIG BROTHER!
... WASABU.
SO YOU WERE CAPTURED AFTER THAT, HUH?
!! YOU KNOW MY NAME?!
I KNOW YOU TWO BECAUSE YOU'RE FAMOUS, BUT...
YOUR COUNTRY WAS DESTROYED BY THE EMPIRE.
SO YOU COULDN'T STAND
BEING ONE OF THEIR UNDERLINGS AND
DOING THE SAME THING TO OTHER COUNTRIES, COULD YOU?
H-HOW DO YOU KNOW ALL THAT?!
KEISHA, HE'S NOT LYING.
...

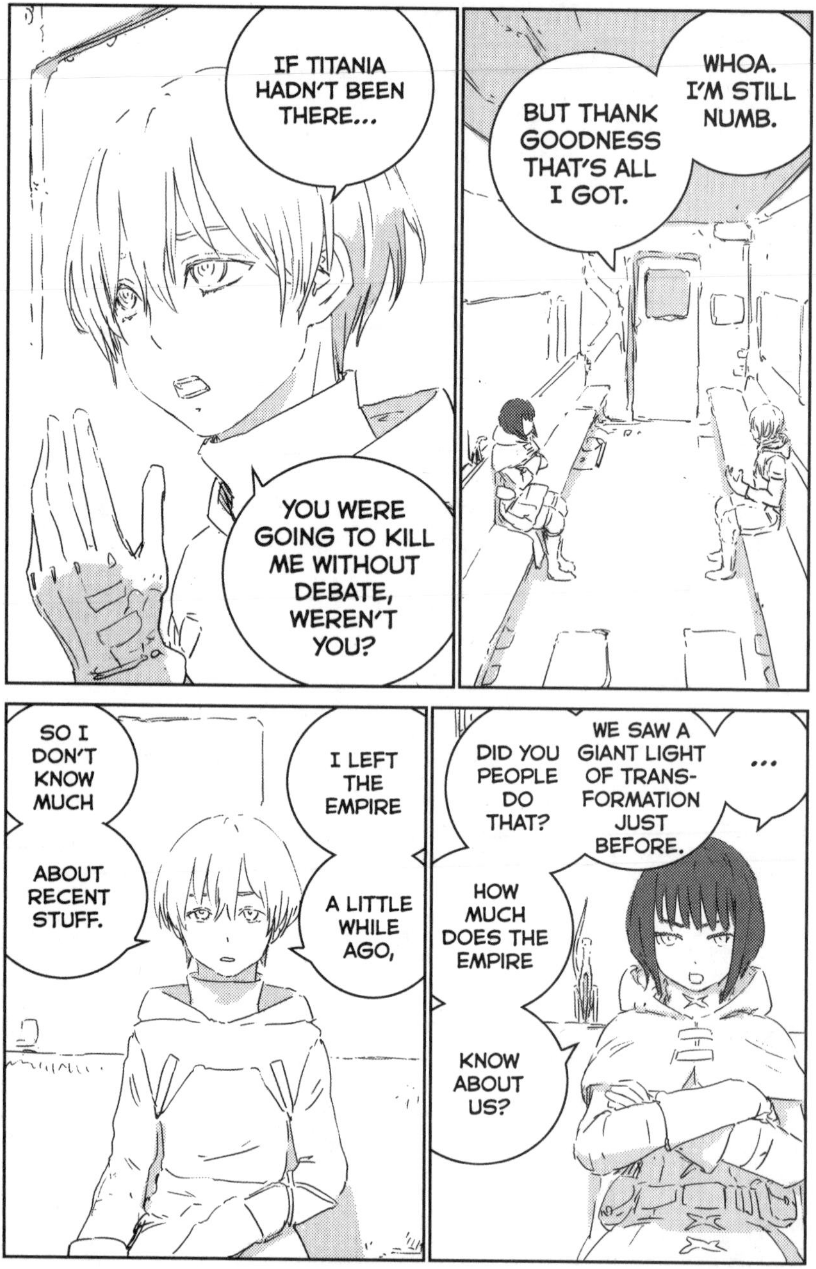
WHOA. I'M STILL NUMB.
BUT THANK GOODNESS THAT'S ALL I GOT.
IF TITANIA HADN'T BEEN THERE...
YOU WERE GOING TO KILL ME WITHOUT DEBATE, WEREN'T YOU?
...
WE SAW A GIANT LIGHT OF TRANS-FORMATION JUST BEFORE.
DID YOU PEOPLE DO THAT?
HOW MUCH DOES THE EMPIRE
KNOW ABOUT US?
I LEFT THE EMPIRE
A LITTLE WHILE AGO,
SO I DON'T KNOW MUCH
ABOUT RECENT STUFF.

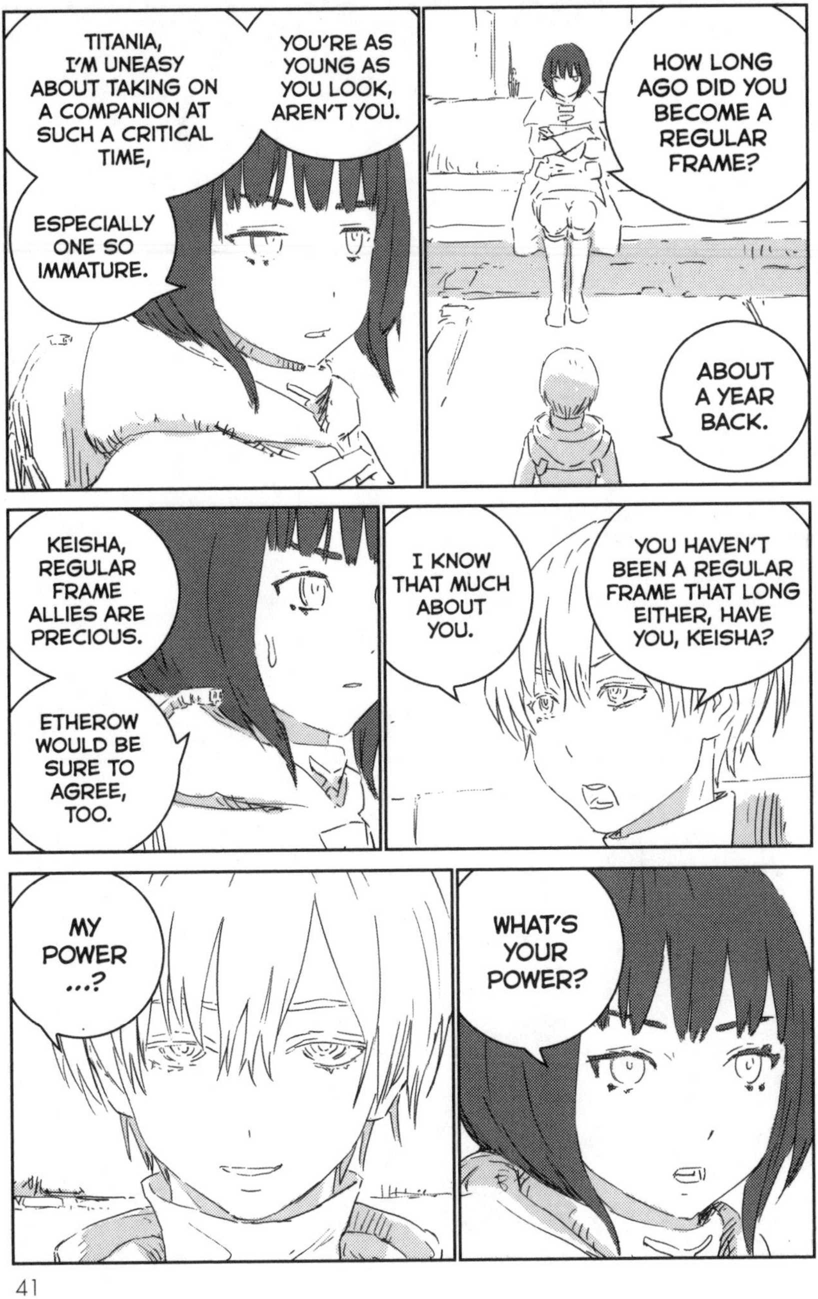
HOW LONG AGO DID YOU BECOME A REGULAR FRAME?
ABOUT A YEAR BACK.
YOU'RE AS YOUNG AS YOU LOOK, AREN'T YOU.
TITANIA, I'M UNEASY ABOUT TAKING ON A COMPANION AT SUCH A CRITICAL TIME,
ESPECIALLY ONE SO IMMATURE.
YOU HAVEN'T BEEN A REGULAR FRAME THAT LONG EITHER, HAVE YOU, KEISHA?
I KNOW THAT MUCH ABOUT YOU.
KEISHA, REGULAR FRAME ALLIES ARE PRECIOUS.
ETHEROW WOULD BE SURE TO AGREE, TOO.
WHAT'S YOUR POWER?
MY POWER ...?

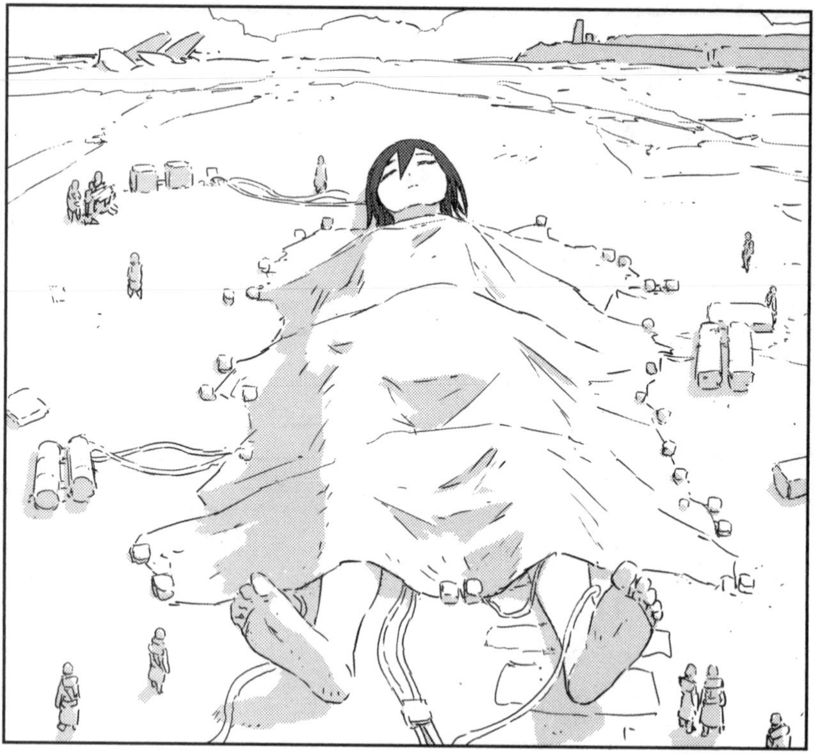

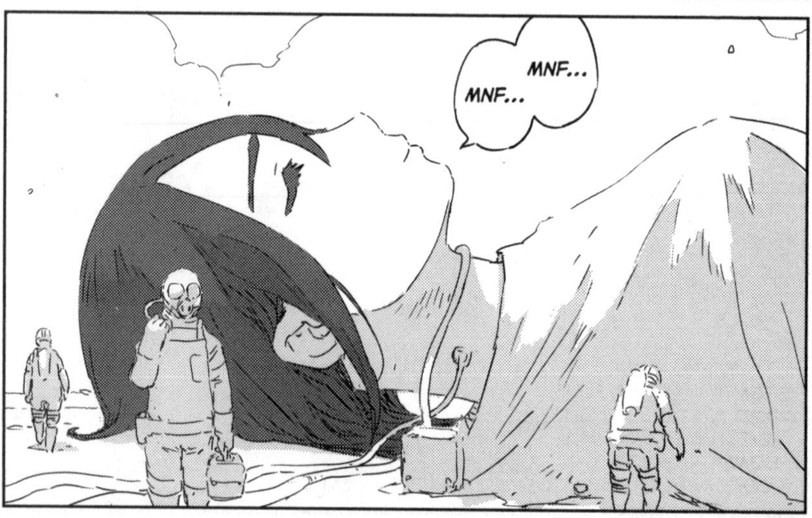
MNF... MNF...

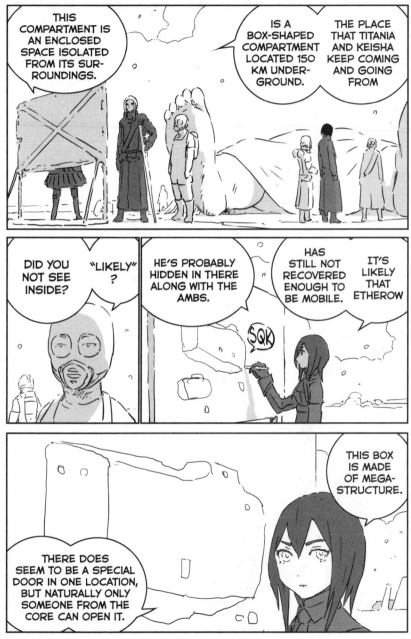

THE PLACE THAT TITANIA AND KEISHA KEEP COMING AND GOING FROM
IS A BOX-SHAPED COMPARTMENT LOCATED 150 KM UNDER-GROUND.
THIS COMPARTMENT IS AN ENCLOSED SPACE ISOLATED FROM ITS SUR-ROUNDINGS.
IT'S LIKELY THAT ETHEROW
HAS STILL NOT RECOVERED ENOUGH TO BE MOBILE.
HE'S PROBABLY HIDDEN IN THERE ALONG WITH THE AMBS.
SQK
"LIKELY"?
DID YOU NOT SEE INSIDE?
THIS BOX IS MADE OF MEGA-STRUCTURE.
THERE DOES SEEM TO BE A SPECIAL DOOR IN ONE LOCATION, BUT NATURALLY ONLY SOMEONE FROM THE CORE CAN OPEN IT.

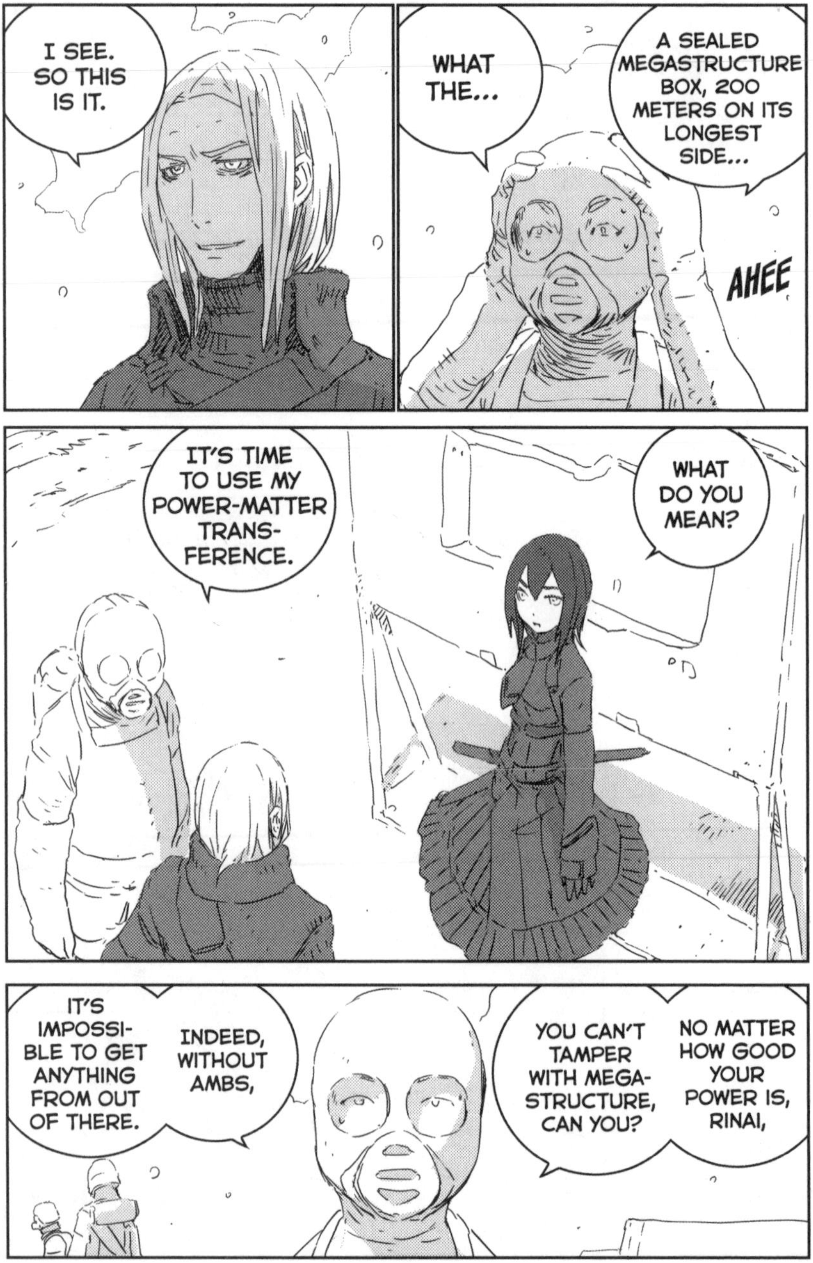
A SEALED MEGASTRUCTURE BOX, 200 METERS ON ITS LONGEST SIDE...
WHAT THE...
AHEE
I SEE. SO THIS IS IT.
WHAT DO YOU MEAN?
IT'S TIME TO USE MY POWER-MATTER TRANSFERENCE.
NO MATTER HOW GOOD YOUR POWER IS, RINAI,
YOU CAN'T TAMPER WITH MEGA-STRUCTURE, CAN YOU?
INDEED, WITHOUT AMBS,
IT'S IMPOSSIBLE TO GET ANYTHING FROM OUT OF THERE.

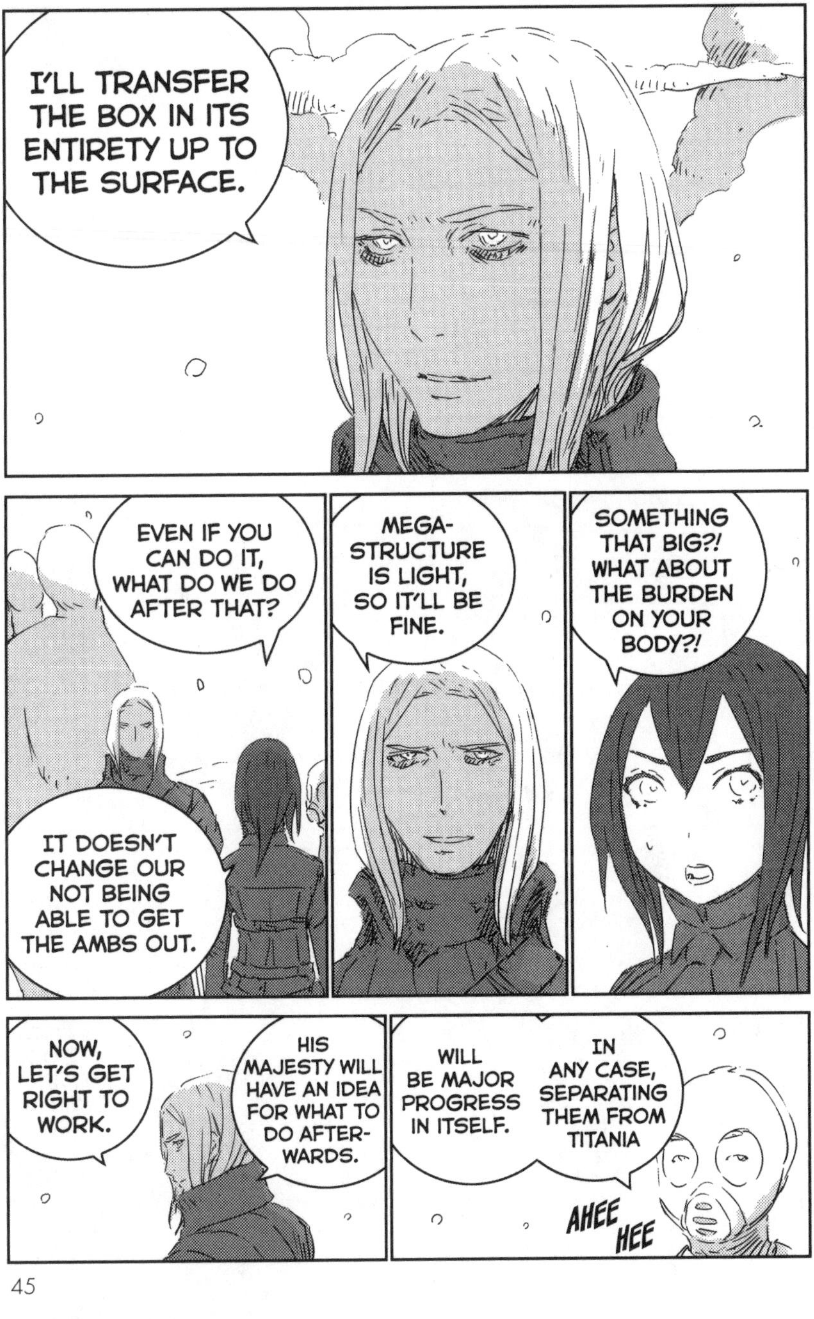
I'LL TRANSFER THE BOX IN ITS ENTIRETY UP TO THE SURFACE.
SOMETHING THAT BIG?! WHAT ABOUT THE BURDEN ON YOUR BODY?!
MEGA-STRUCTURE IS LIGHT, SO IT'LL BE FINE.
EVEN IF YOU CAN DO IT, WHAT DO WE DO AFTER THAT?
IT DOESN'T CHANGE OUR NOT BEING ABLE TO GET THE AMBS OUT.
IN ANY CASE, SEPARATING THEM FROM TITANIA
WILL BE MAJOR PROGRESS IN ITSELF.
AHEE HEE
HIS MAJESTY WILL HAVE AN IDEA FOR WHAT TO DO AFTER-WARDS.
NOW, LET'S GET RIGHT TO WORK.

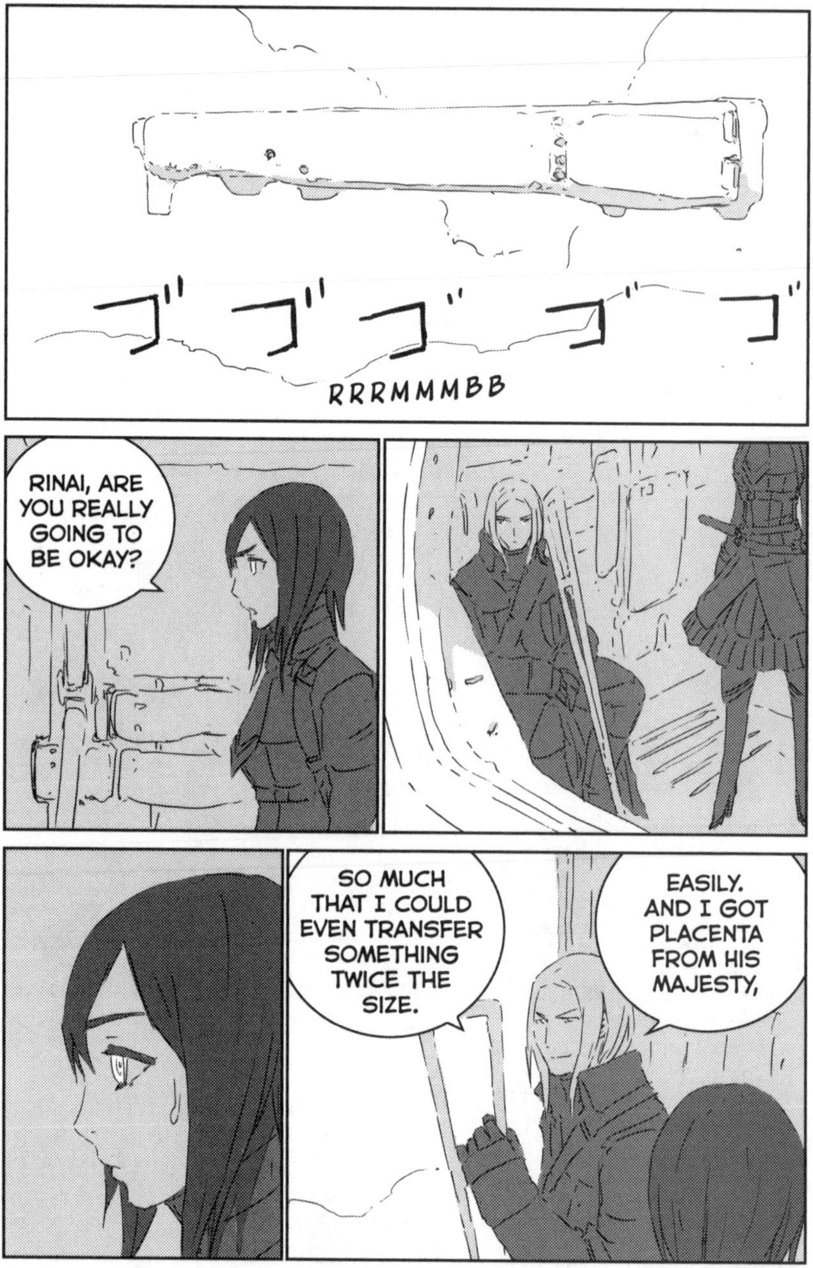
ゴゴゴゴゴ
RRRMMMBB
RINAI, ARE YOU REALLY GOING TO BE OKAY?
EASILY. AND I GOT PLACENTA FROM HIS MAJESTY,
SO MUCH THAT I COULD EVEN TRANSFER SOMETHING TWICE THE SIZE.

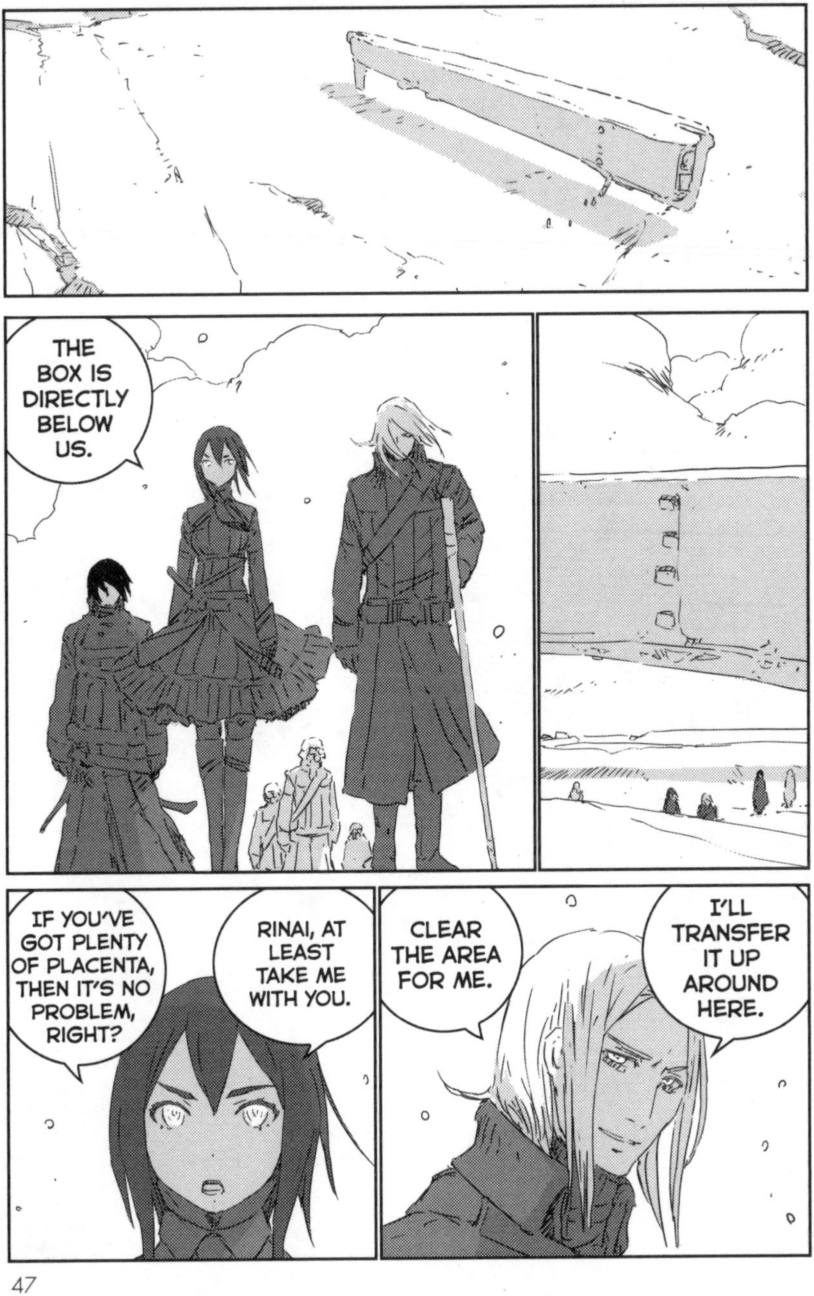
THE BOX IS DIRECTLY BELOW US.
I'LL TRANSFER IT UP AROUND HERE.
CLEAR THE AREA FOR ME.
RINAI, AT LEAST TAKE ME WITH YOU.
IF YOU'VE GOT PLENTY OF PLACENTA, THEN IT'S NO PROBLEM, RIGHT?

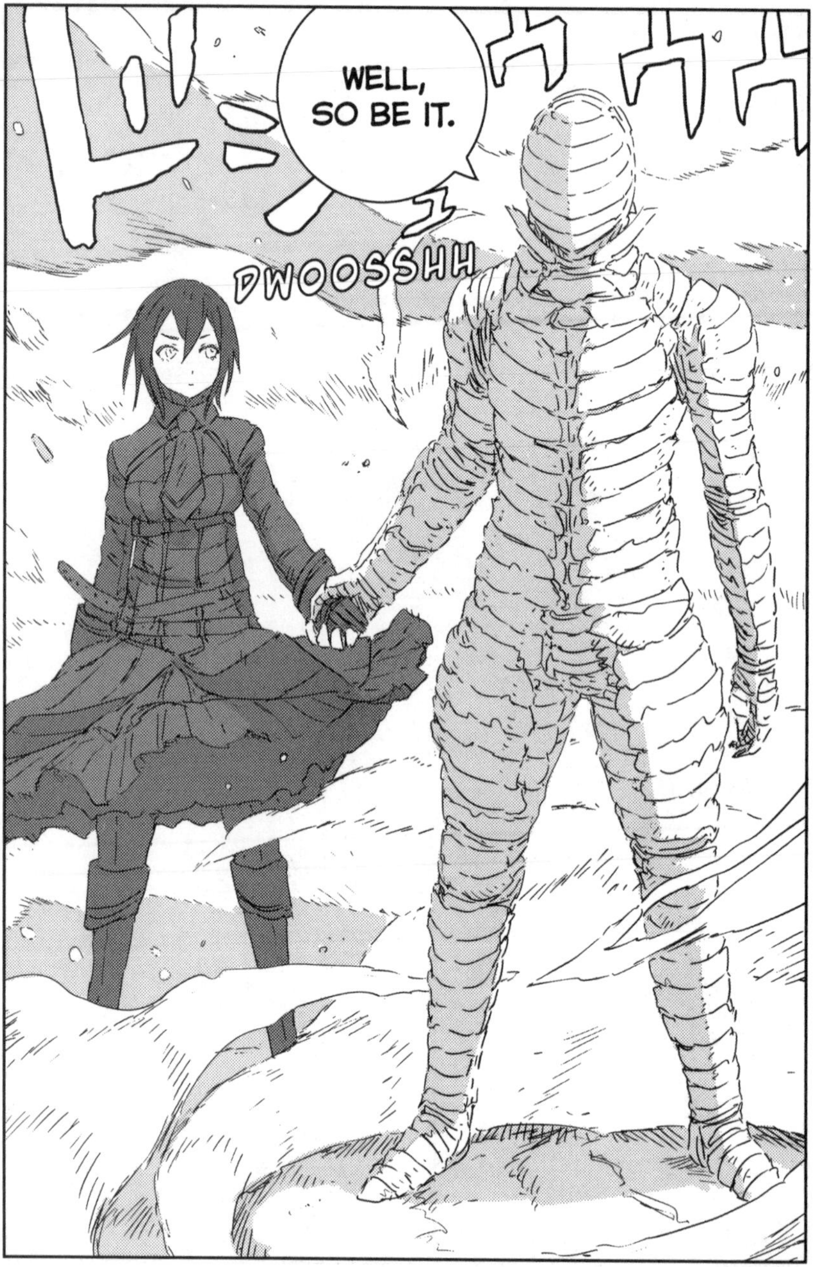
WELL, SO BE IT.
DWOOSSHH

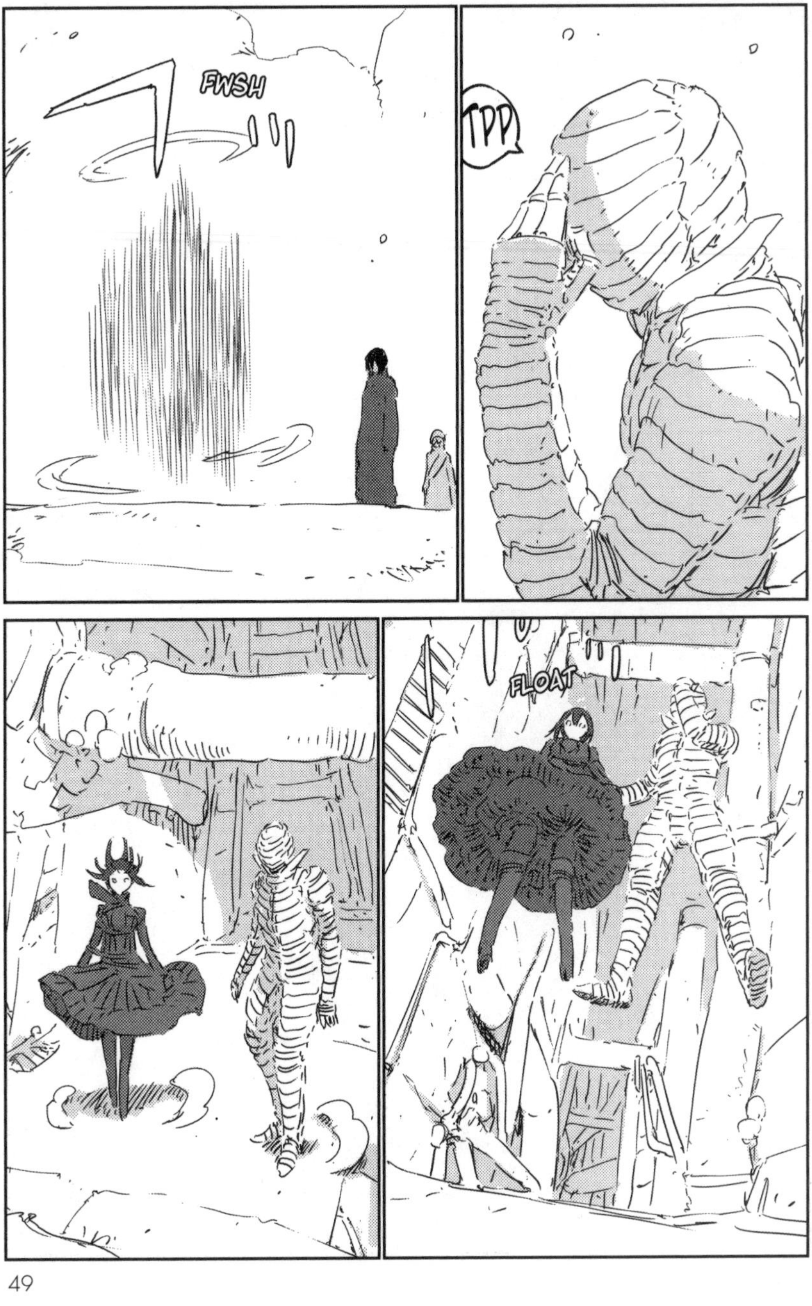
TPP
FWSH
FLOAT

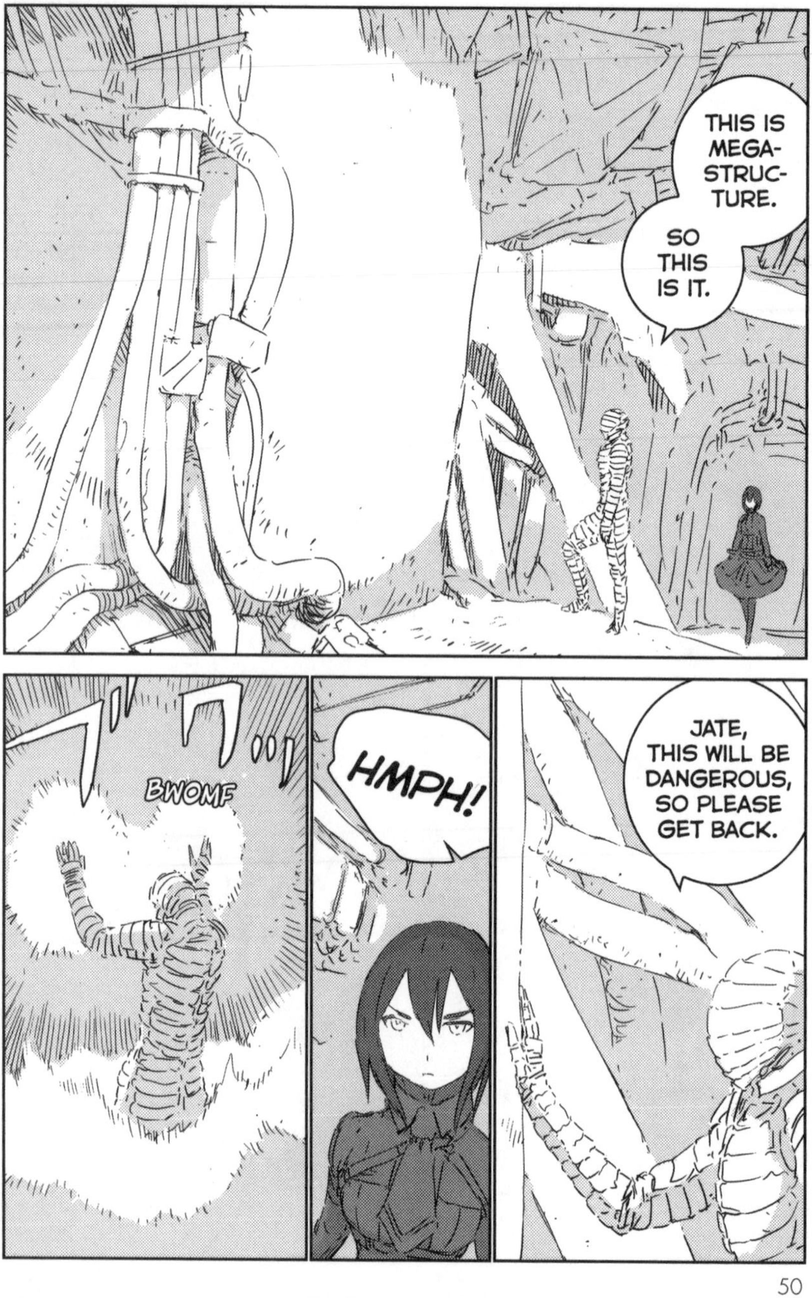
THIS IS MEGA-STRUCTURE.
SO THIS IS IT.
JATE, THIS WILL BE DANGEROUS, SO PLEASE GET BACK.
HMPH!
BWOMF

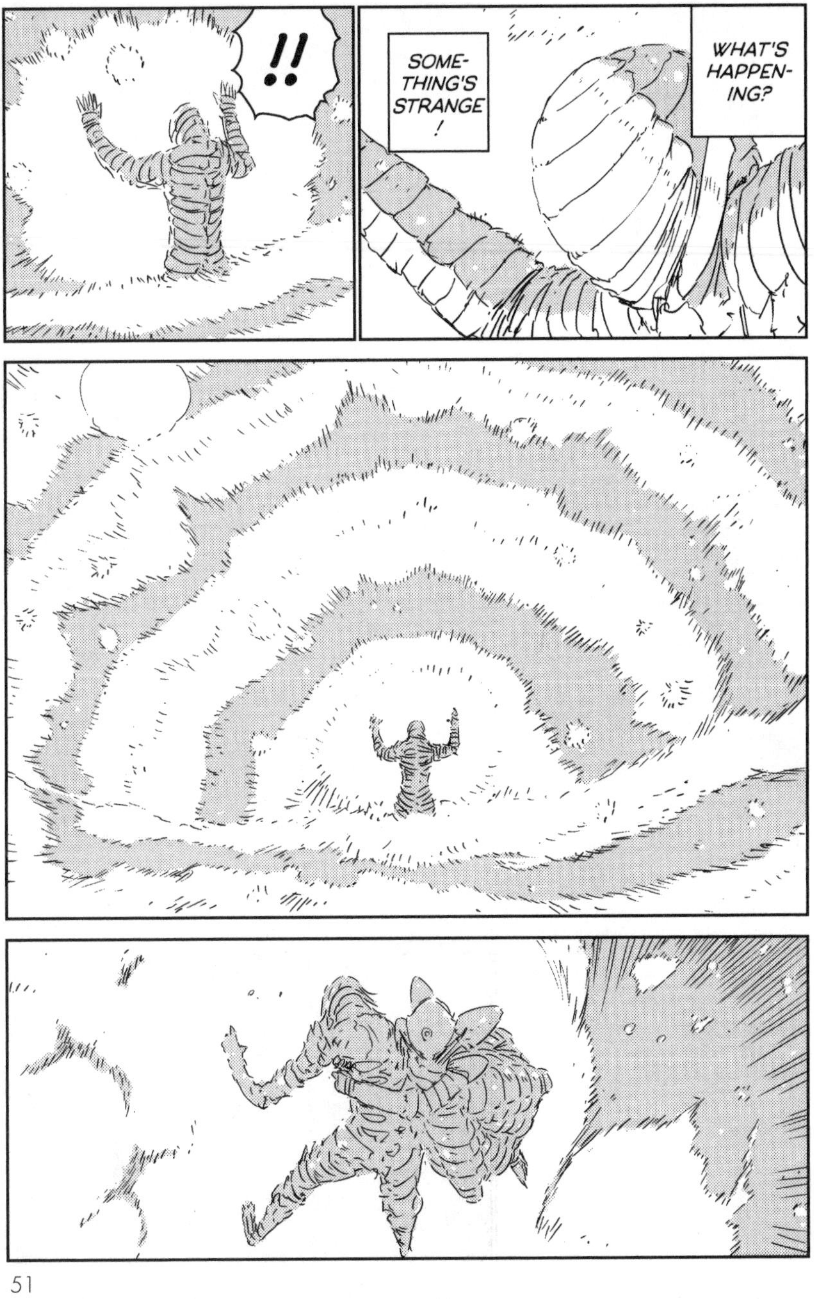
WHAT'S HAPPEN-ING?
SOME-THING'S STRANGE !
!!

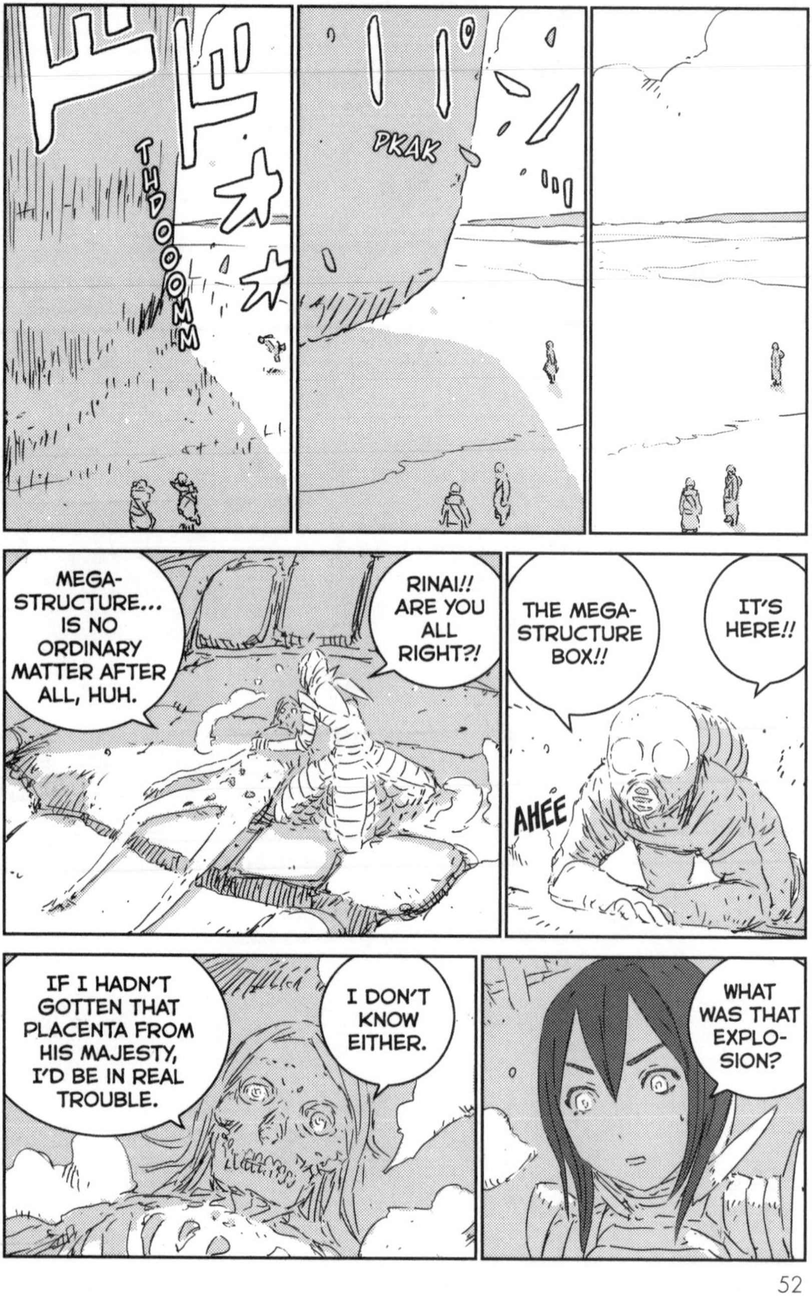
PKAK
ドドオオ
THDOOOOMM
IT'S HERE!!
THE MEGA-STRUCTURE BOX!!
AHEE
RINAI!! ARE YOU ALL RIGHT?!
MEGA-STRUCTURE... IS NO ORDINARY MATTER AFTER ALL, HUH.
WHAT WAS THAT EXPLOSION?
I DON'T KNOW EITHER.
IF I HADN'T GOTTEN THAT PLACENTA FROM HIS MAJESTY, I'D BE IN REAL TROUBLE.

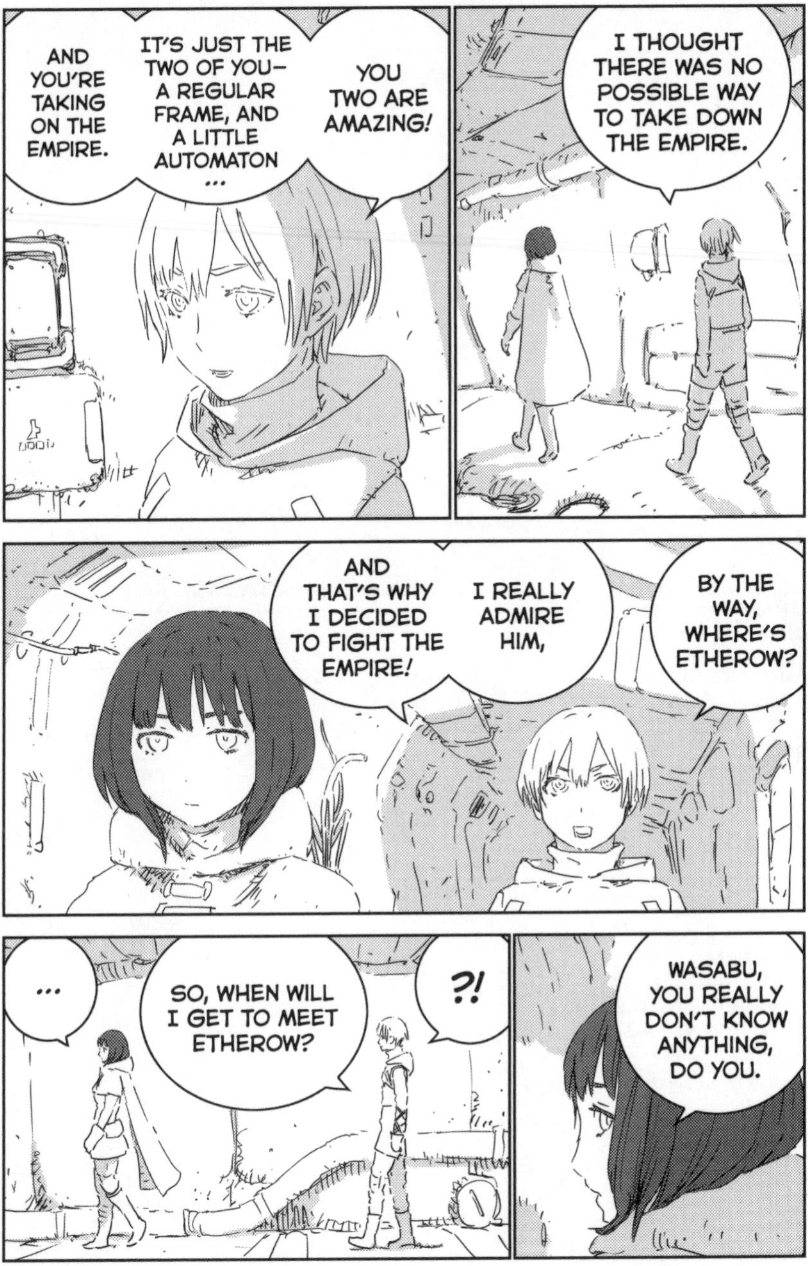
I THOUGHT THERE WAS NO POSSIBLE WAY TO TAKE DOWN THE EMPIRE.
YOU TWO ARE AMAZING!
IT'S JUST THE TWO OF YOU— A REGULAR FRAME, AND A LITTLE AUTOMATON ...
AND YOU'RE TAKING ON THE EMPIRE.
BY THE WAY, WHERE'S ETHEROW?
I REALLY ADMIRE HIM,
AND THAT'S WHY I DECIDED TO FIGHT THE EMPIRE!
WASABU, YOU REALLY DON'T KNOW ANYTHING, DO YOU.
?!
SO, WHEN WILL I GET TO MEET ETHEROW?
...

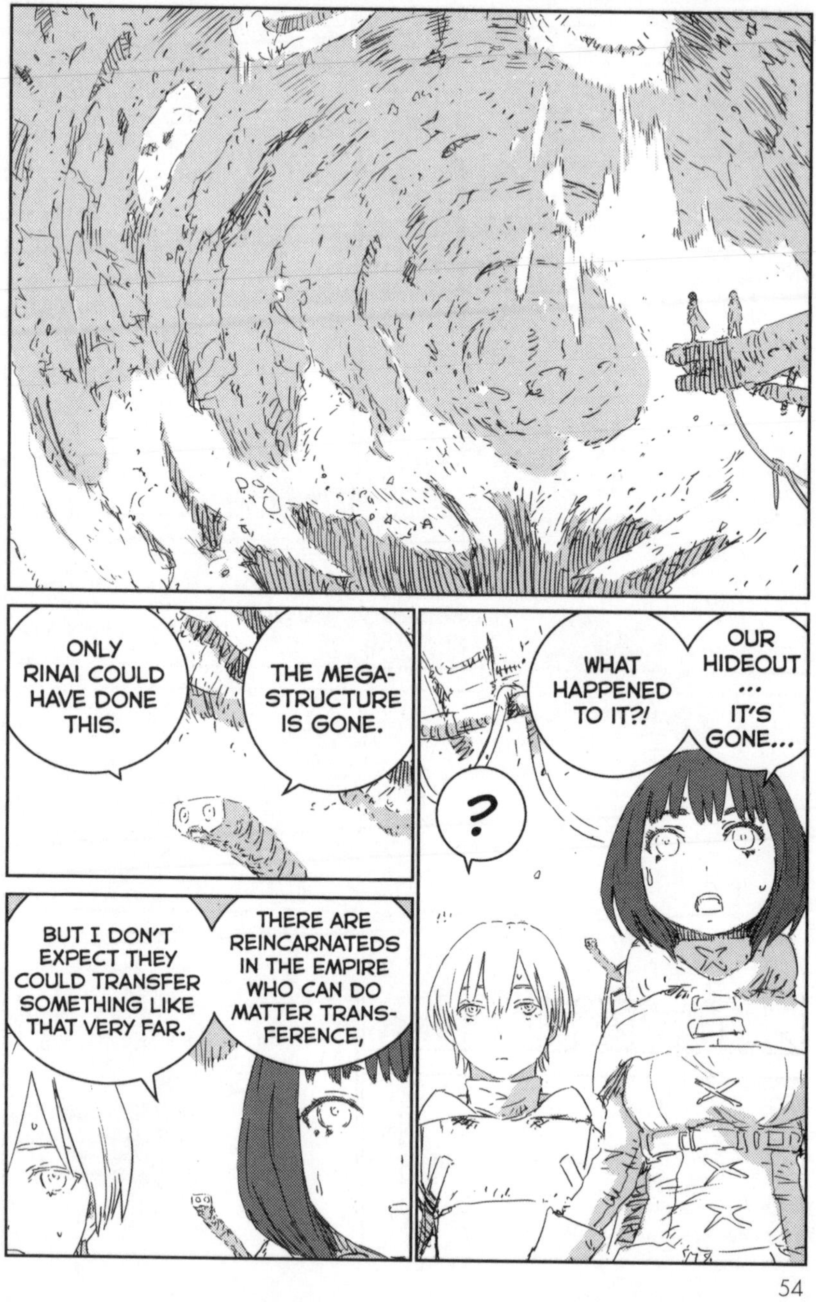
OUR HIDEOUT... IT'S GONE...
WHAT HAPPENED TO IT?!
?
THE MEGA-STRUCTURE IS GONE.
ONLY RINAI COULD HAVE DONE THIS.
THERE ARE REINCARNATEDS IN THE EMPIRE WHO CAN DO MATTER TRANS-FERENCE,
BUT I DON'T EXPECT THEY COULD TRANSFER SOMETHING LIKE THAT VERY FAR.

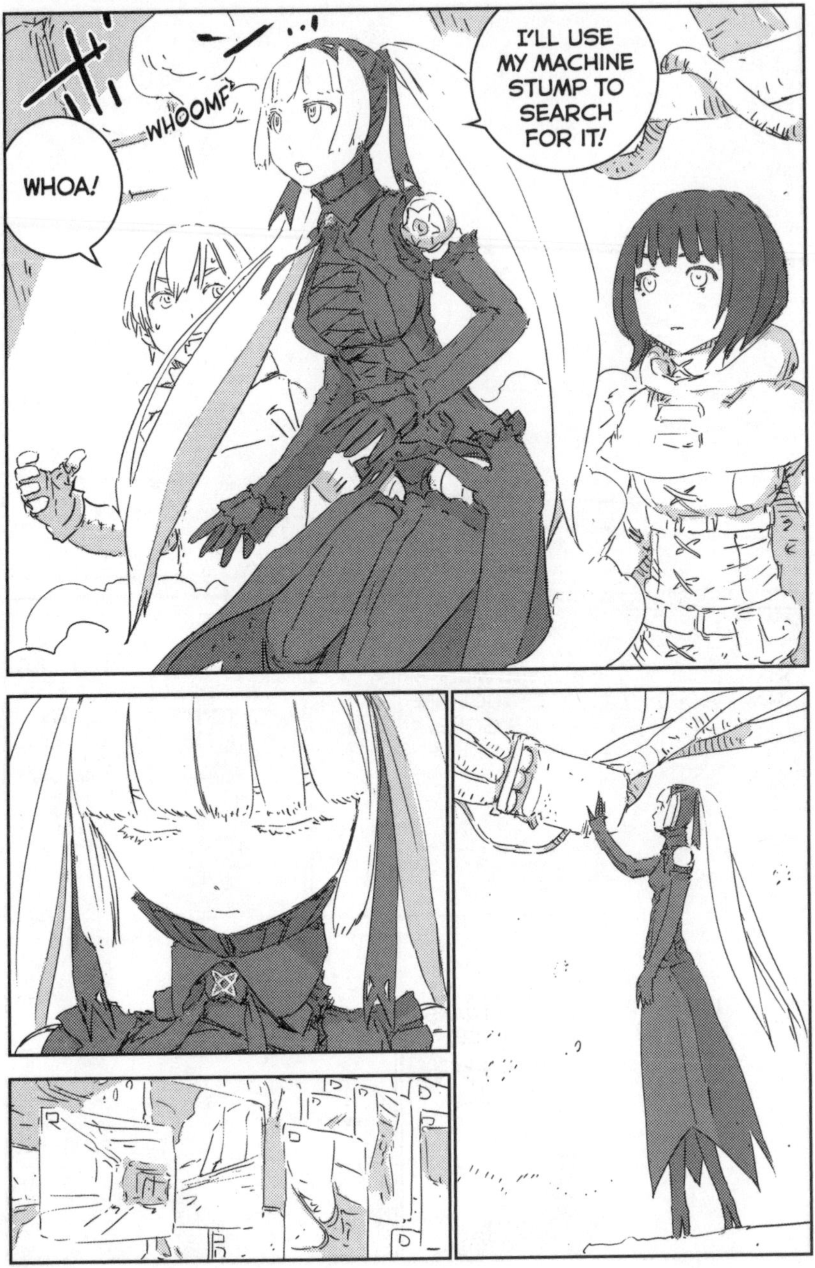
I'LL USE MY MACHINE STUMP TO SEARCH FOR IT!
WHOOMF
WHOA!

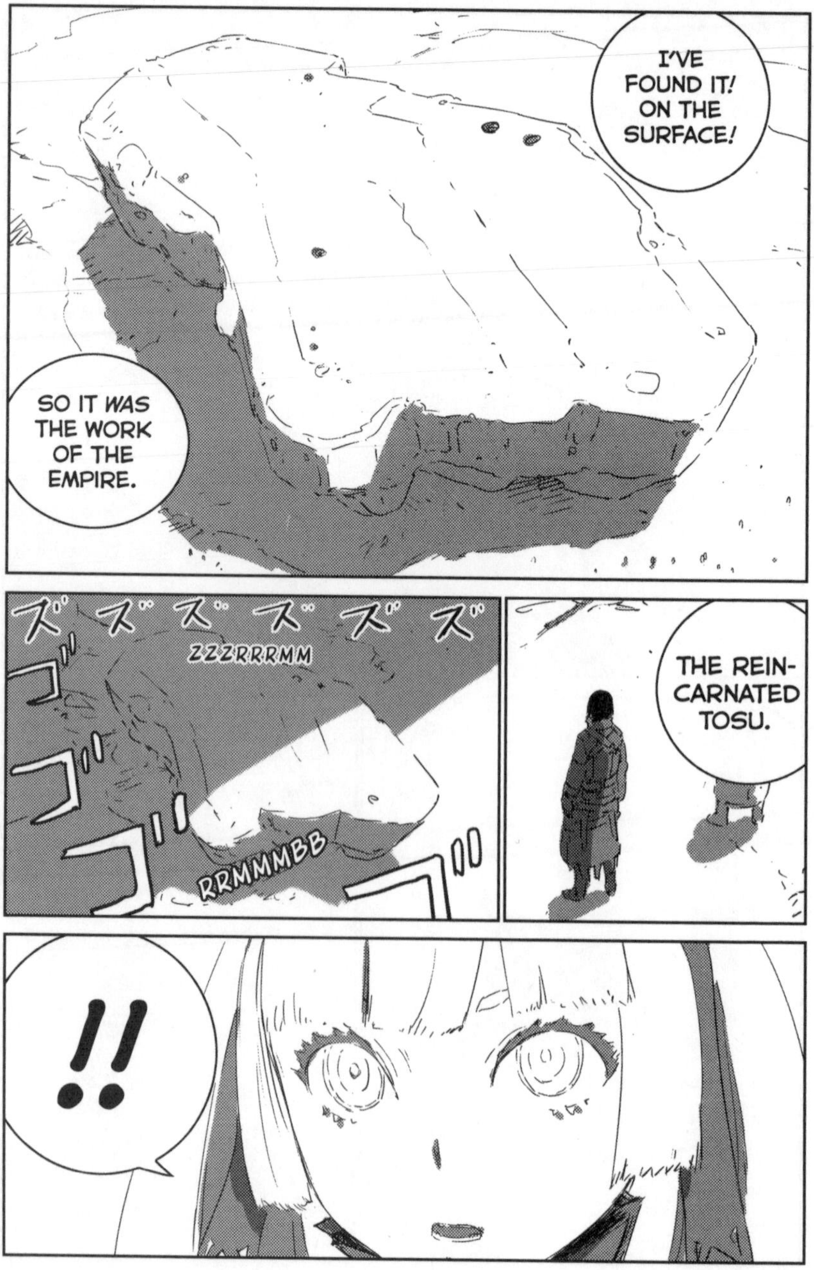
I'VE FOUND IT! ON THE SURFACE!
SO IT WAS THE WORK OF THE EMPIRE.
THE REIN-CARNATED TOSU.
ズズズズズズ
ZZZRRRMM
ゴゴゴゴ
RRMMMBB
!!

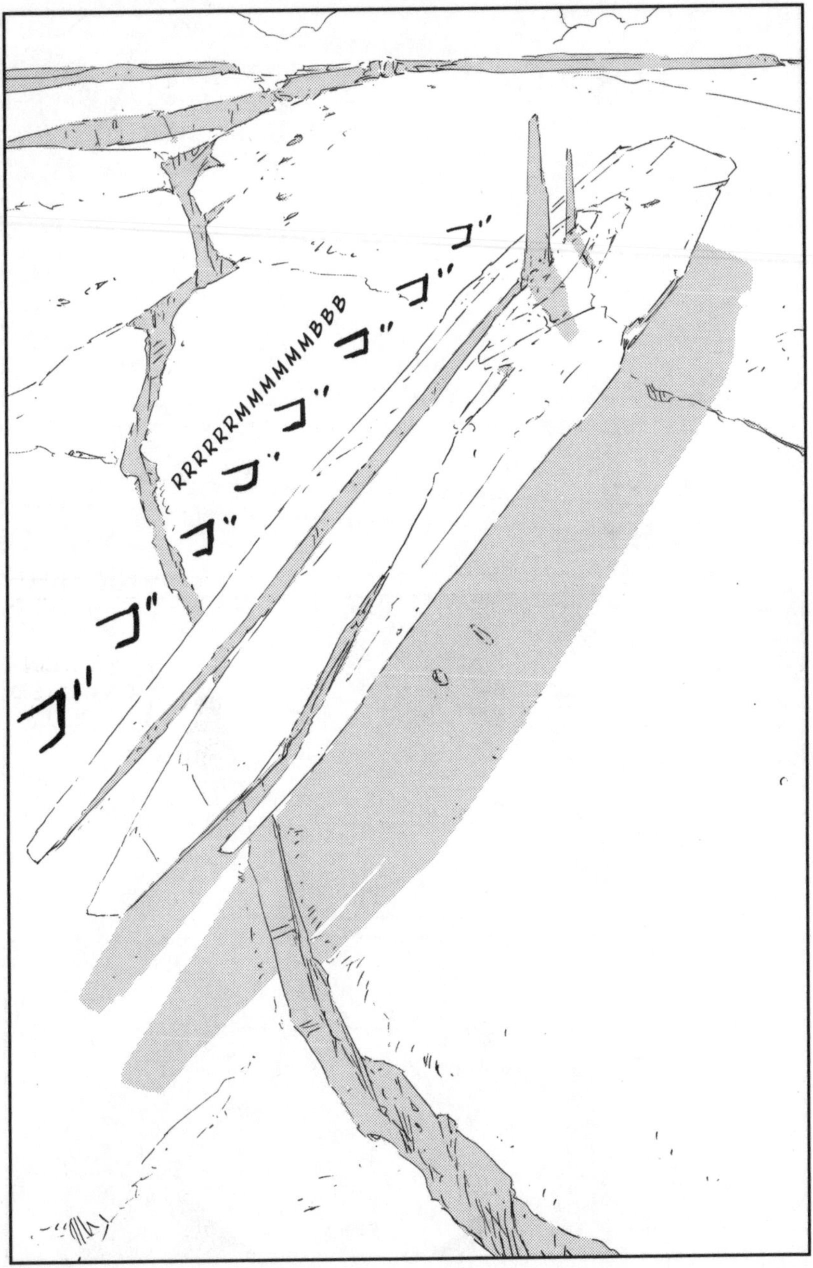
ゴゴゴゴゴゴゴゴ
RRRRRRMMMMMMBBB

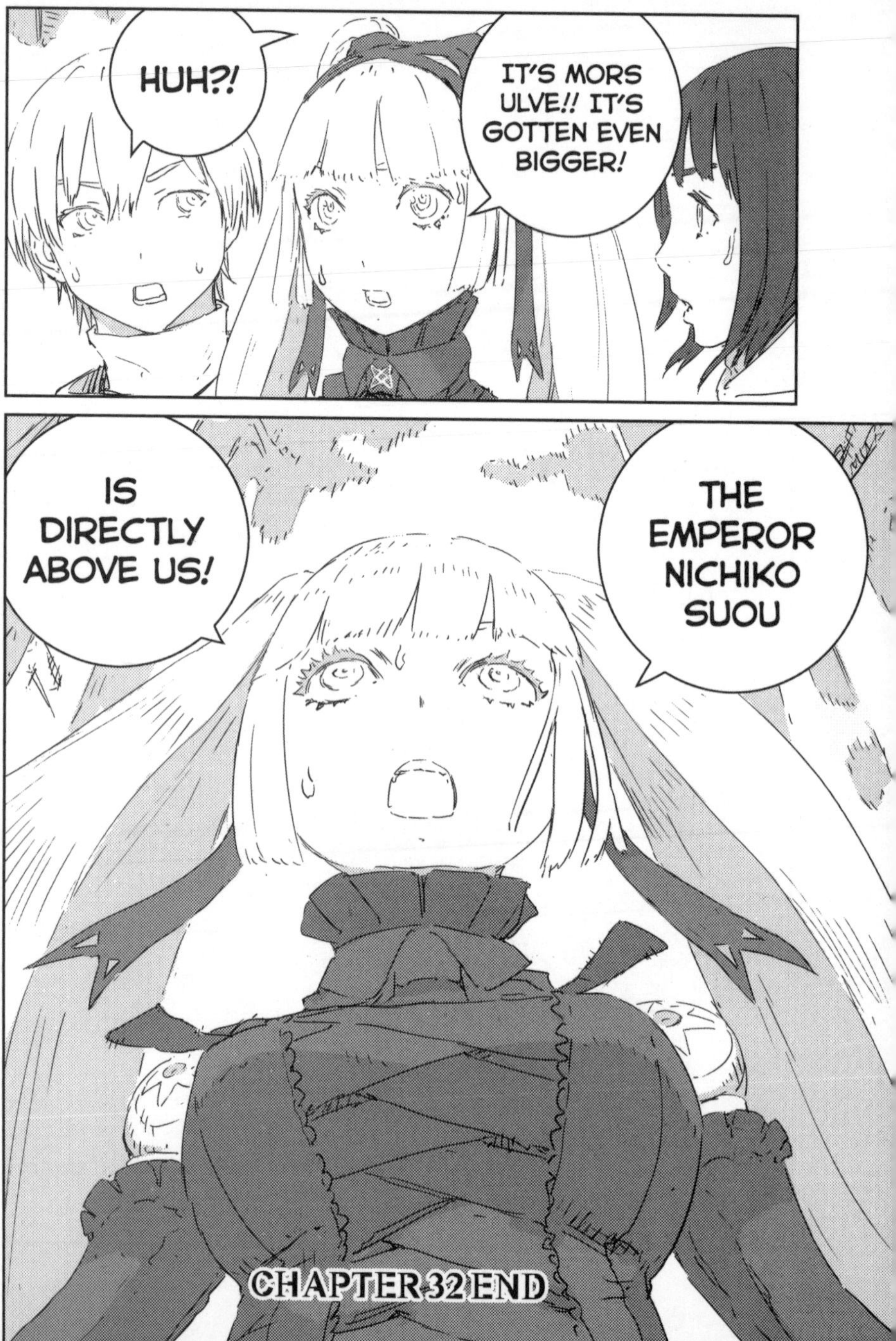
IT'S MORS ULVE!! IT'S GOTTEN EVEN BIGGER!
HUH?!
THE EMPEROR NICHIKO SUOU
IS DIRECTLY ABOVE US!
CHAPTER 32 END

APOSIMZ

X

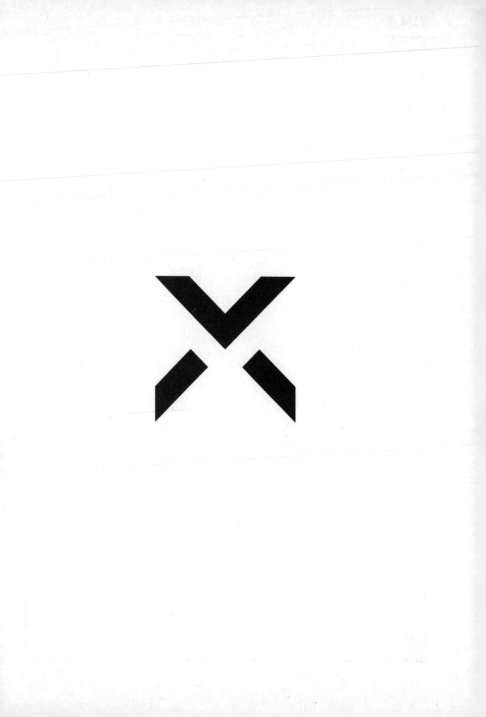

CHAPTER 33

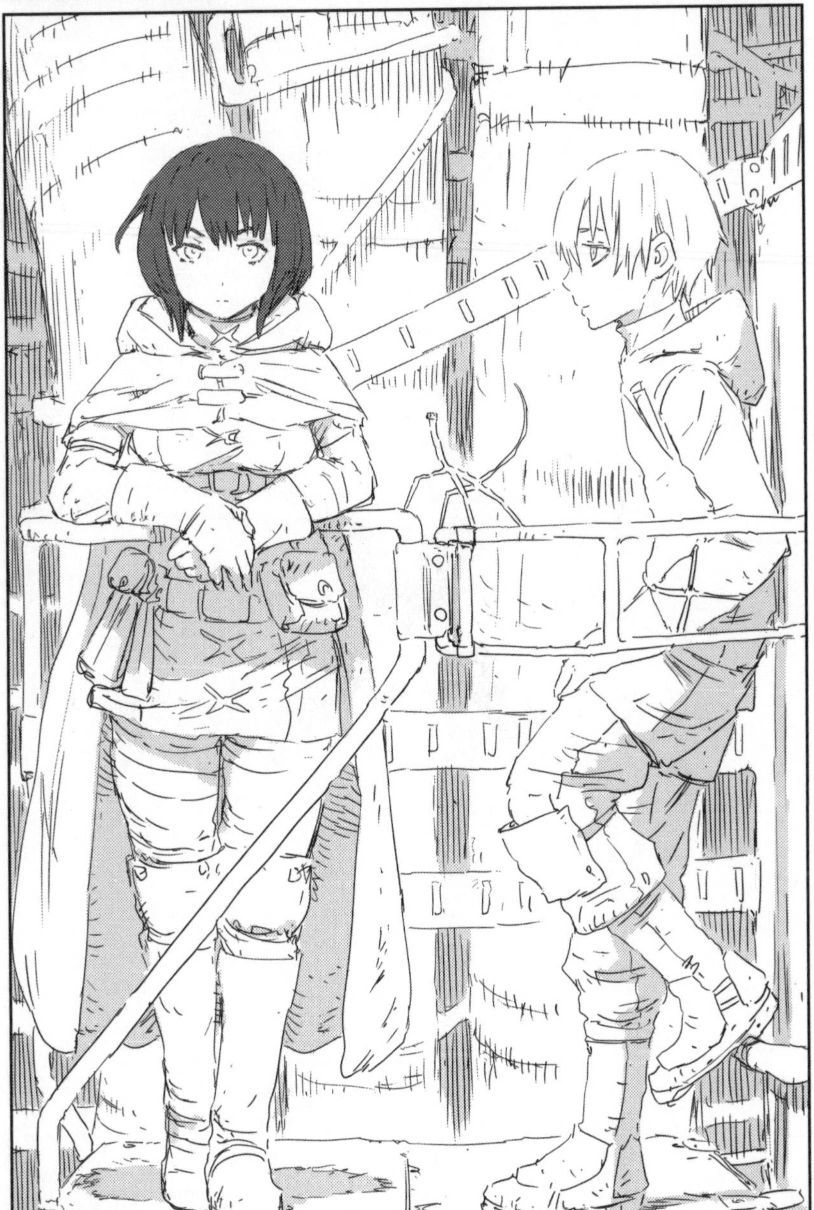

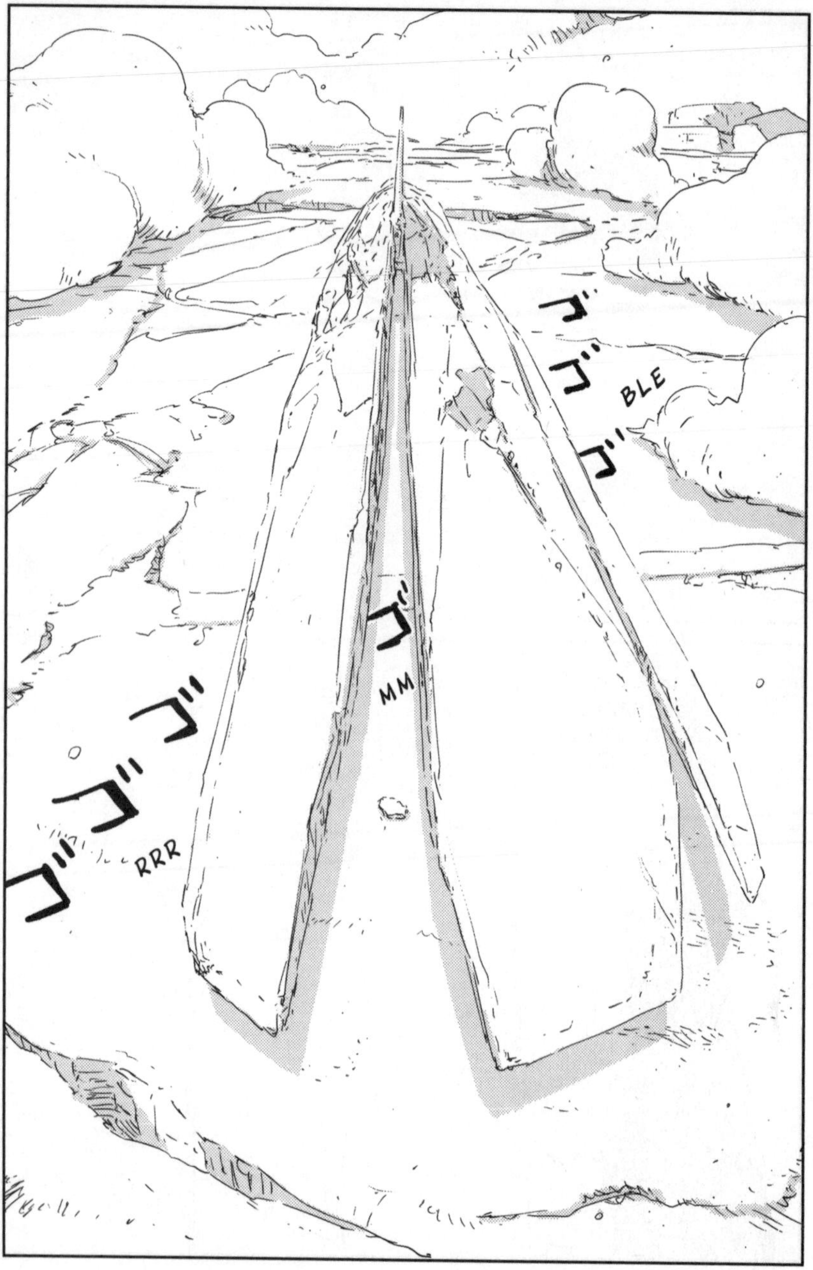
ゴゴ
BLE
ゴ
MM
ゴゴゴ
RRR

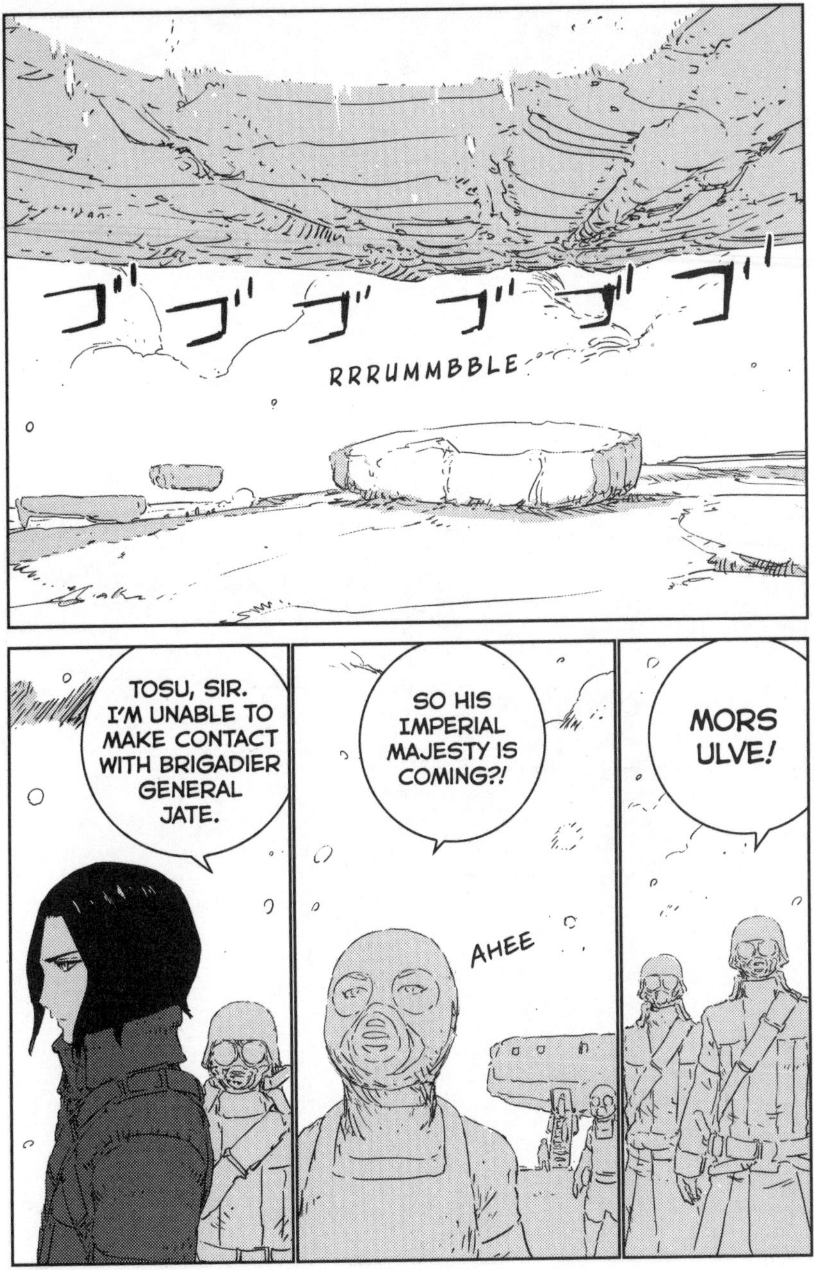
ゴゴゴゴゴゴ
RRRUMMBBLE
MORS ULVE!
SO HIS IMPERIAL MAJESTY IS COMING?!
AHEE
TOSU, SIR. I'M UNABLE TO MAKE CONTACT WITH BRIGADIER GENERAL JATE.

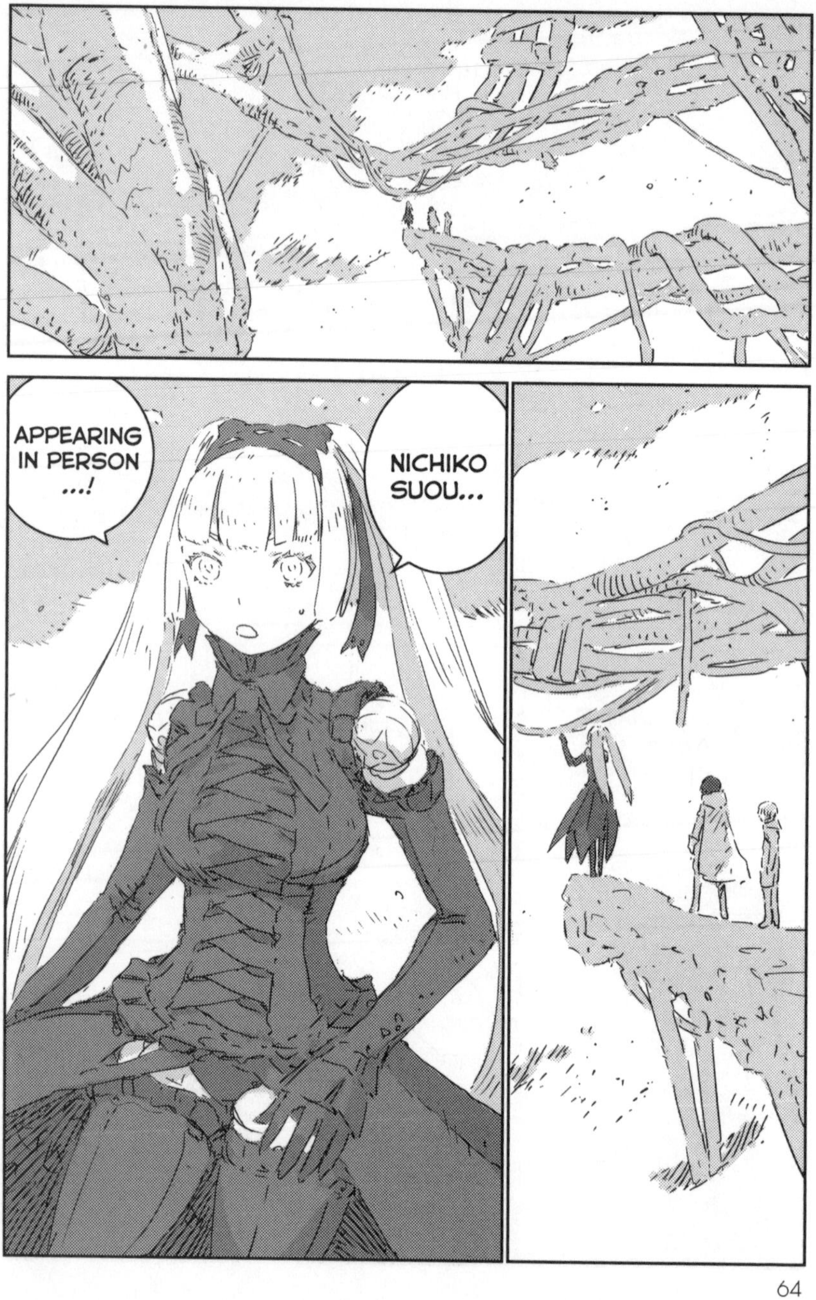
NICHIKO SUOU...
APPEARING IN PERSON ...!

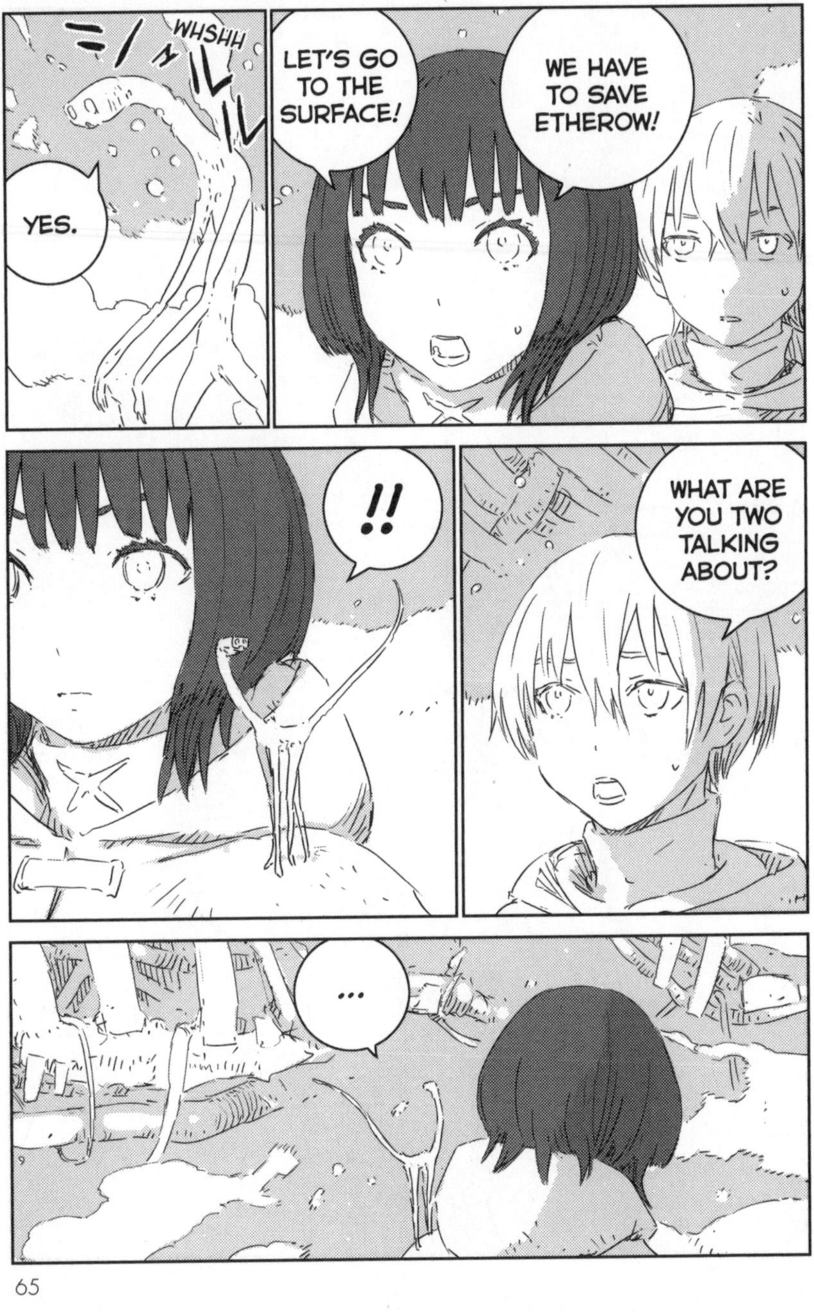
WE HAVE TO SAVE ETHEROW!
LET'S GO TO THE SURFACE!
WHSHH
YES.
WHAT ARE YOU TWO TALKING ABOUT?
!!
...

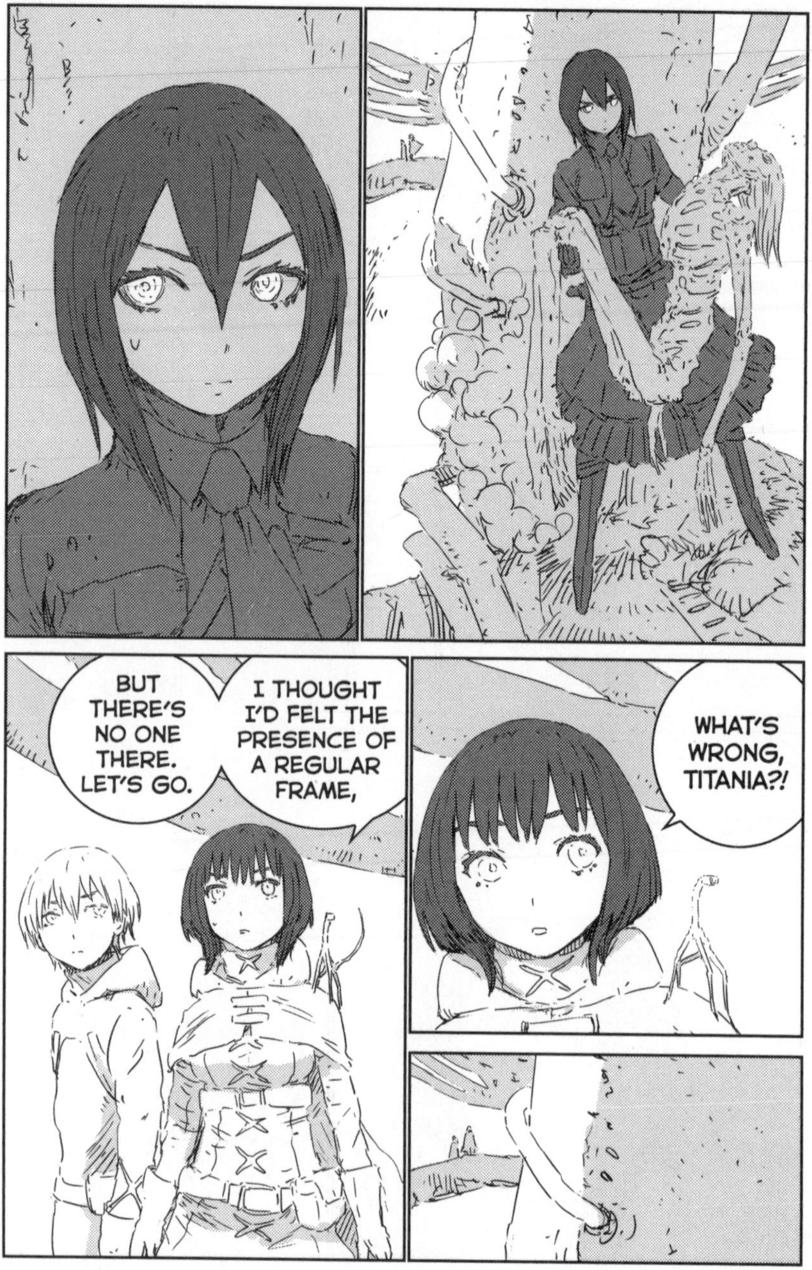
WHAT'S WRONG, TITANIA?!
I THOUGHT I'D FELT THE PRESENCE OF A REGULAR FRAME,
BUT THERE'S NO ONE THERE. LET'S GO.

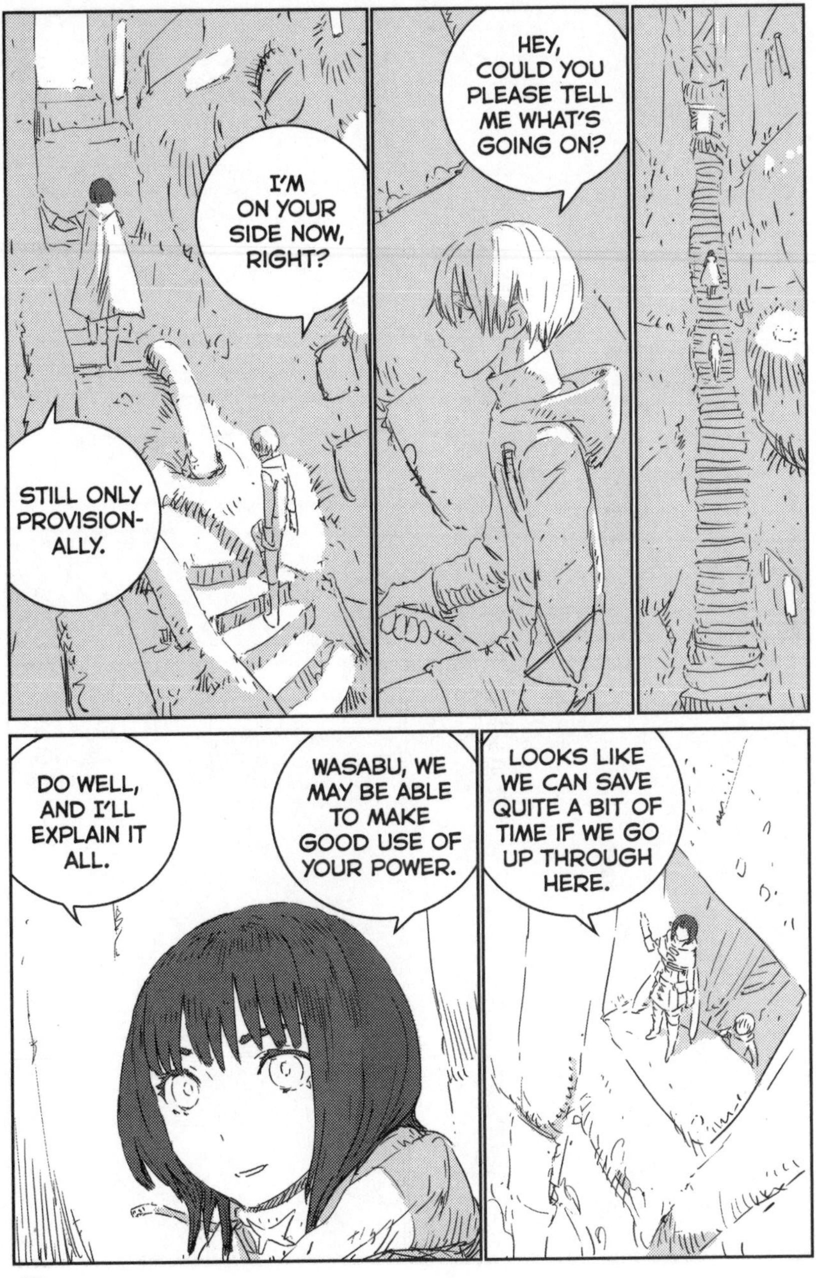
HEY, COULD YOU PLEASE TELL ME WHAT'S GOING ON?
I'M ON YOUR SIDE NOW, RIGHT?
STILL ONLY PROVISION-ALLY.
LOOKS LIKE WE CAN SAVE QUITE A BIT OF TIME IF WE GO UP THROUGH HERE.
WASABU, WE MAY BE ABLE TO MAKE GOOD USE OF YOUR POWER.
DO WELL, AND I'LL EXPLAIN IT ALL.

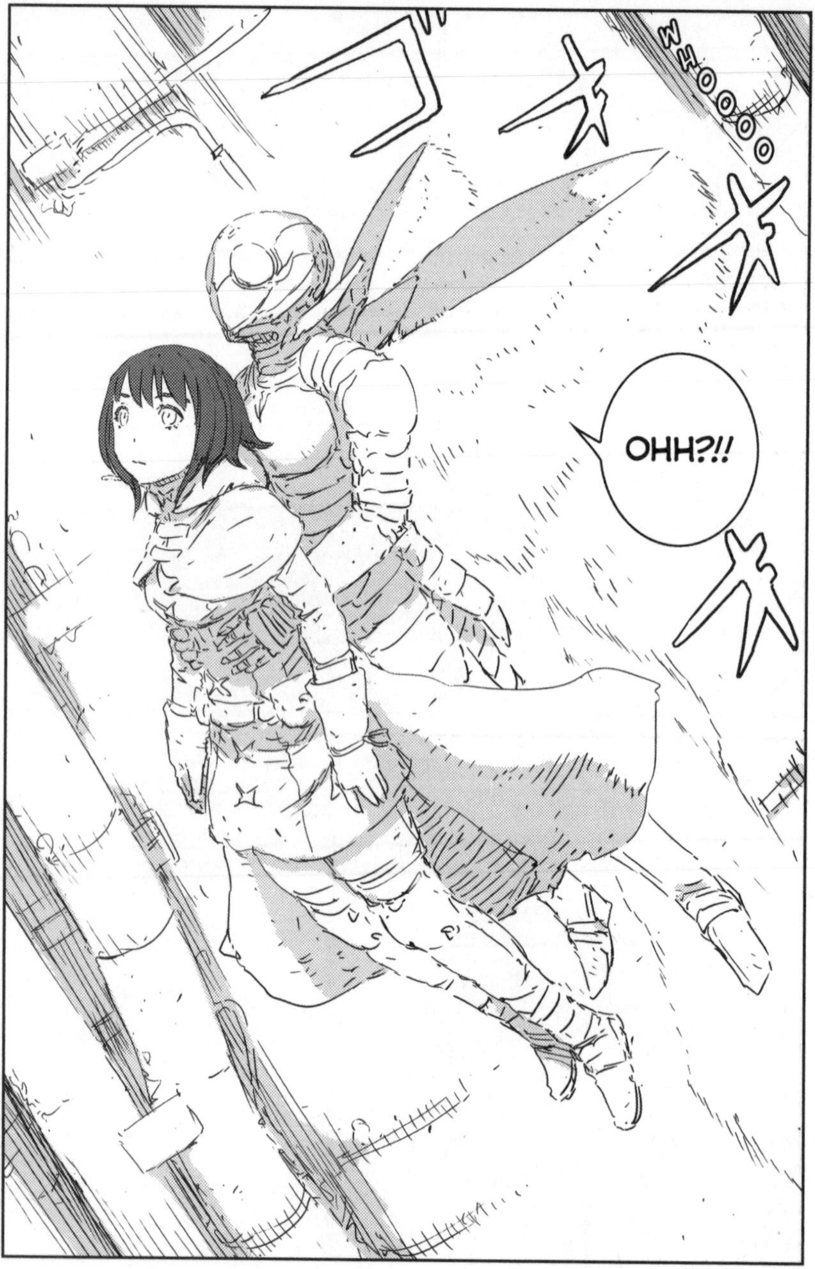
WHOOOOO
OHH?!!

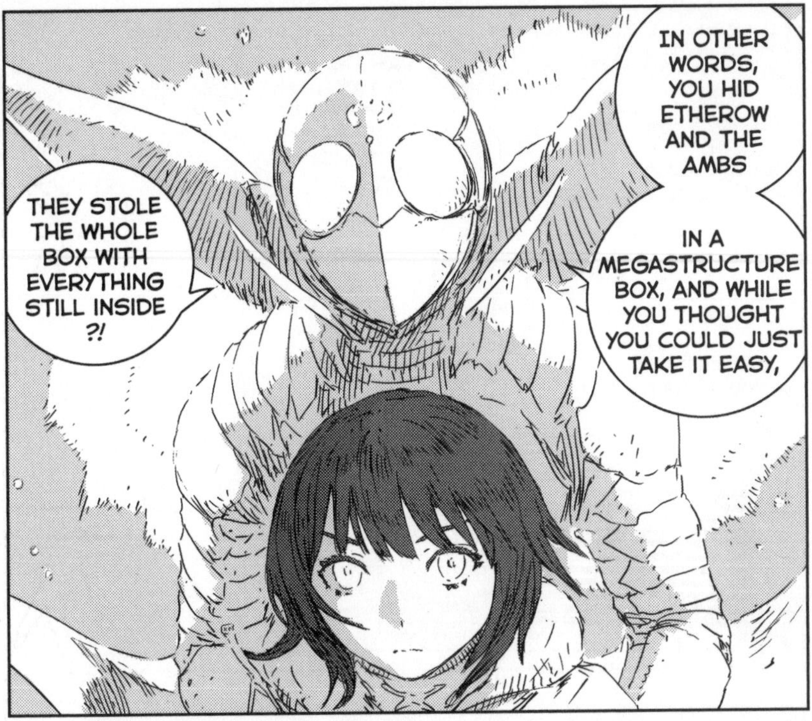
IN OTHER WORDS, YOU HID ETHEROW AND THE AMBS
IN A MEGASTRUCTURE BOX, AND WHILE YOU THOUGHT YOU COULD JUST TAKE IT EASY,
THEY STOLE THE WHOLE BOX WITH EVERYTHING STILL INSIDE ?!

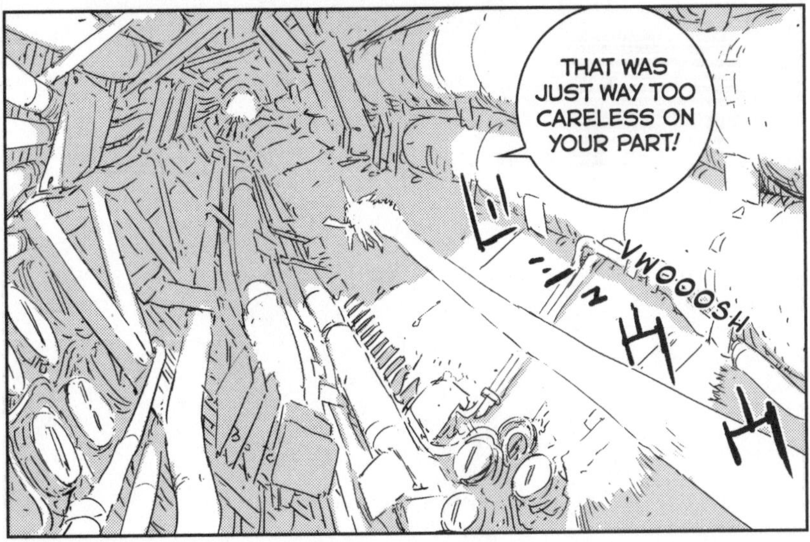
THAT WAS JUST WAY TOO CARELESS ON YOUR PART!
VWOOOSH

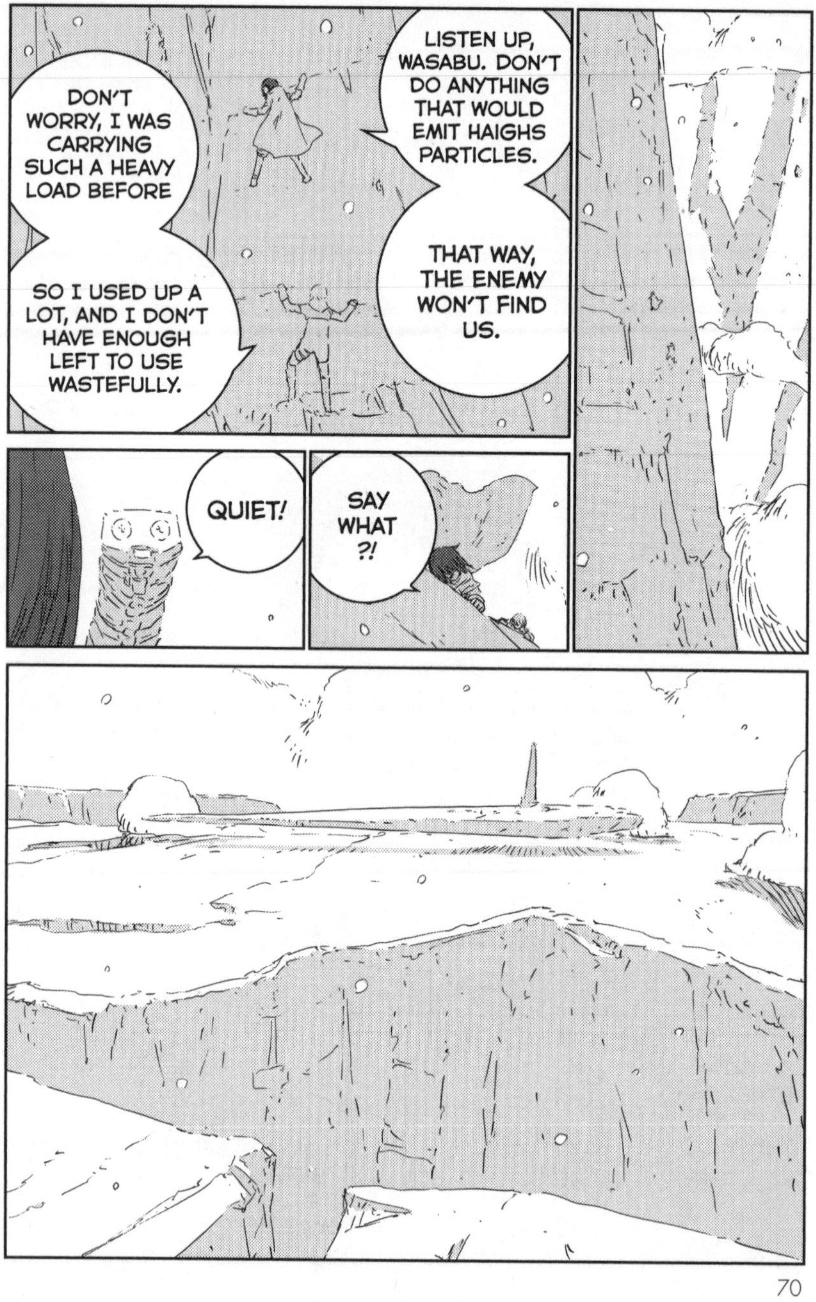
LISTEN UP, WASABU. DON'T DO ANYTHING THAT WOULD EMIT HAIGHS PARTICLES.
THAT WAY, THE ENEMY WON'T FIND US.
DON'T WORRY, I WAS CARRYING SUCH A HEAVY LOAD BEFORE
SO I USED UP A LOT, AND I DON'T HAVE ENOUGH LEFT TO USE WASTEFULLY.
SAY WHAT?!
QUIET!

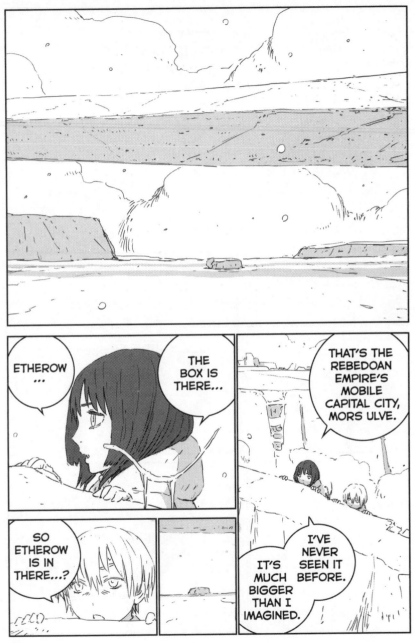

THAT'S THE REBEDOAN EMPIRE'S MOBILE CAPITAL CITY, MORS ULVE.
I'VE NEVER SEEN IT BEFORE.
IT'S MUCH BIGGER THAN I IMAGINED.
THE BOX IS THERE...
ETHEROW...
SO ETHEROW IS IN THERE...?

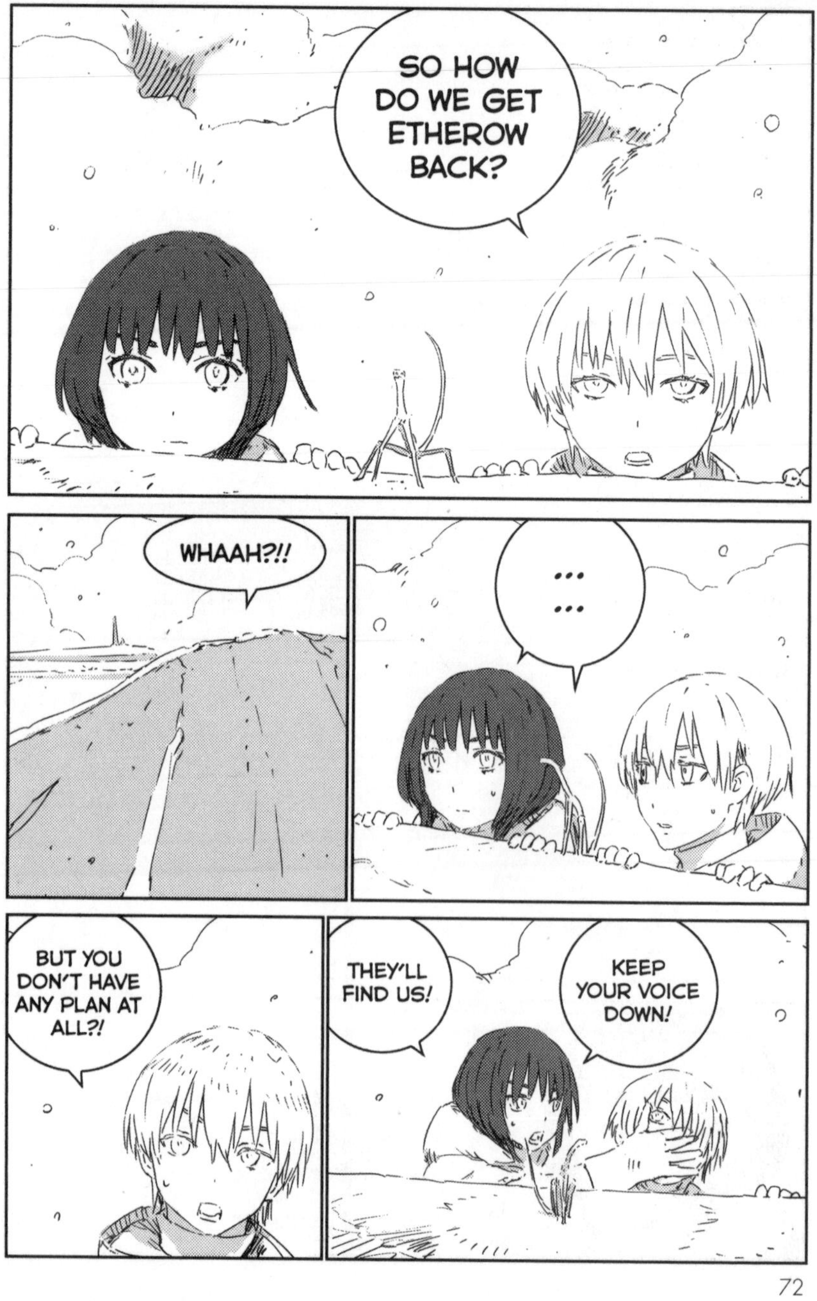
SO HOW DO WE GET ETHEROW BACK?
...
...
WHAAH?!!
KEEP YOUR VOICE DOWN!
THEY'LL FIND US!
BUT YOU DON'T HAVE ANY PLAN AT ALL?!

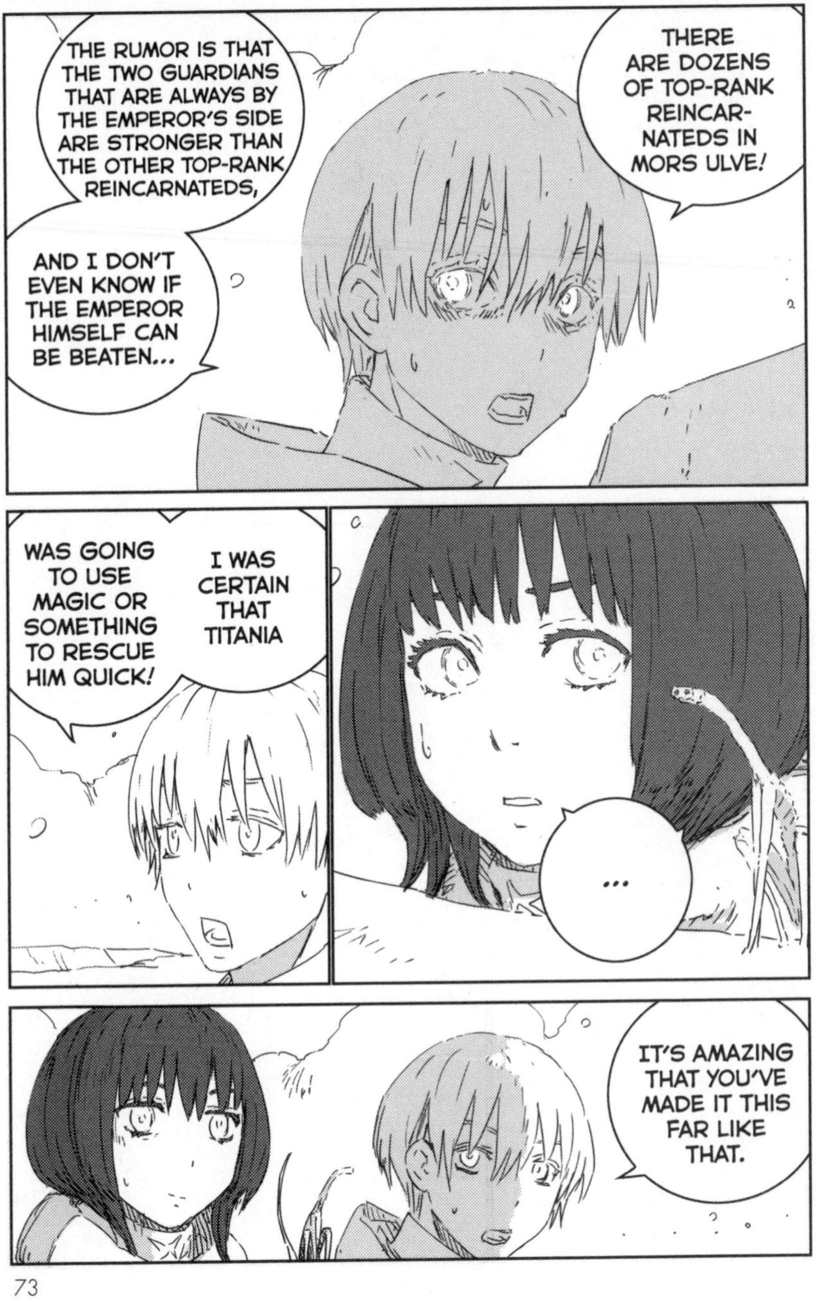
THERE ARE DOZENS OF TOP-RANK REINCAR-NATEDS IN MORS ULVE!
THE RUMOR IS THAT THE TWO GUARDIANS THAT ARE ALWAYS BY THE EMPEROR'S SIDE ARE STRONGER THAN THE OTHER TOP-RANK REINCARNATEDS,
AND I DON'T EVEN KNOW IF THE EMPEROR HIMSELF CAN BE BEATEN...
...
I WAS CERTAIN THAT TITANIA
WAS GOING TO USE MAGIC OR SOMETHING TO RESCUE HIM QUICK!
IT'S AMAZING THAT YOU'VE MADE IT THIS FAR LIKE THAT.

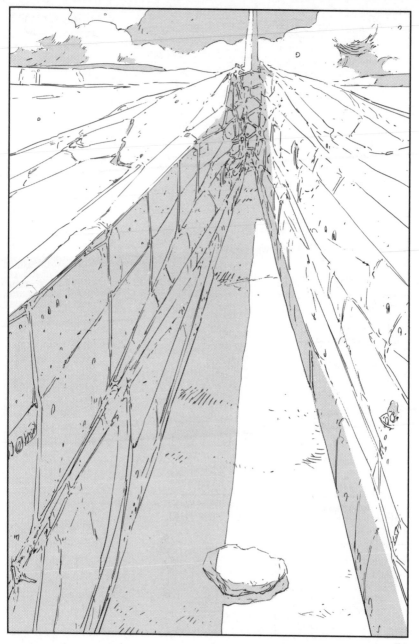

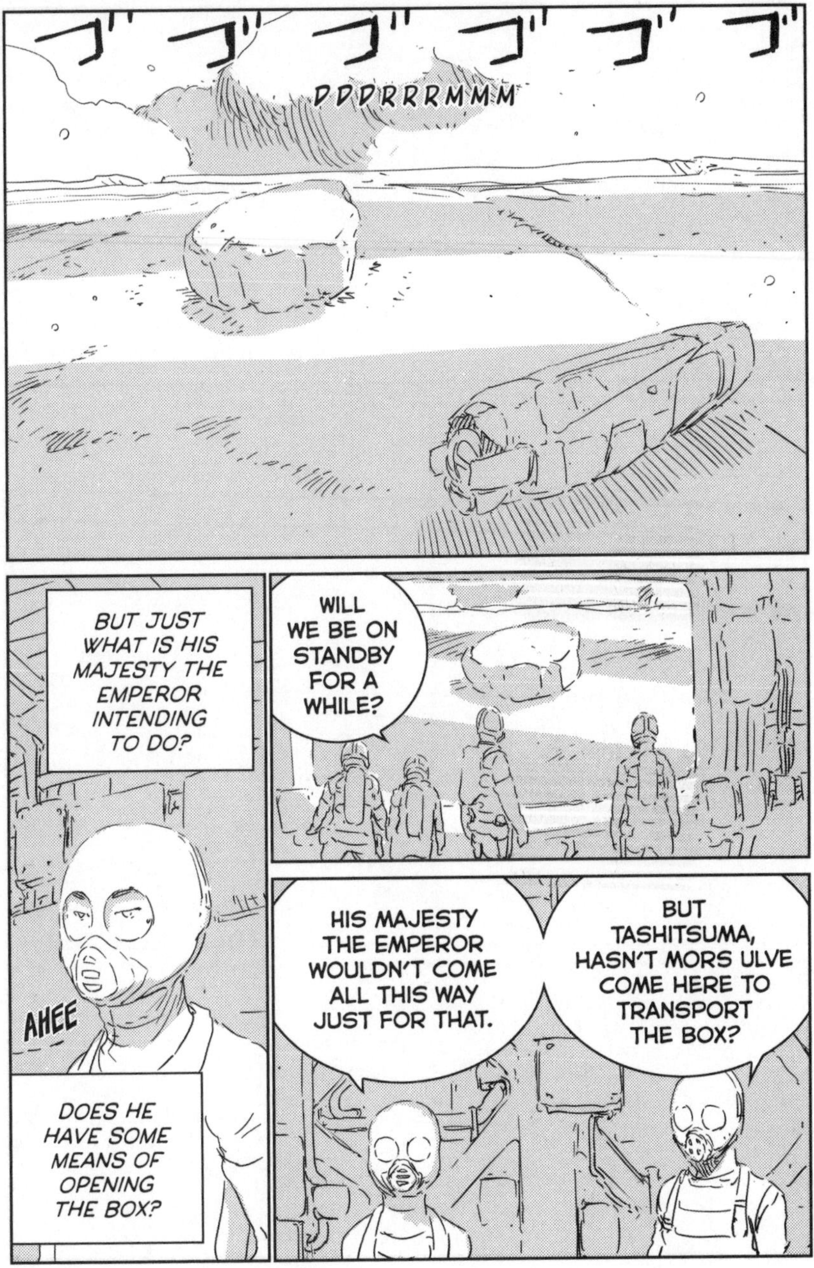
ゴ ゴ ゴ ゴ ゴ ゴ
DDDRRRMMM
WILL WE BE ON STANDBY FOR A WHILE?
BUT TASHITSUMA, HASN'T MORS ULVE COME HERE TO TRANSPORT THE BOX?
HIS MAJESTY THE EMPEROR WOULDN'T COME ALL THIS WAY JUST FOR THAT.
BUT JUST WHAT IS HIS MAJESTY THE EMPEROR INTENDING TO DO?
AHEE
DOES HE HAVE SOME MEANS OF OPENING THE BOX?

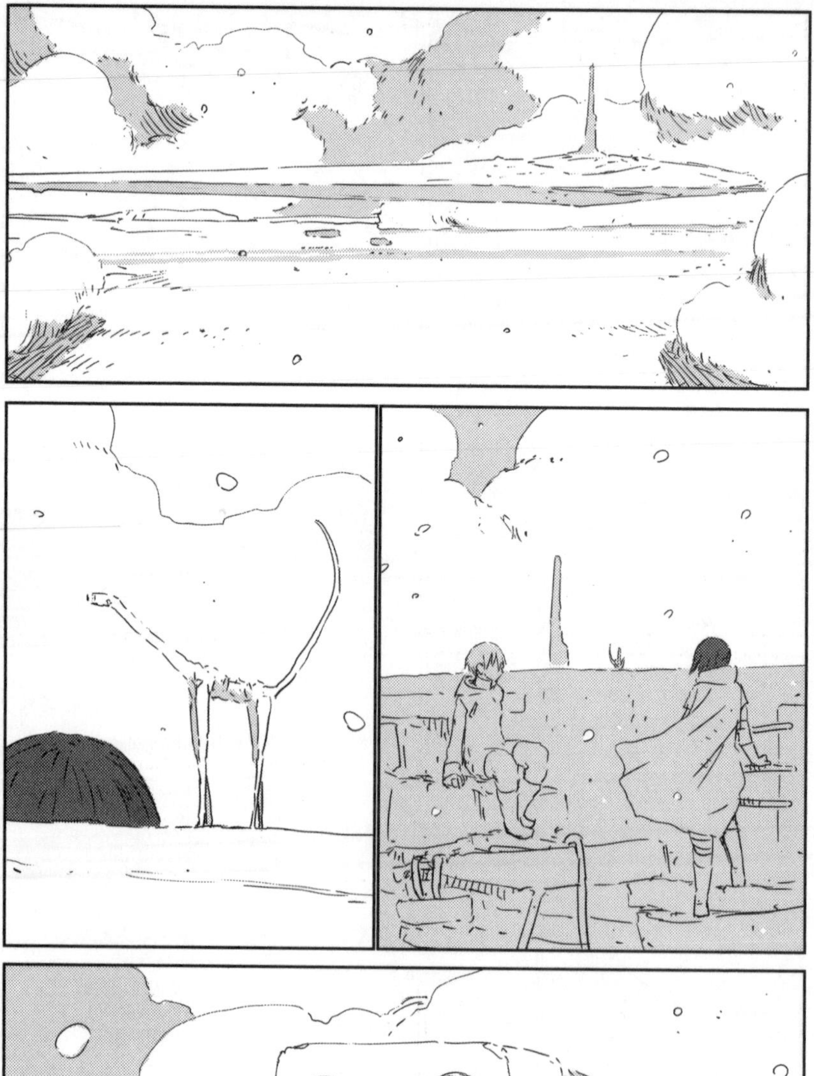

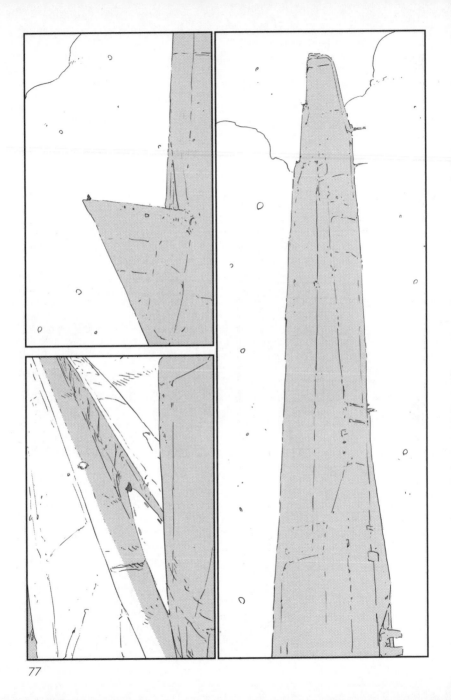

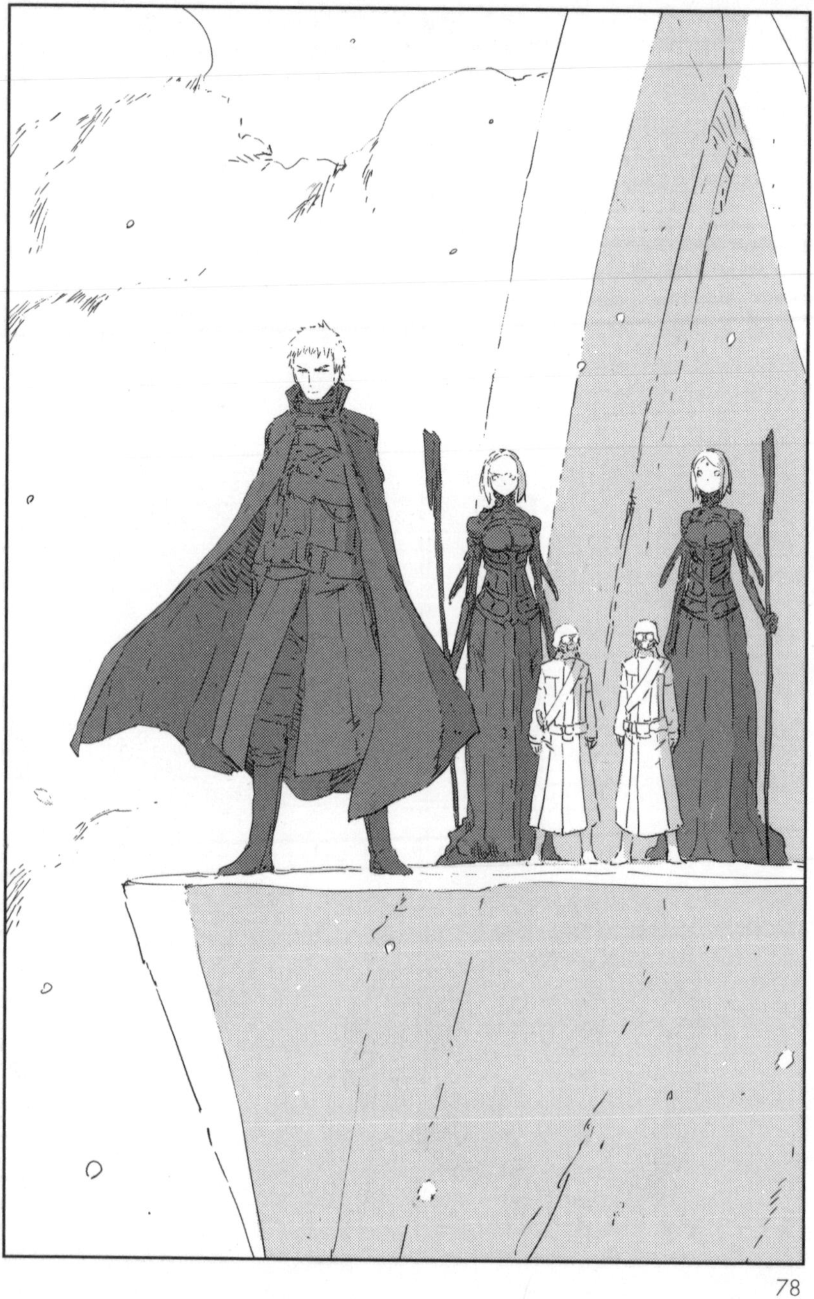

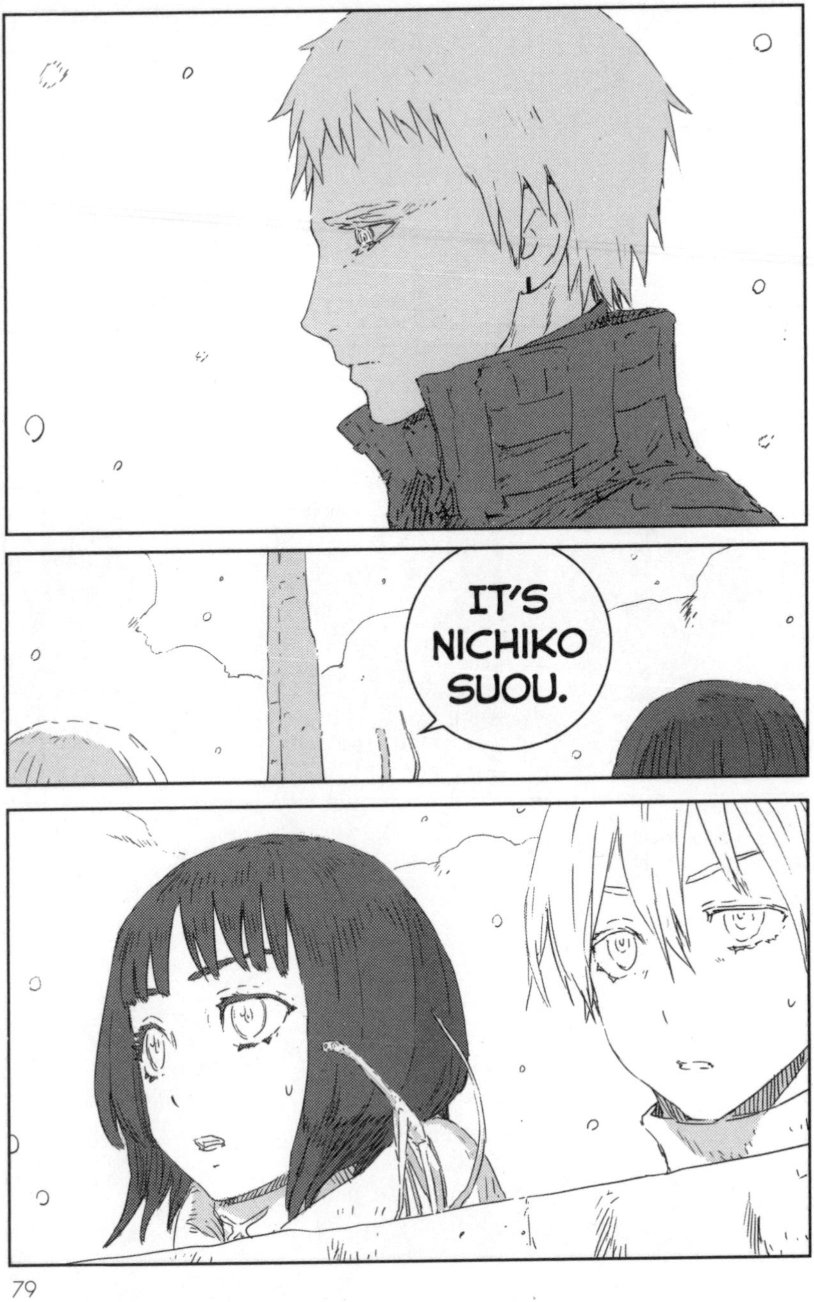
IT'S NICHIKO SUOU.

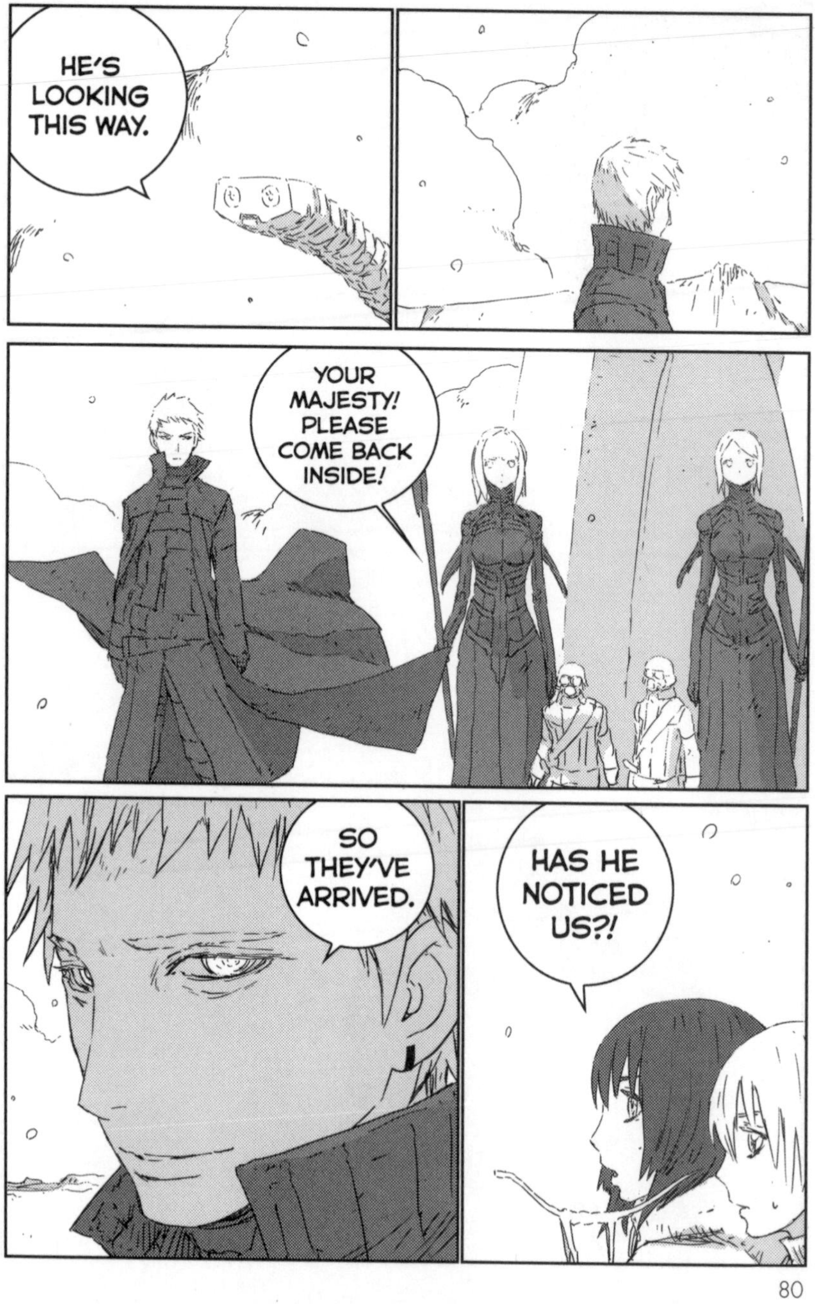
HE'S LOOKING THIS WAY.
YOUR MAJESTY! PLEASE COME BACK INSIDE!
HAS HE NOTICED US?!
SO THEY'VE ARRIVED.

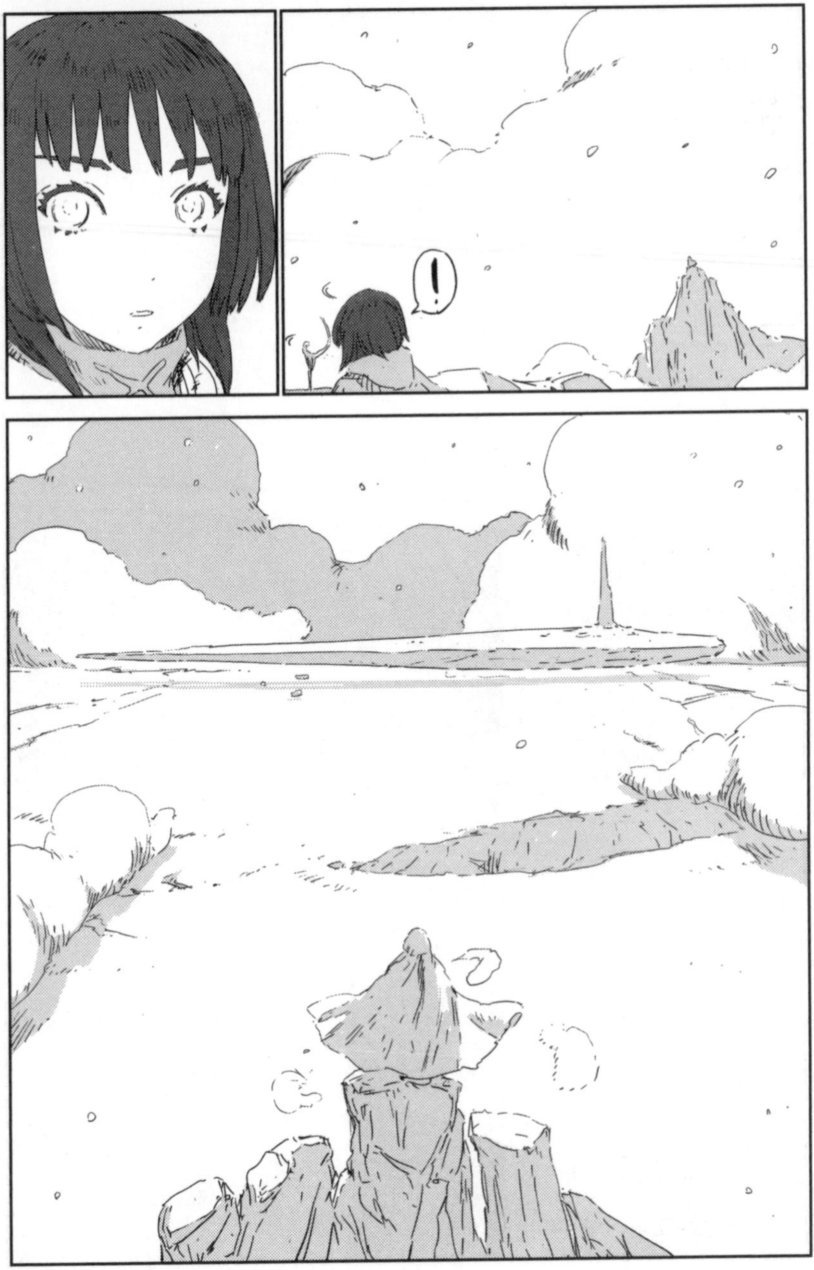
!

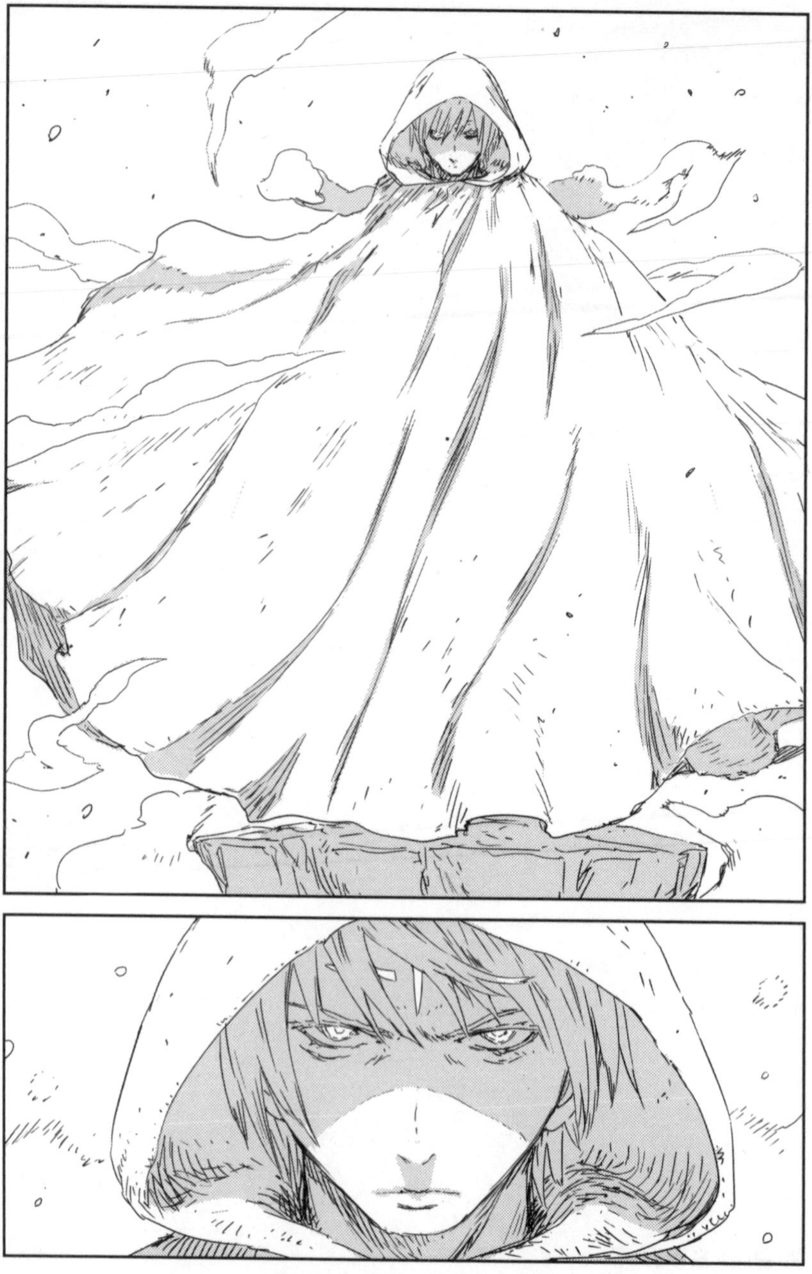

CHAPTER 33 END

APOSIMZ

CHAPTER 34

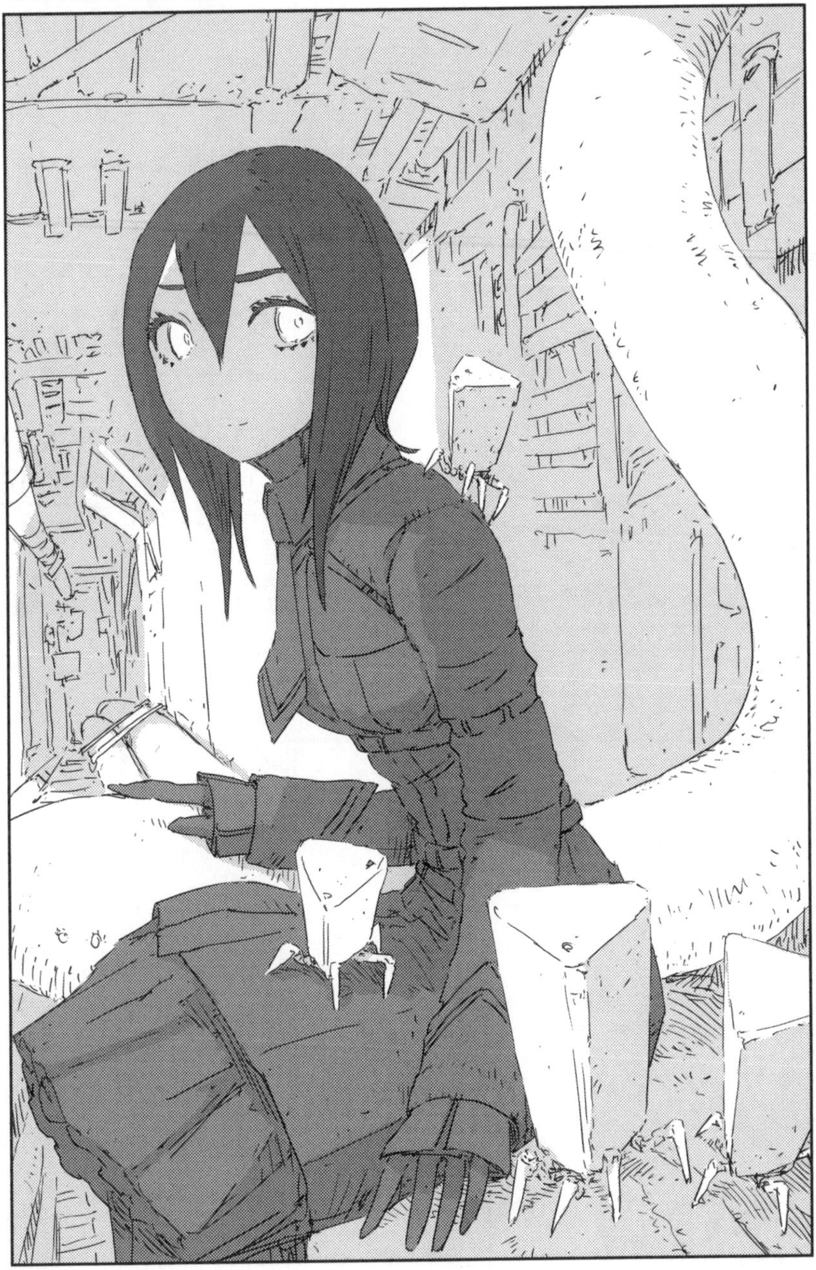

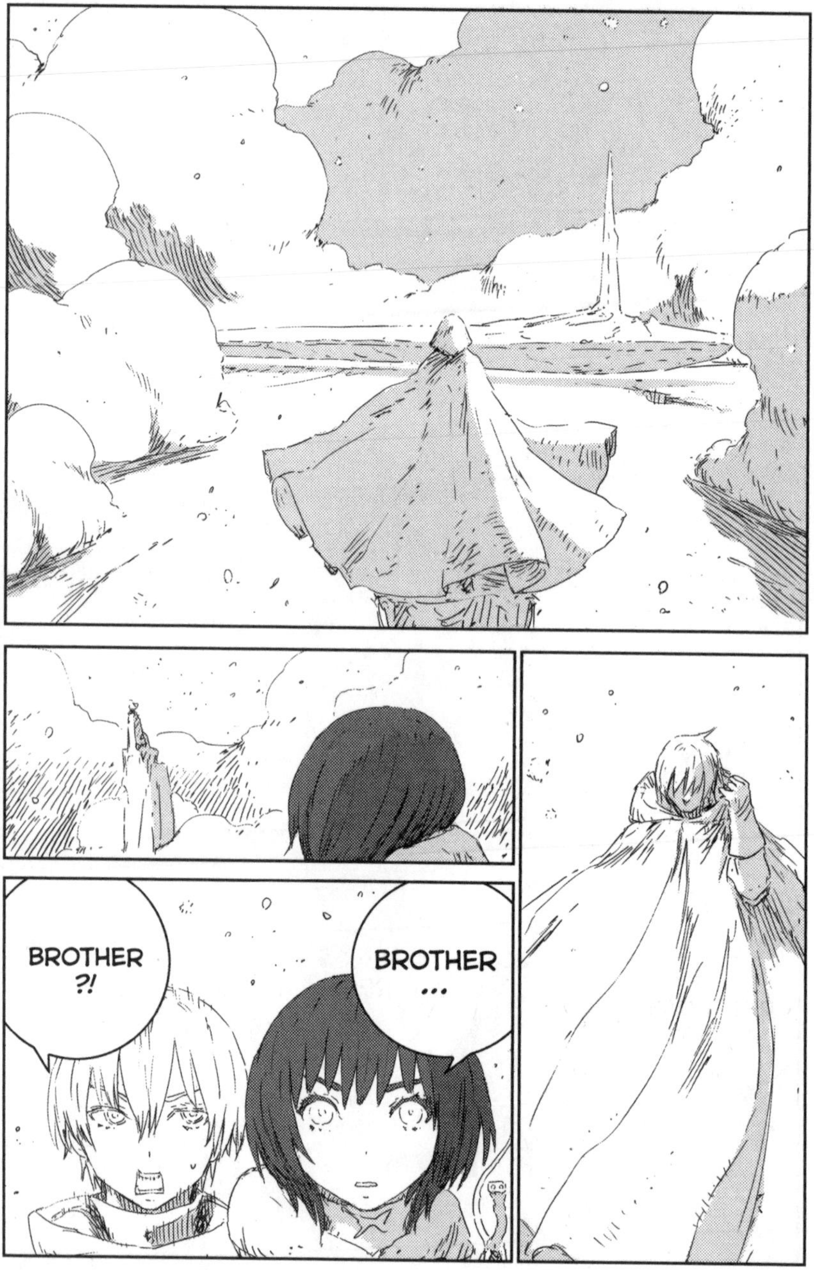
BROTHER ...
BROTHER ?!

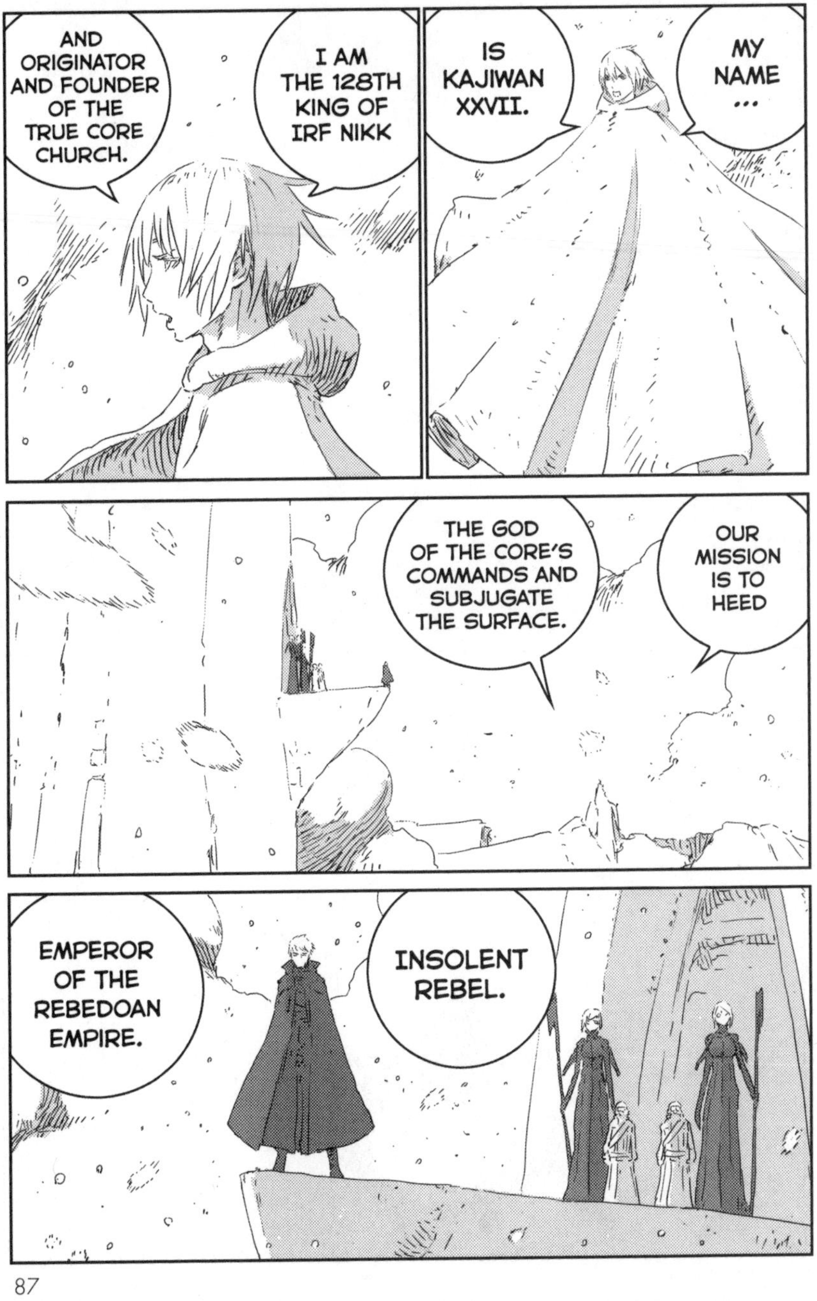
MY NAME ...
IS KAJIWAN XXVII.
I AM THE 128TH KING OF IRF NIKK
AND ORIGINATOR AND FOUNDER OF THE TRUE CORE CHURCH.
OUR MISSION IS TO HEED
THE GOD OF THE CORE'S COMMANDS AND SUBJUGATE THE SURFACE.
INSOLENT REBEL.
EMPEROR OF THE REBEDOAN EMPIRE.

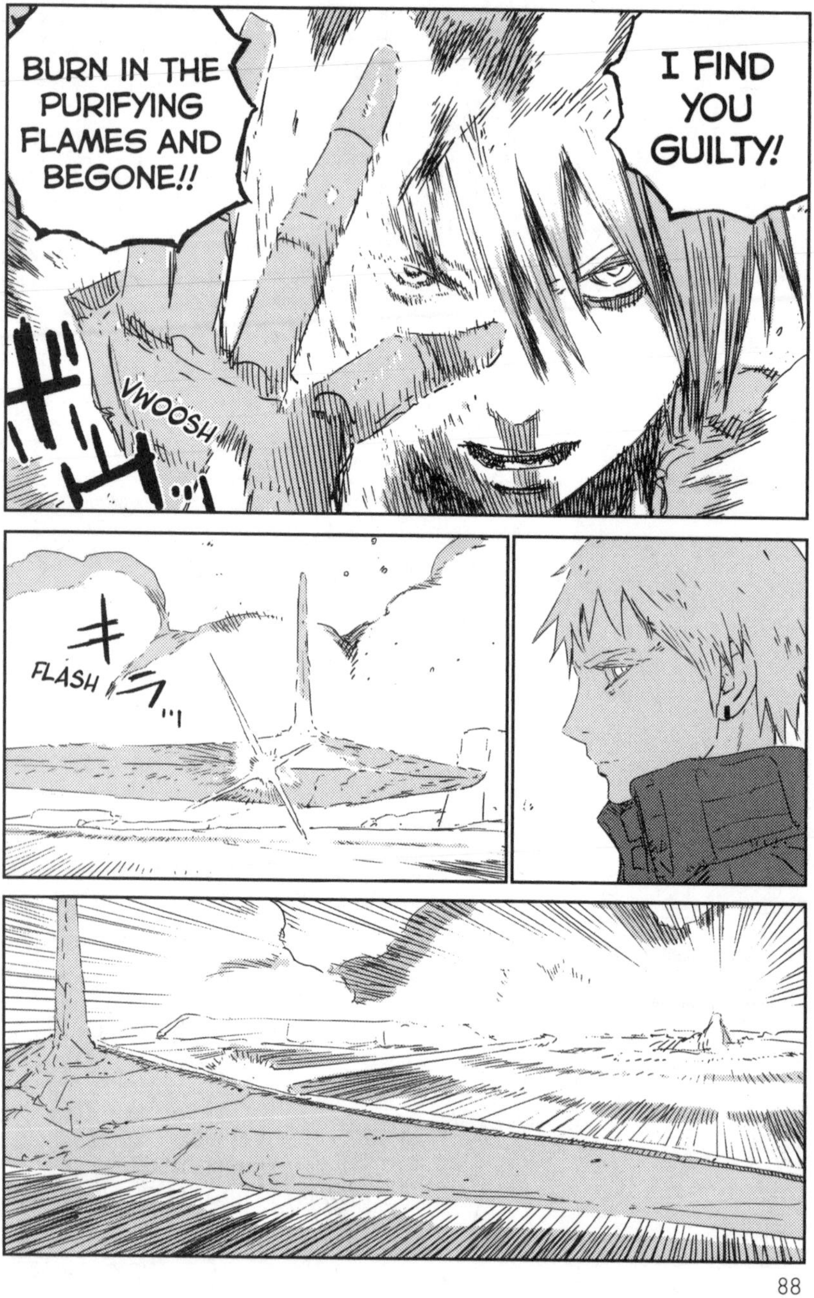
I FIND YOU GUILTY!
BURN IN THE PURIFYING FLAMES AND BEGONE!!
VWOOSH
FLASH

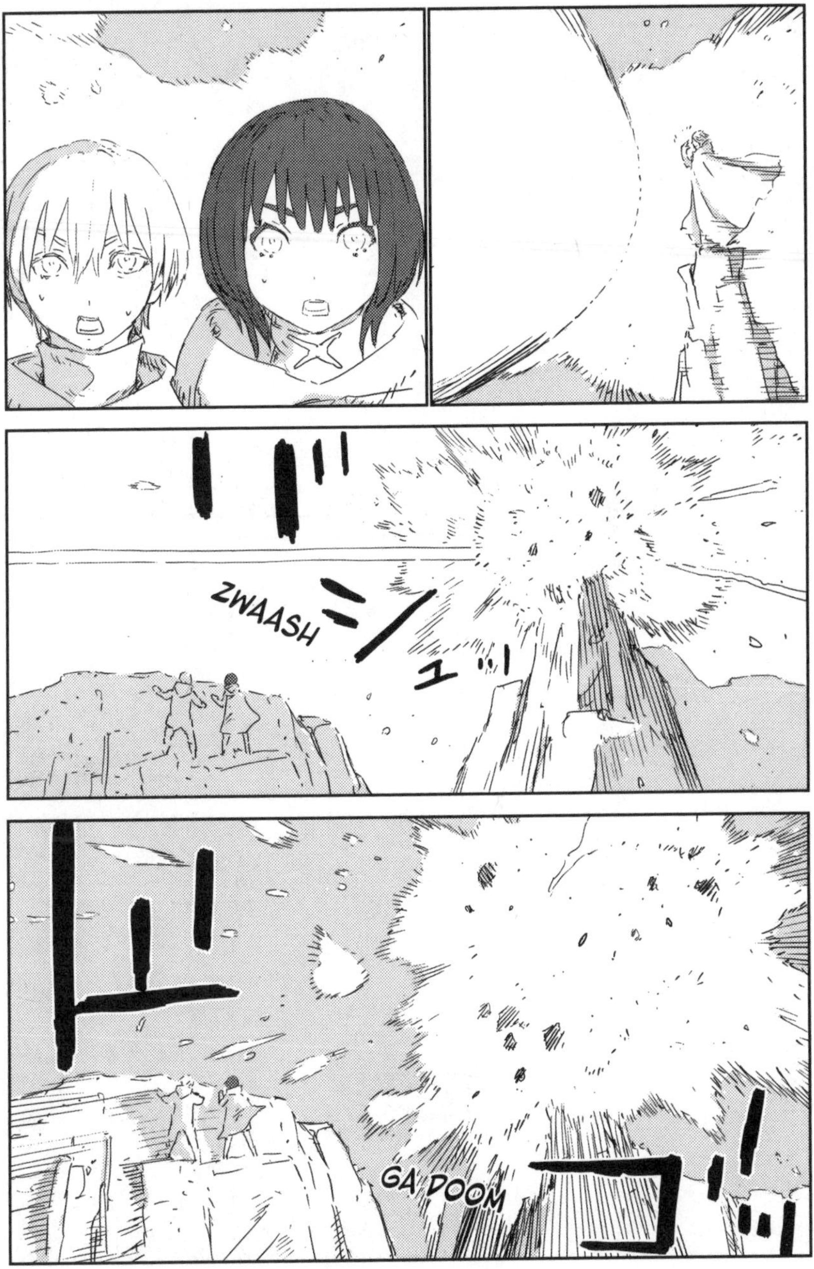
ZWAASH
GA DOOM

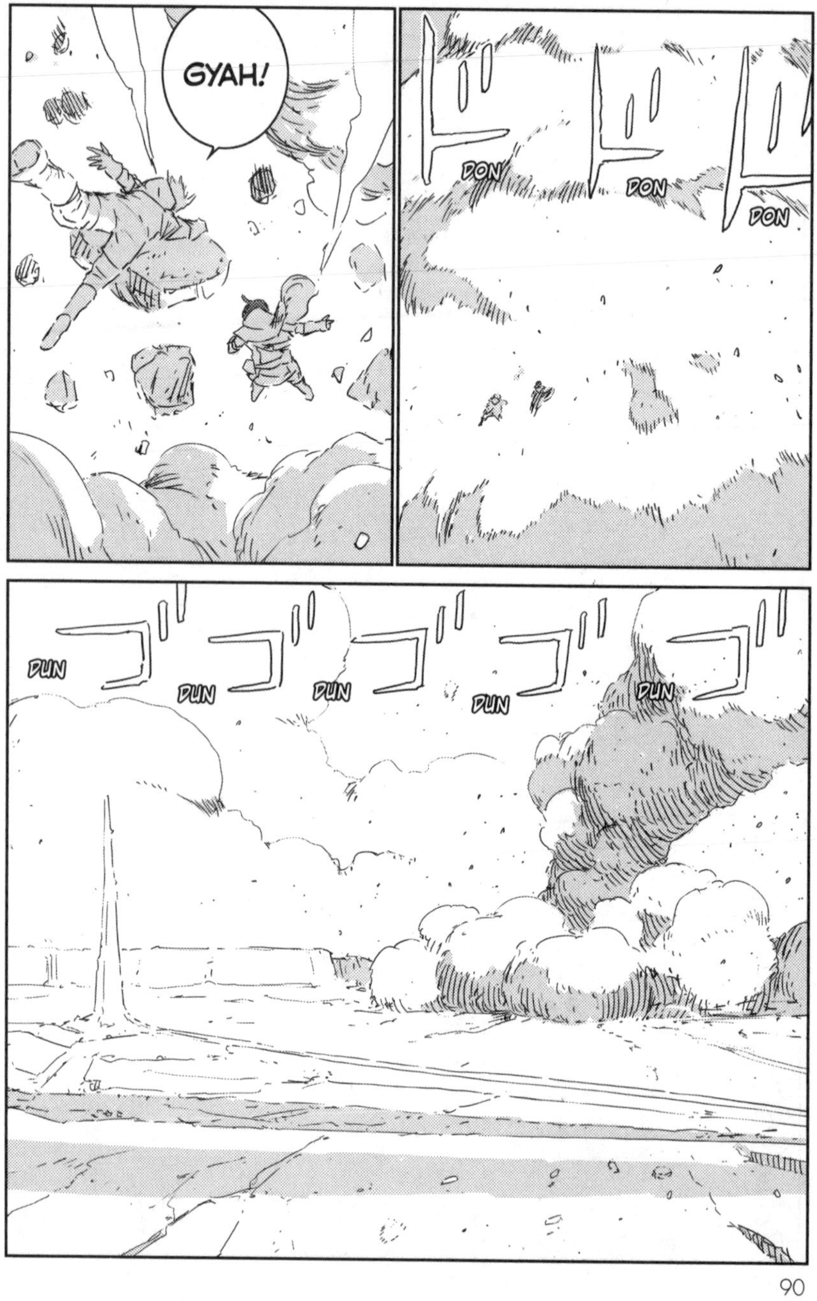
ドドド
DON
DON
DON
GYAH!
ゴゴゴゴゴ
DUN
DUN
DUN
DUN
DUN

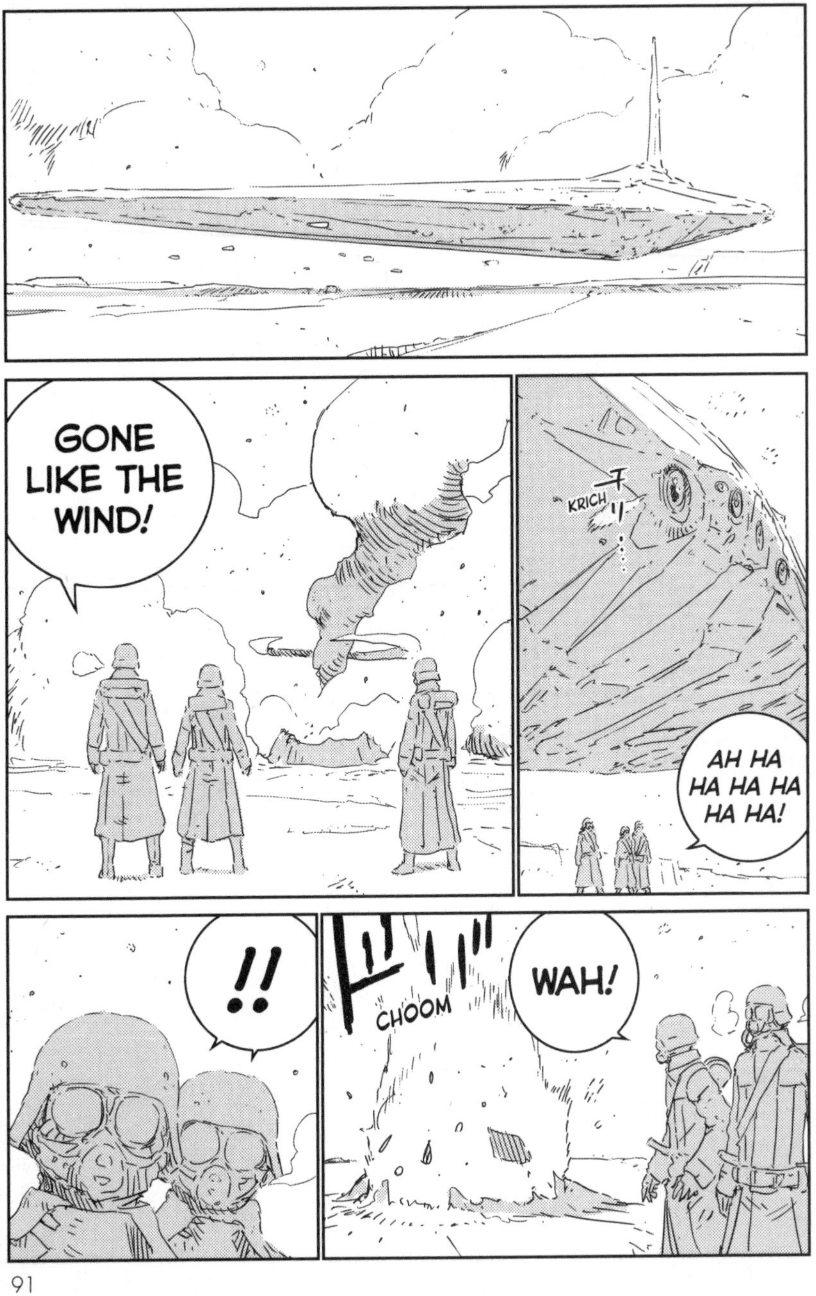
KRICH
AH HA HA HA HA HA HA!
GONE LIKE THE WIND!
WAH!
CHOOM
!!

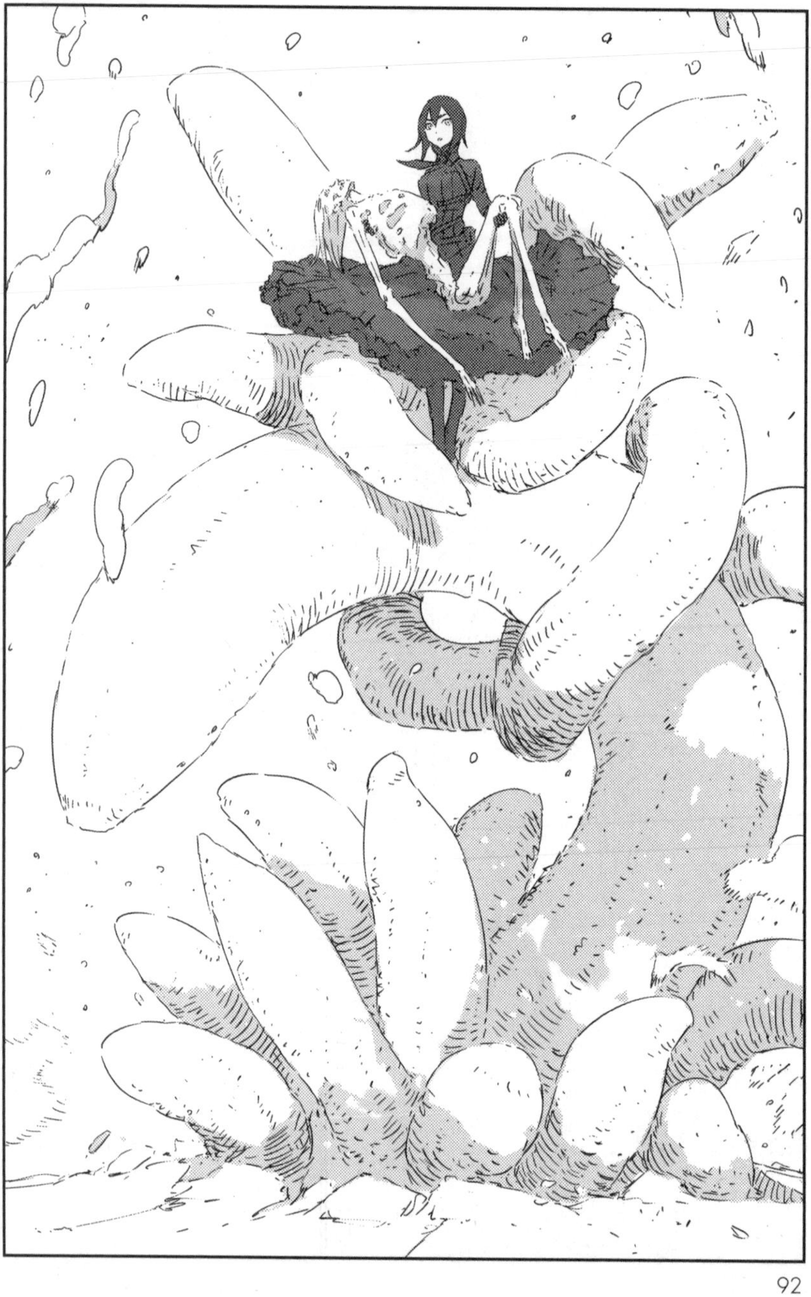

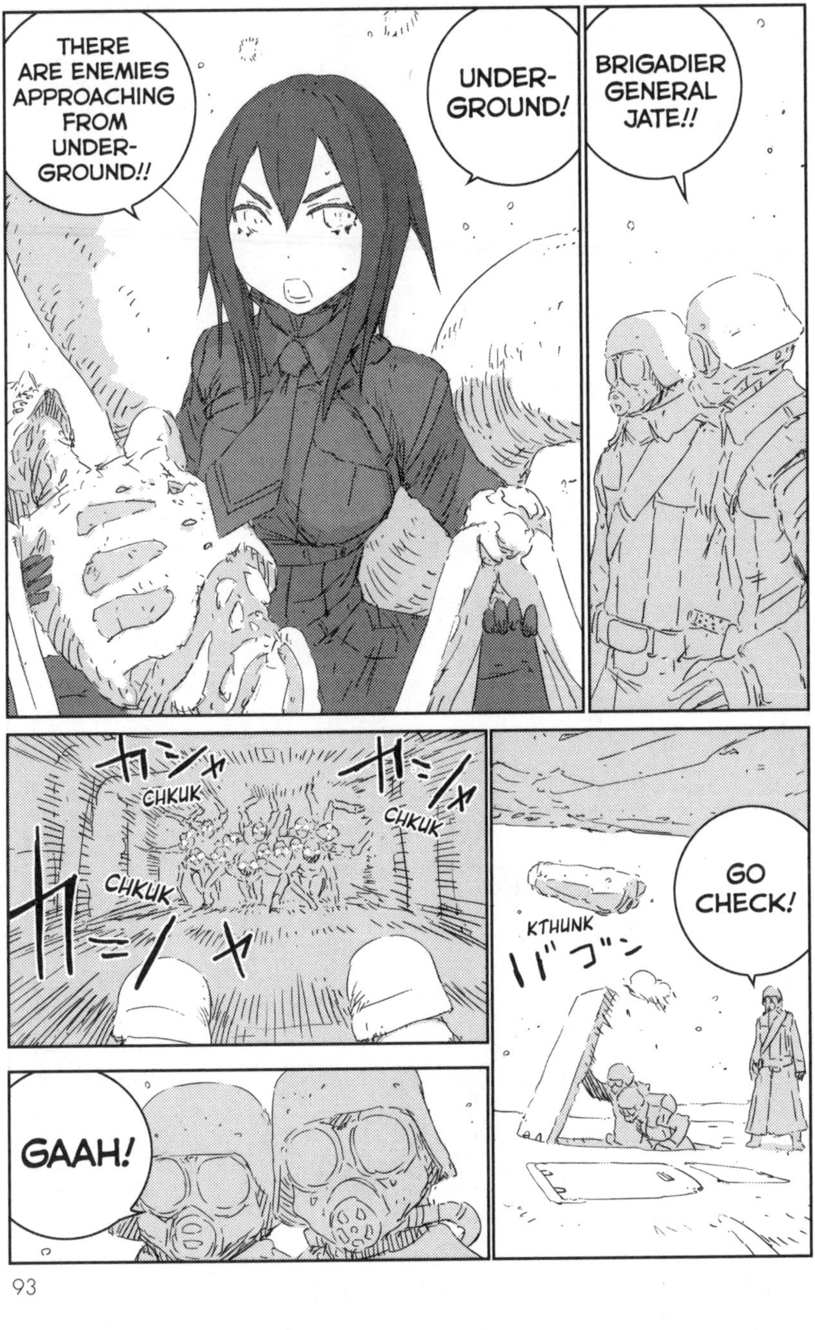
BRIGADIER GENERAL JATE!!
UNDER-GROUND!
THERE ARE ENEMIES APPROACHING FROM UNDER-GROUND!!
GO CHECK!
KTHUNK
バゴン
ガシャ
CHKUK
ガシャ
CHKUK
CHKUK
ガシャ
GAAH!

DWOMMF
CHKUK
CHKUK
HRRRMM
PKAK
PZAAK
GKUNG
VWMMM
FRAME DISEASE SUFFERERS! A HORDE OF THEM!
KRIK
KRAK

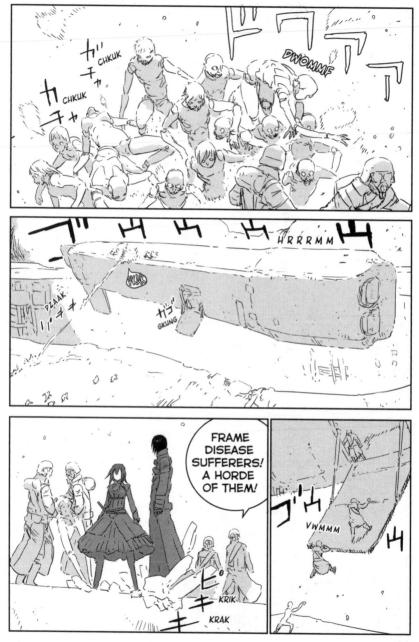

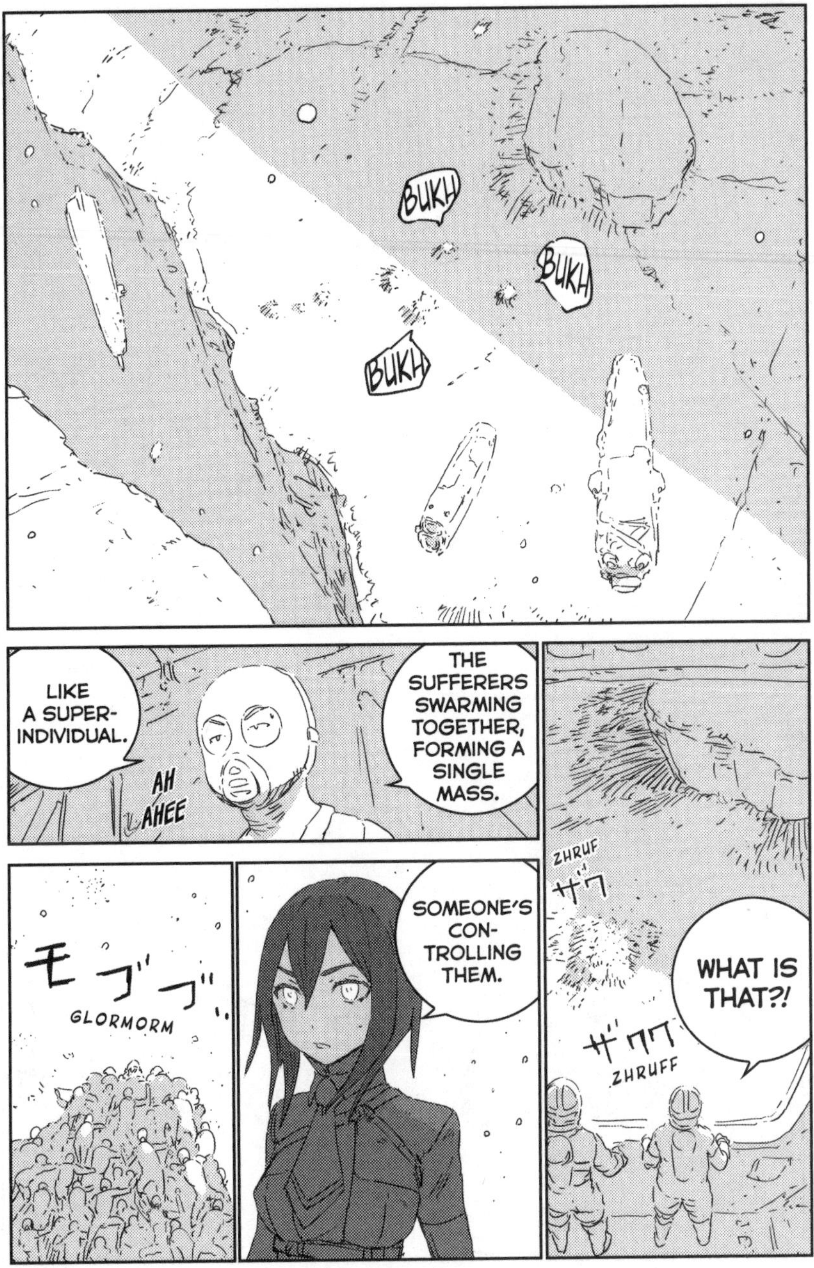
BUKH
BUKH
BUKH
ZHRUF
ザワ
WHAT IS THAT?!
ザワワ
ZHRUFF
THE SUFFERERS SWARMING TOGETHER, FORMING A SINGLE MASS.
LIKE A SUPER-INDIVIDUAL.
AH AHEE
SOMEONE'S CON-TROLLING THEM.
モゴゴ
GLORMORM

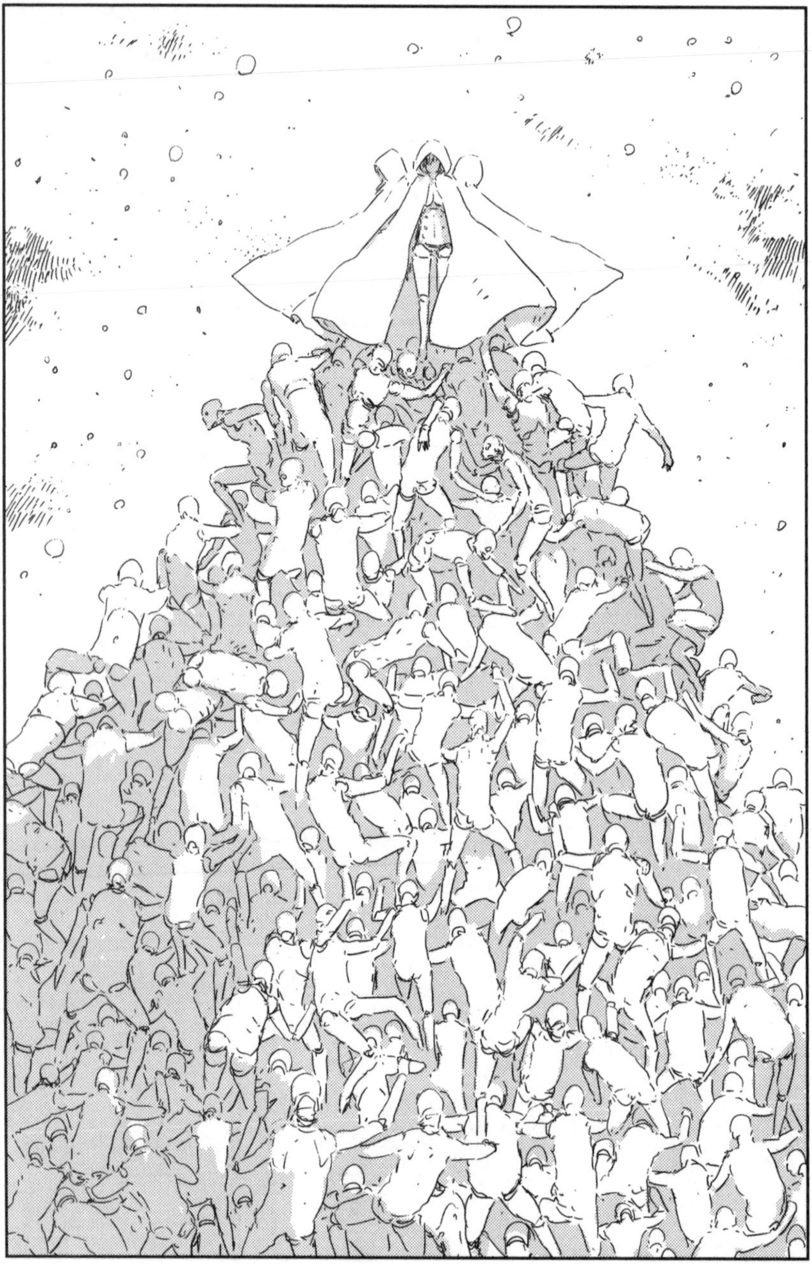

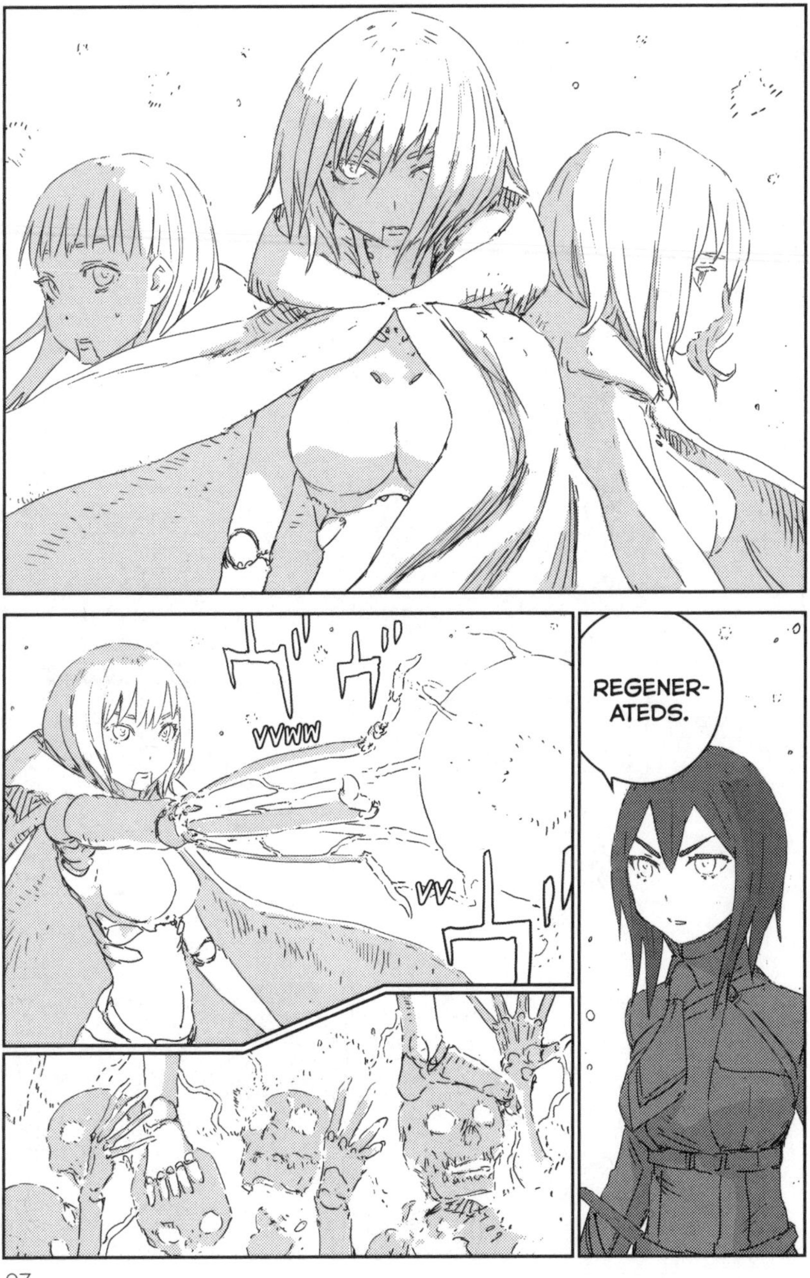
REGENER-
ATEDS.
VVWW
VV

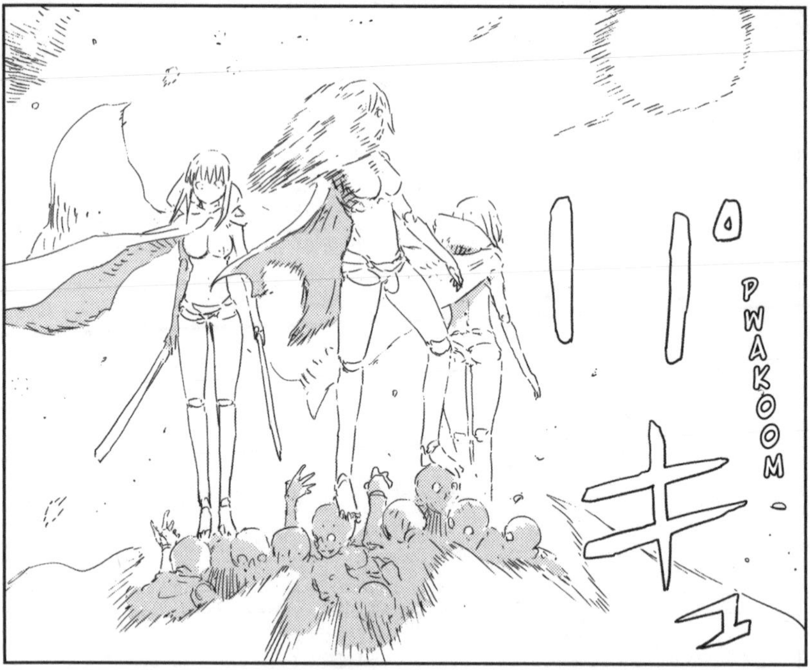
PWAKOOM
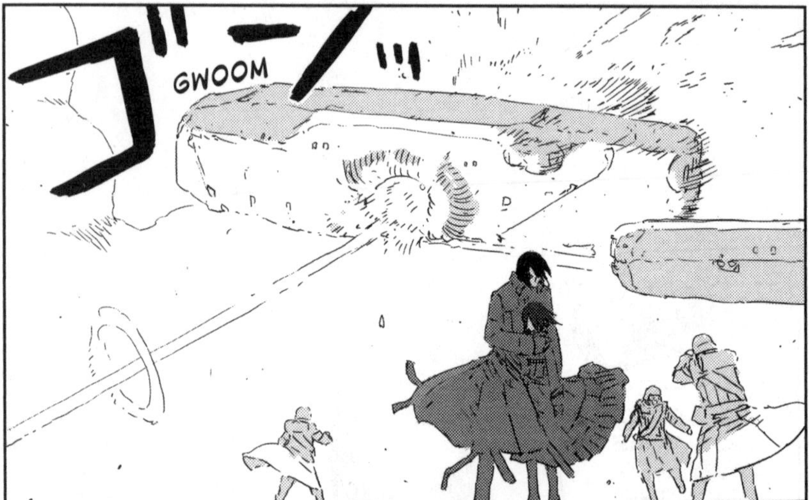
GWOOM

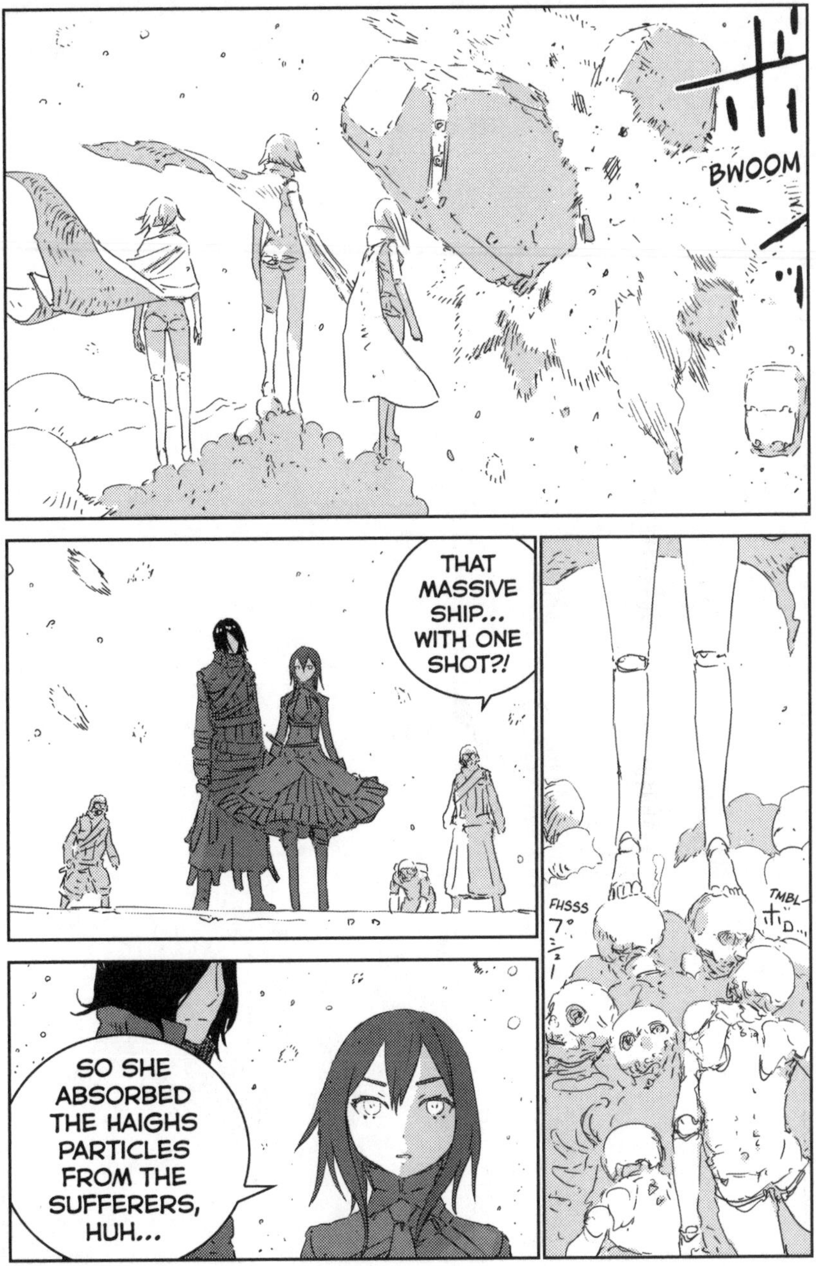
BWOOM
TMBL
FHSSS
THAT MASSIVE SHIP... WITH ONE SHOT?!
SO SHE ABSORBED THE HAIGHS PARTICLES FROM THE SUFFERERS, HUH...

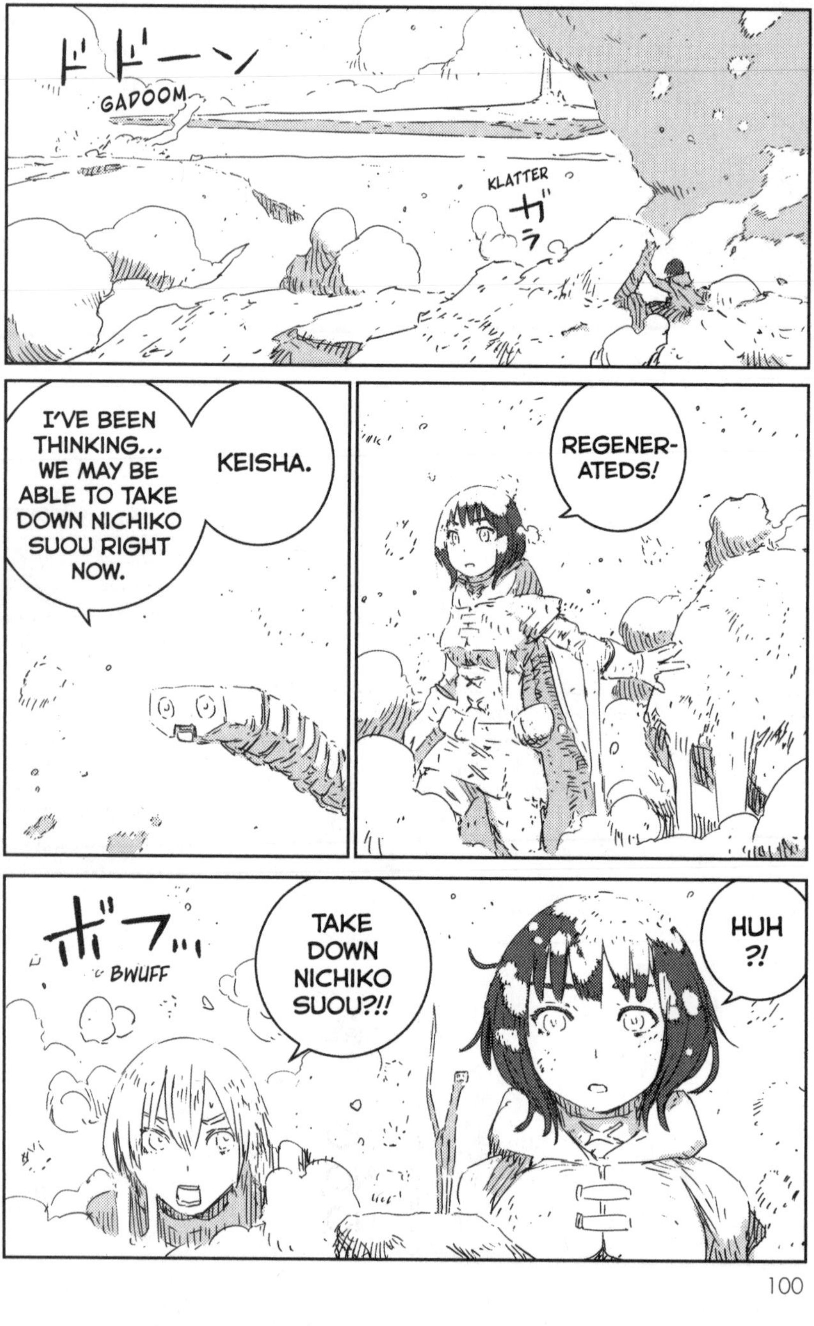
ドドーン
GADOOM
ガラ
KLATTER
REGENERATEDS!
KEISHA.
I'VE BEEN THINKING... WE MAY BE ABLE TO TAKE DOWN NICHIKO SUOU RIGHT NOW.
HUH ?!
TAKE DOWN NICHIKO SUOU?!!
ボフッ
BWUFF

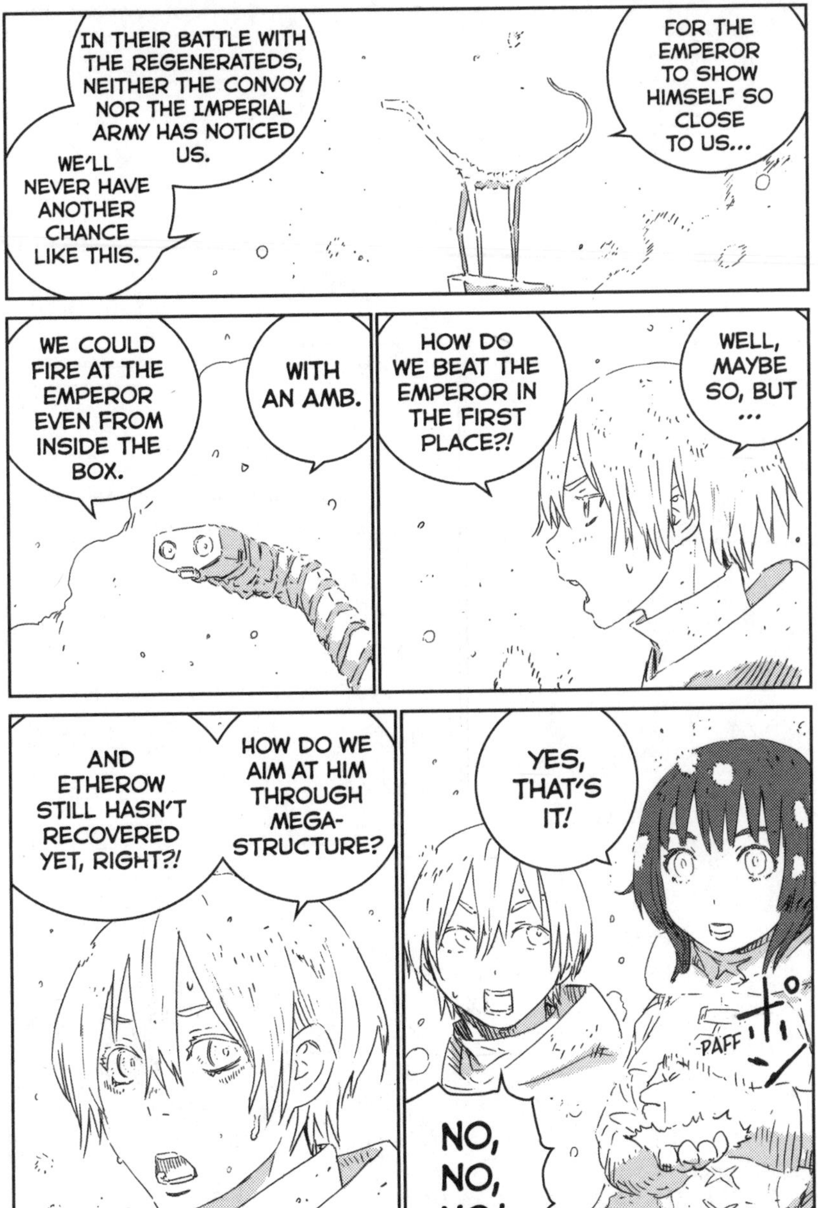
FOR THE EMPEROR TO SHOW HIMSELF SO CLOSE TO US...
IN THEIR BATTLE WITH THE REGENERATEDS, NEITHER THE CONVOY NOR THE IMPERIAL ARMY HAS NOTICED US.
WE'LL NEVER HAVE ANOTHER CHANCE LIKE THIS.
WELL, MAYBE SO, BUT ...
HOW DO WE BEAT THE EMPEROR IN THE FIRST PLACE?!
WITH AN AMB.
WE COULD FIRE AT THE EMPEROR EVEN FROM INSIDE THE BOX.
YES, THAT'S IT!
PAFF
NO, NO, NO!
HOW DO WE AIM AT HIM THROUGH MEGA-STRUCTURE?
AND ETHEROW STILL HASN'T RECOVERED YET, RIGHT?!

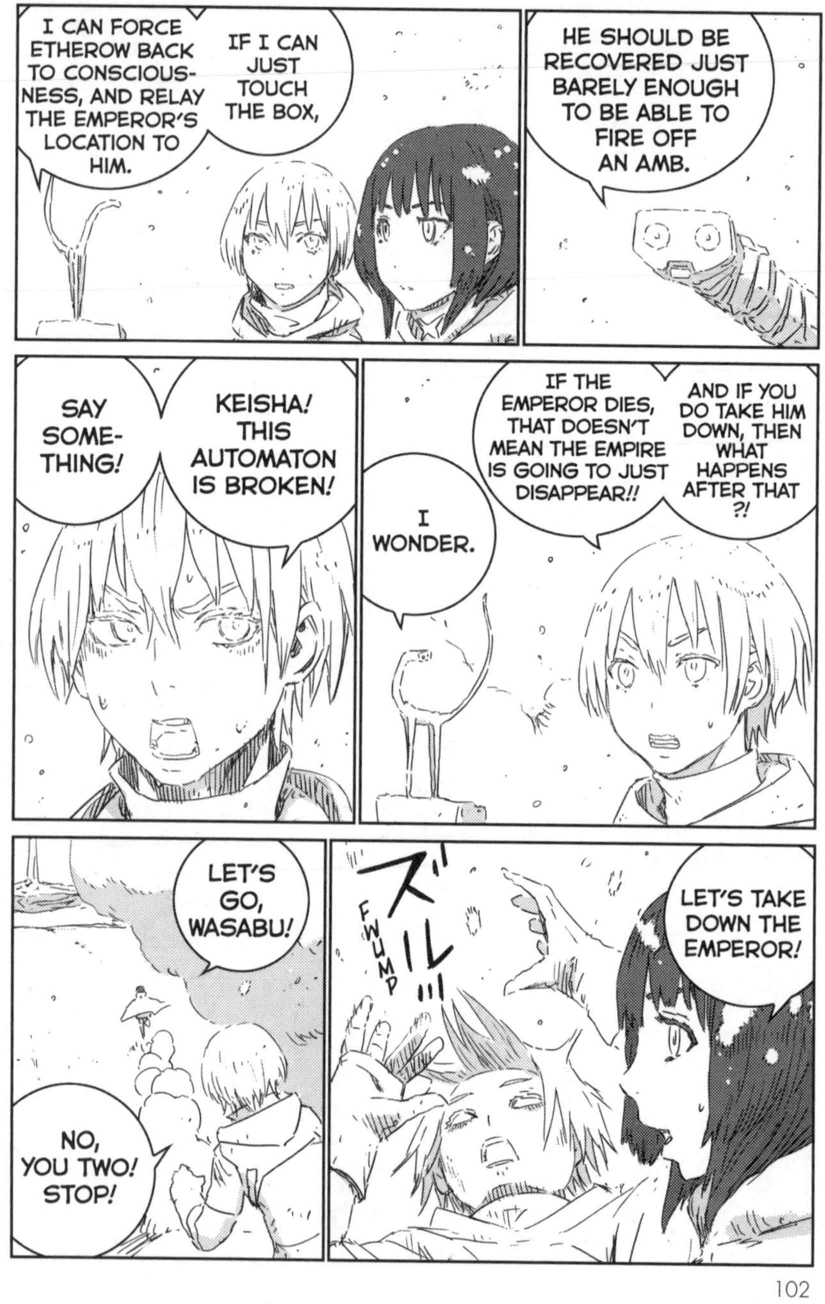
HE SHOULD BE RECOVERED JUST BARELY ENOUGH TO BE ABLE TO FIRE OFF AN AMB.
IF I CAN JUST TOUCH THE BOX,
I CAN FORCE ETHEROW BACK TO CONSCIOUS-NESS, AND RELAY THE EMPEROR'S LOCATION TO HIM.
AND IF YOU DO TAKE HIM DOWN, THEN WHAT HAPPENS AFTER THAT?!
IF THE EMPEROR DIES, THAT DOESN'T MEAN THE EMPIRE IS GOING TO JUST DISAPPEAR!!
I WONDER.
KEISHA! THIS AUTOMATON IS BROKEN!
SAY SOME-THING!
LET'S TAKE DOWN THE EMPEROR!
ズル
FWUMP
LET'S GO, WASABU!
NO, YOU TWO! STOP!

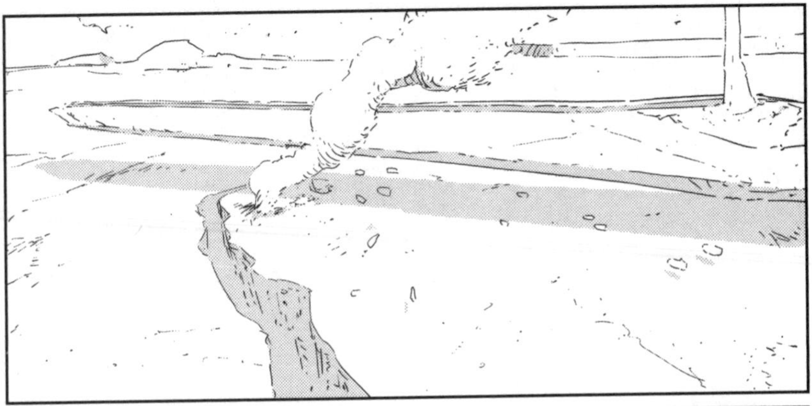

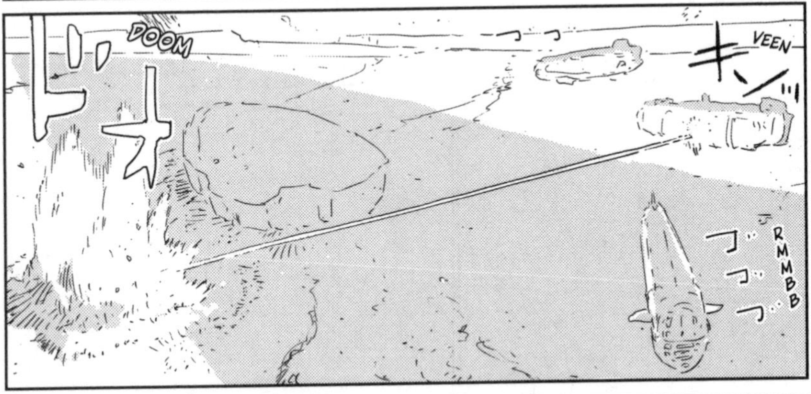
DOOM
VEEN
RMMBB

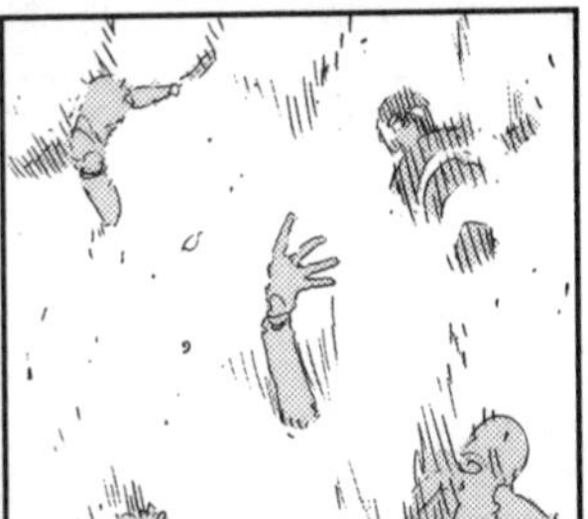

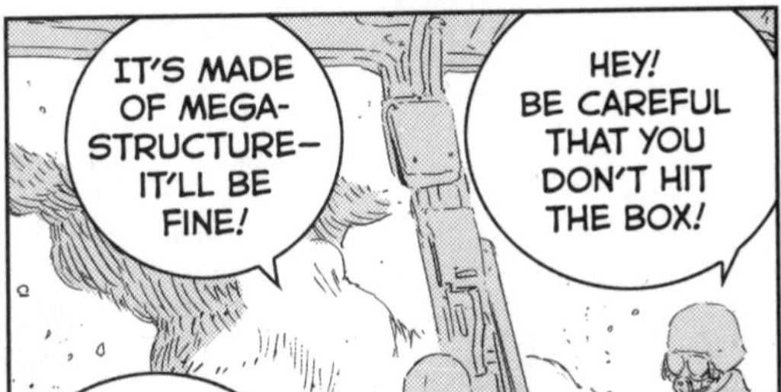
HEY! BE CAREFUL THAT YOU DON'T HIT THE BOX!
IT'S MADE OF MEGA-STRUCTURE— IT'LL BE FINE!
EITHER WAY, ORDERS ARE TO NOT CAUSE ANY IMPACT TO THE BOX!

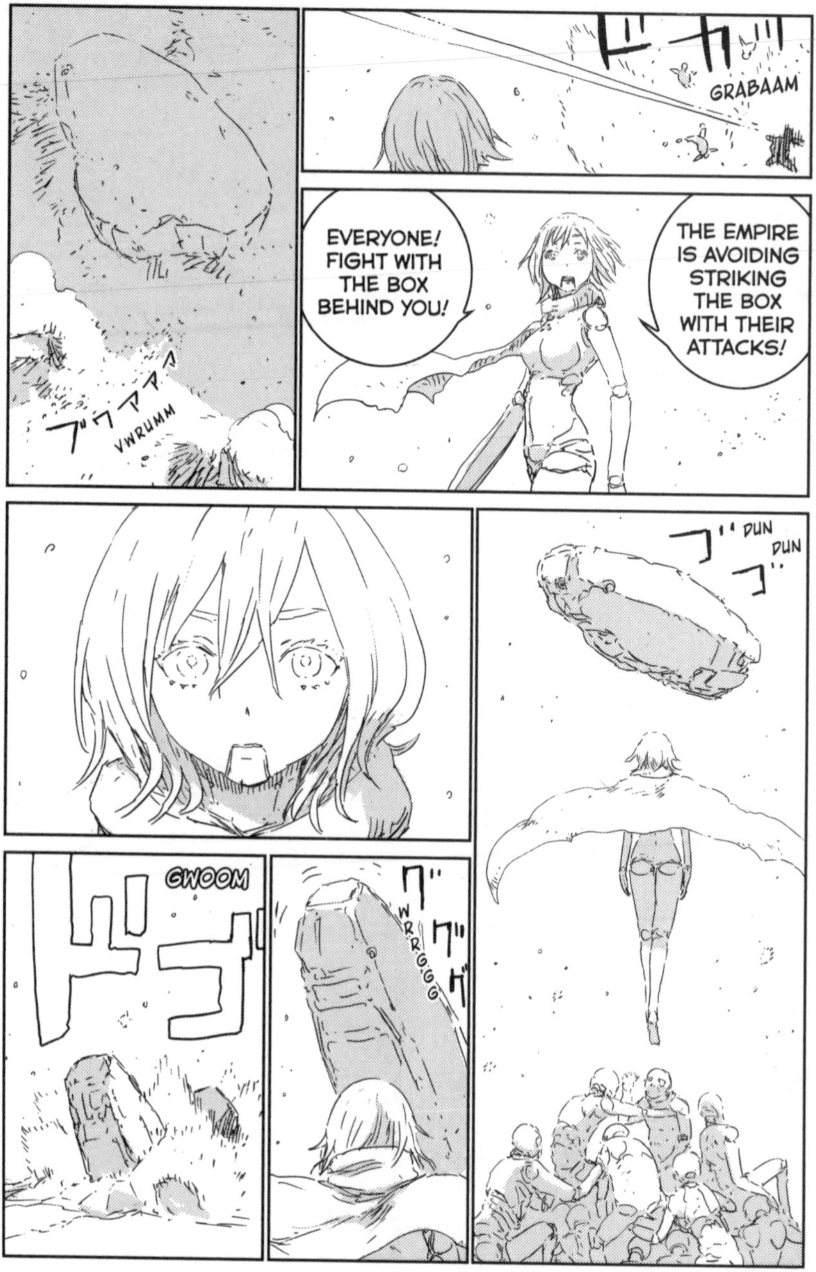

ドガッ
GRABAAM
THE EMPIRE IS AVOIDING STRIKING THE BOX WITH THEIR ATTACKS!
EVERYONE! FIGHT WITH THE BOX BEHIND YOU!
ブワァァ
VWRUMM
ゴゴ
DUN DUN
グググ
WRRGGG
ドゴ
GWOOM

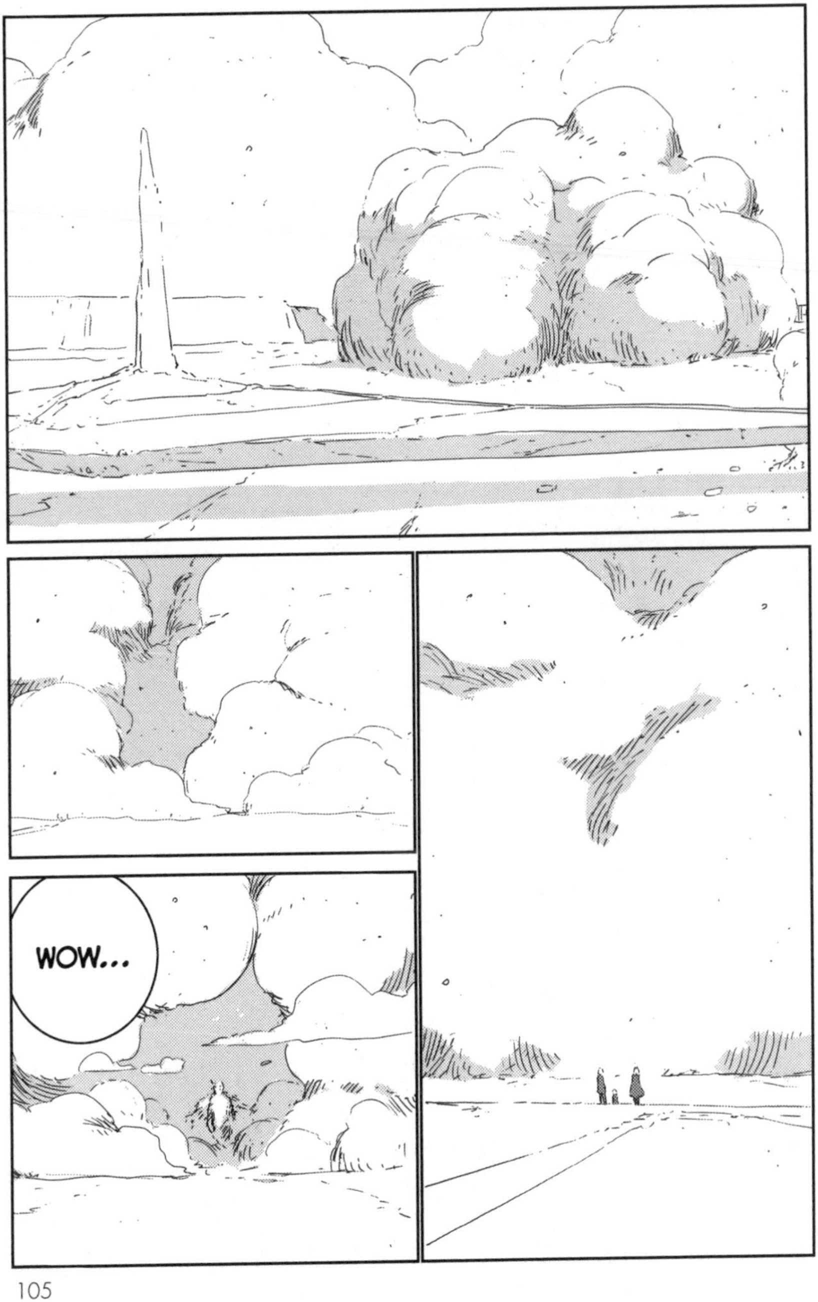
WOW...

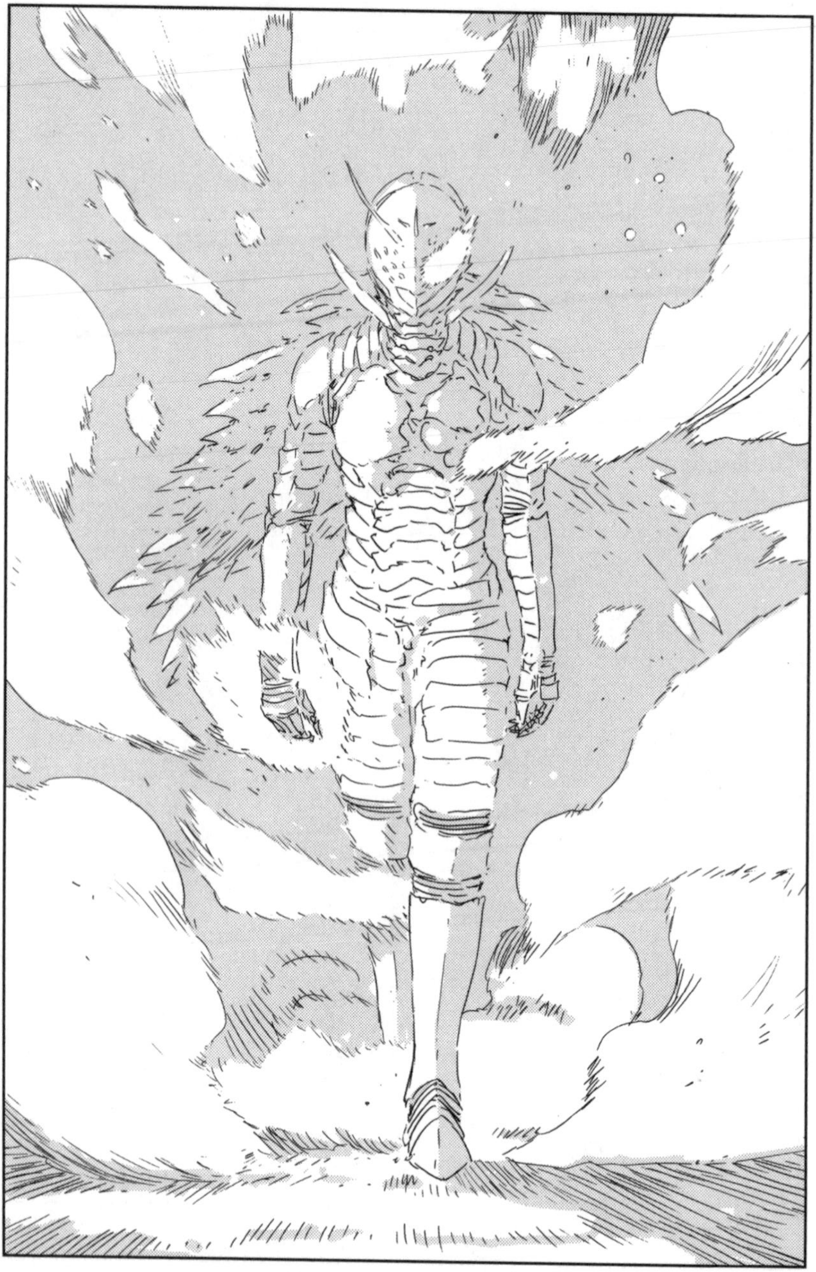

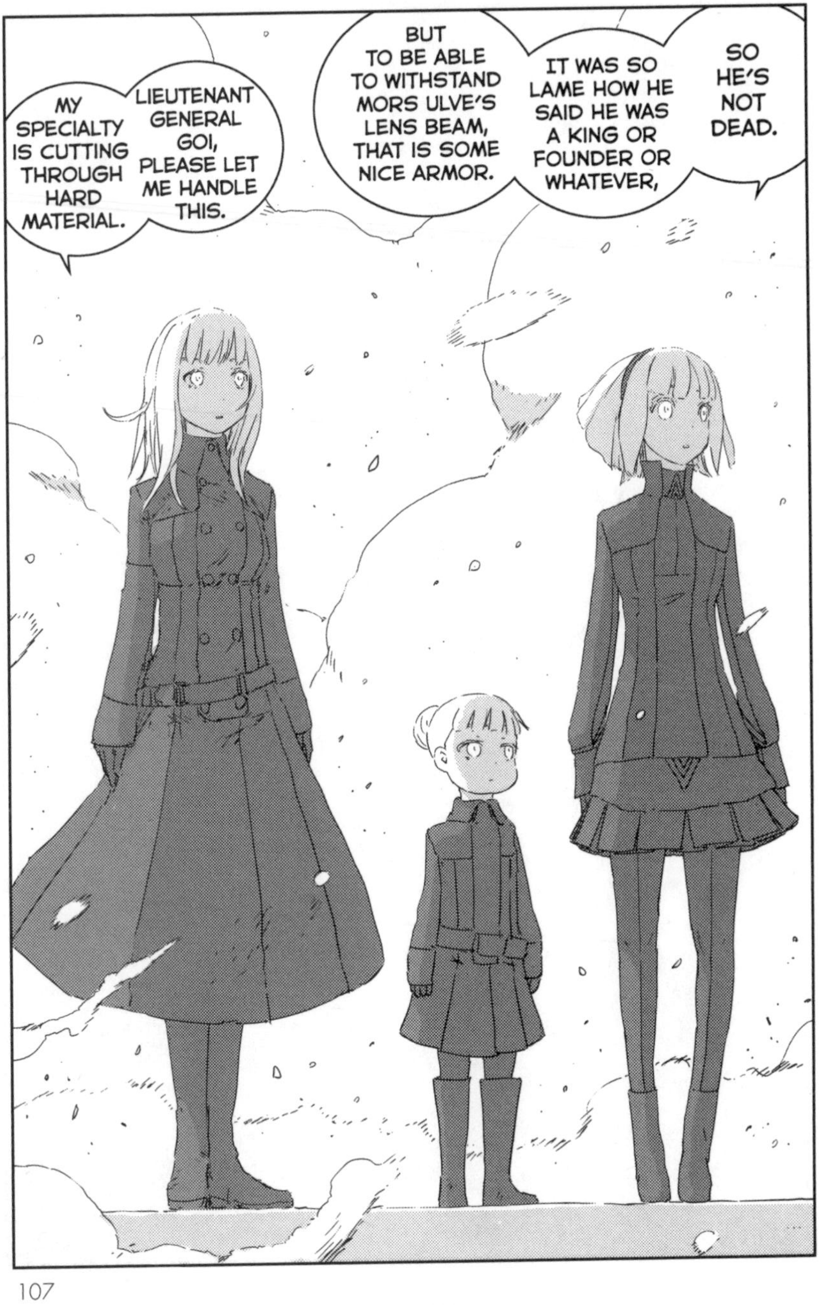
SO HE'S NOT DEAD.
IT WAS SO LAME HOW HE SAID HE WAS A KING OR FOUNDER OR WHATEVER,
BUT TO BE ABLE TO WITHSTAND MORS ULVE'S LENS BEAM, THAT IS SOME NICE ARMOR.
LIEUTENANT GENERAL GOI, PLEASE LET ME HANDLE THIS.
MY SPECIALTY IS CUTTING THROUGH HARD MATERIAL.

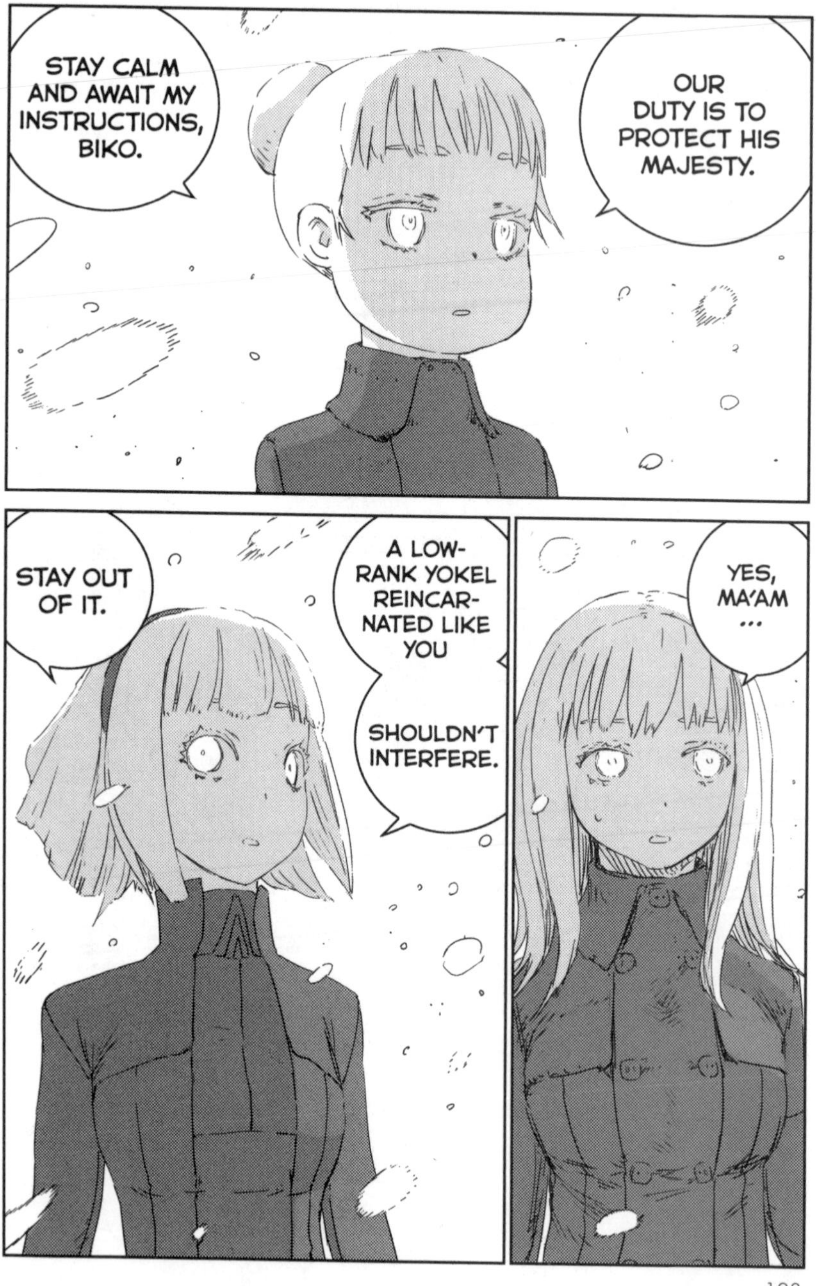
OUR DUTY IS TO PROTECT HIS MAJESTY.
STAY CALM AND AWAIT MY INSTRUCTIONS, BIKO.
YES, MA'AM ...
A LOW-RANK YOKEL REINCARNATED LIKE YOU
SHOULDN'T INTERFERE.
STAY OUT OF IT.

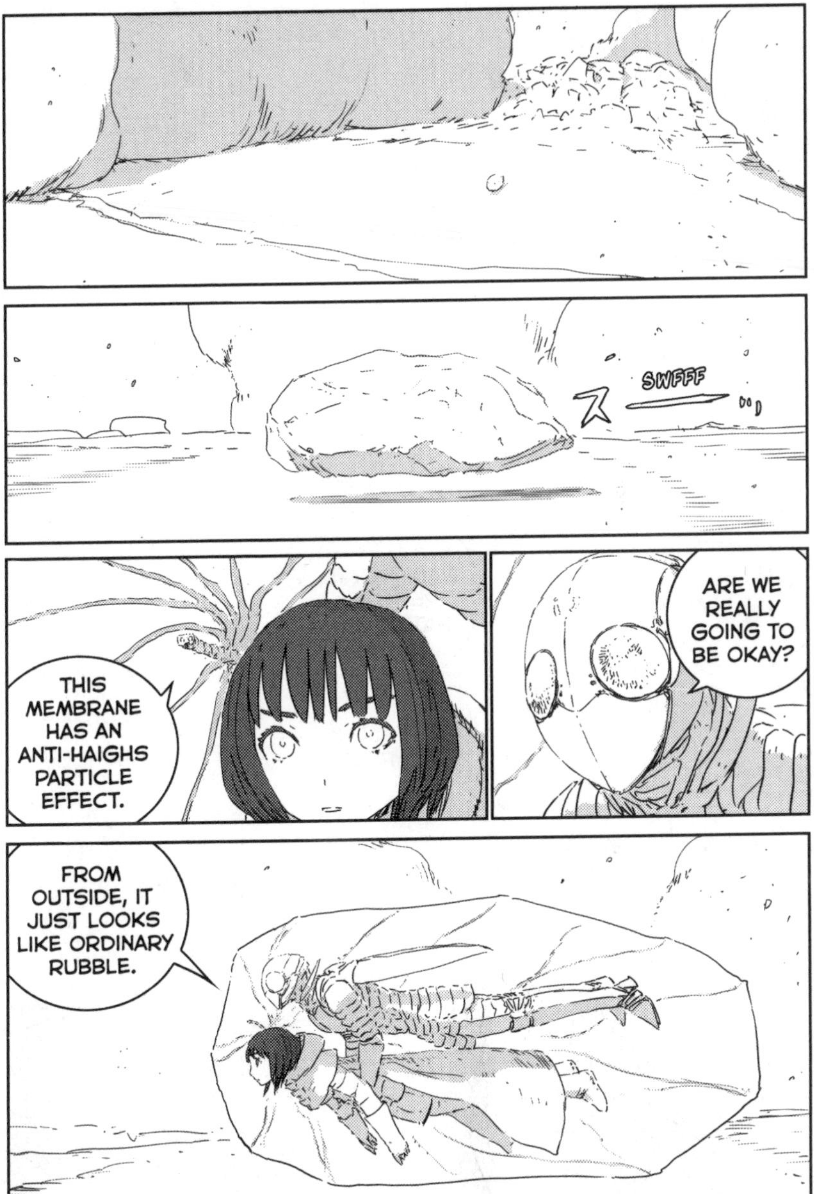
ス
SWFFF
ARE WE REALLY GOING TO BE OKAY?
THIS MEMBRANE HAS AN ANTI-HAIGHS PARTICLE EFFECT.
FROM OUTSIDE, IT JUST LOOKS LIKE ORDINARY RUBBLE.

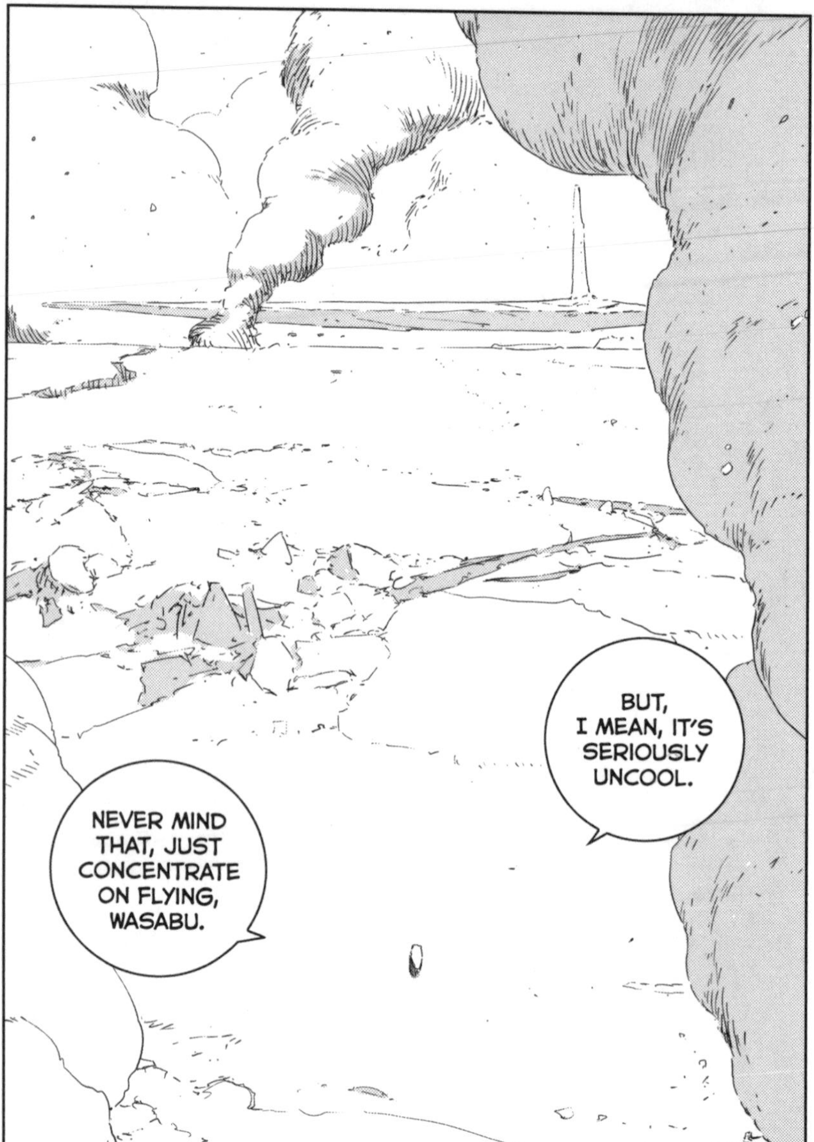
BUT, I MEAN, IT'S SERIOUSLY UNCOOL.
NEVER MIND THAT, JUST CONCENTRATE ON FLYING, WASABU.

CHAPTER 34 END

APOSIMZ

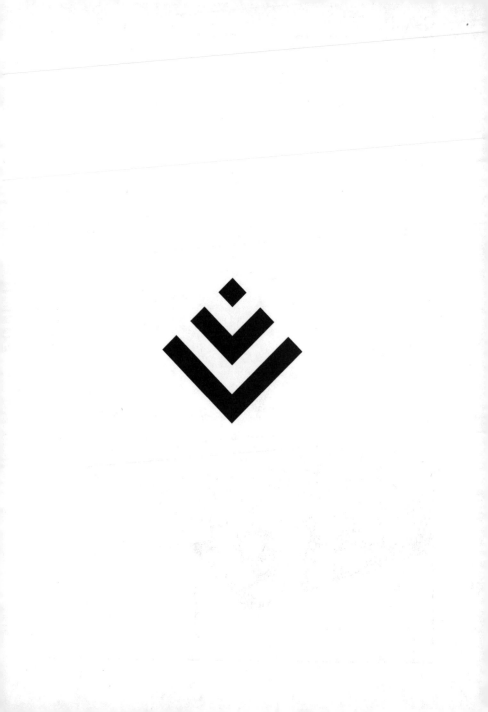

CHAPTER 35

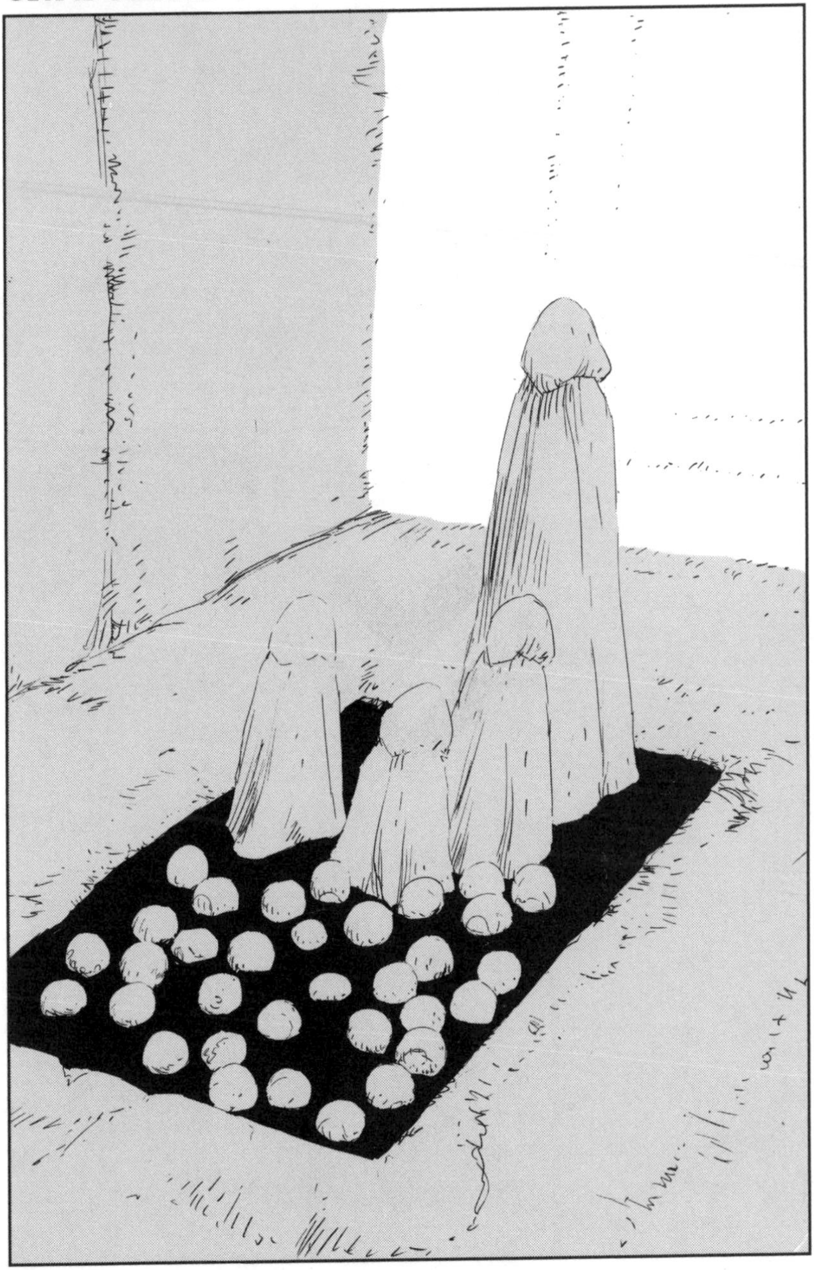

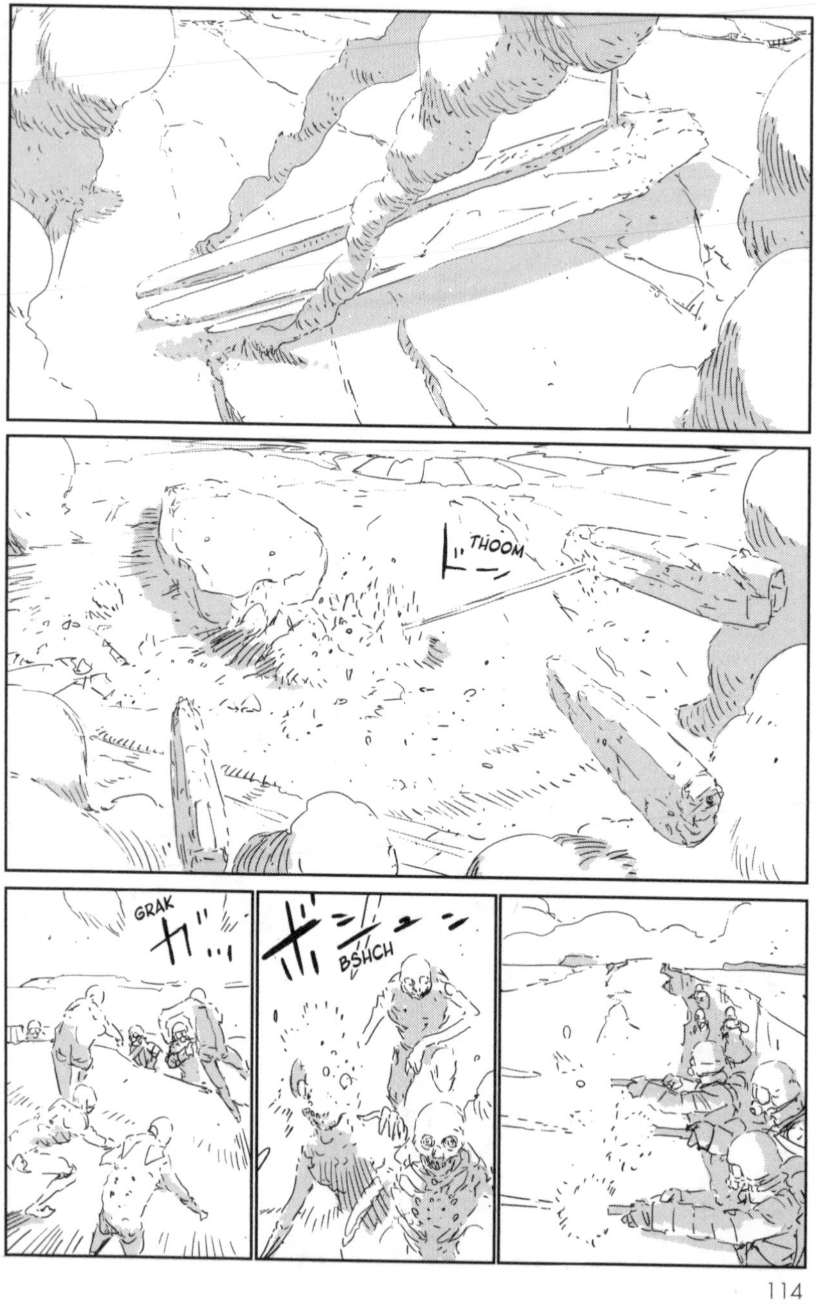
THOOM
BSHCH
GRAK

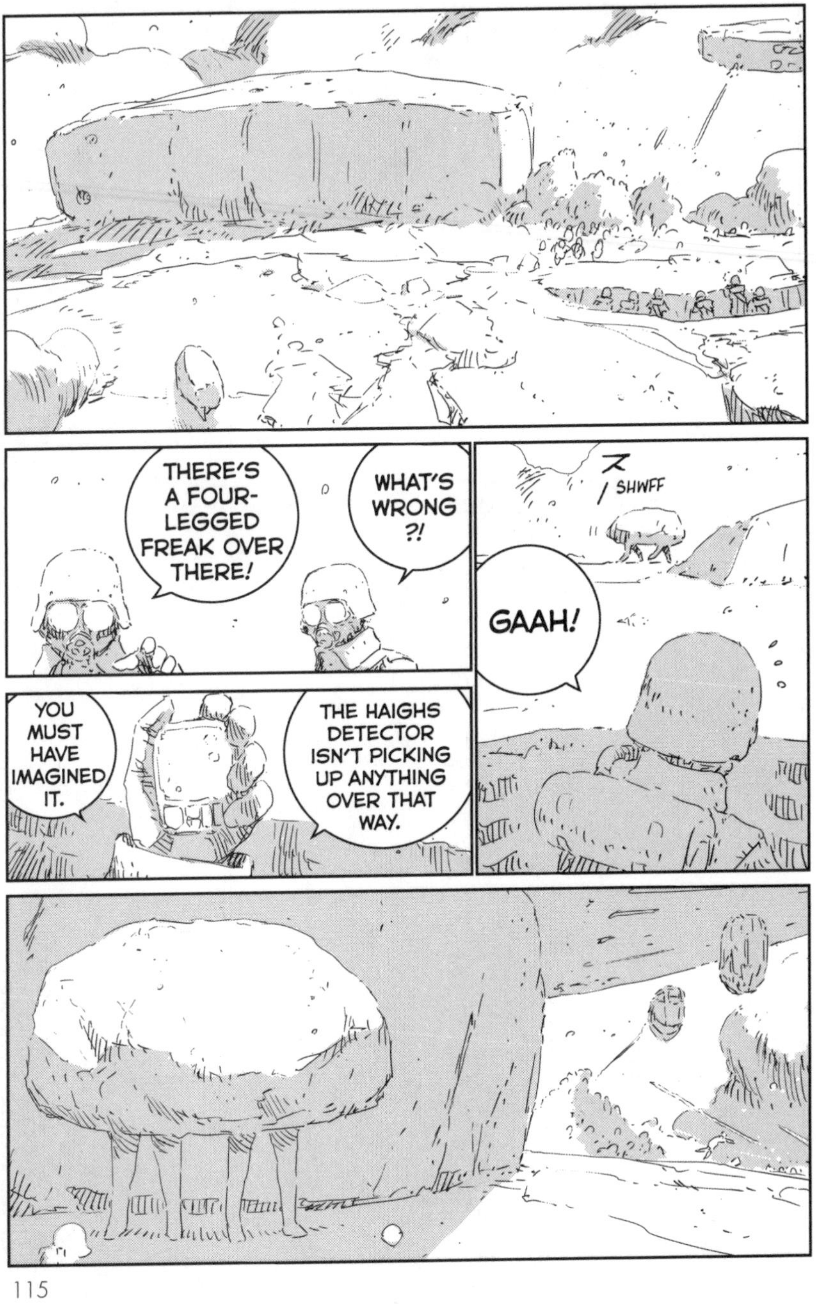
SHWFF
GAAH!
WHAT'S WRONG ?!
THERE'S A FOUR-LEGGED FREAK OVER THERE!
THE HAIGHS DETECTOR ISN'T PICKING UP ANYTHING OVER THAT WAY.
YOU MUST HAVE IMAGINED IT.

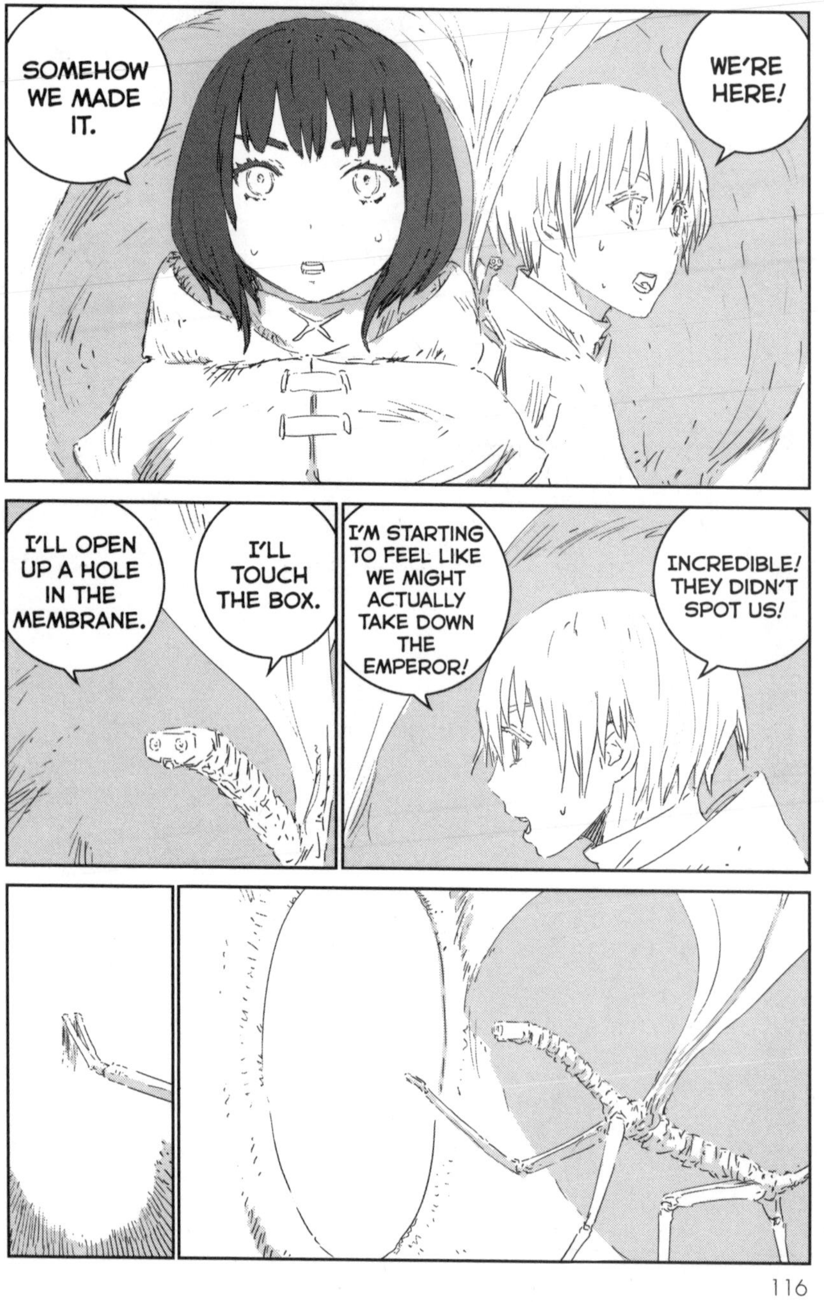
WE'RE HERE!
SOMEHOW WE MADE IT.
INCREDIBLE! THEY DIDN'T SPOT US!
I'M STARTING TO FEEL LIKE WE MIGHT ACTUALLY TAKE DOWN THE EMPEROR!
I'LL TOUCH THE BOX.
I'LL OPEN UP A HOLE IN THE MEMBRANE.

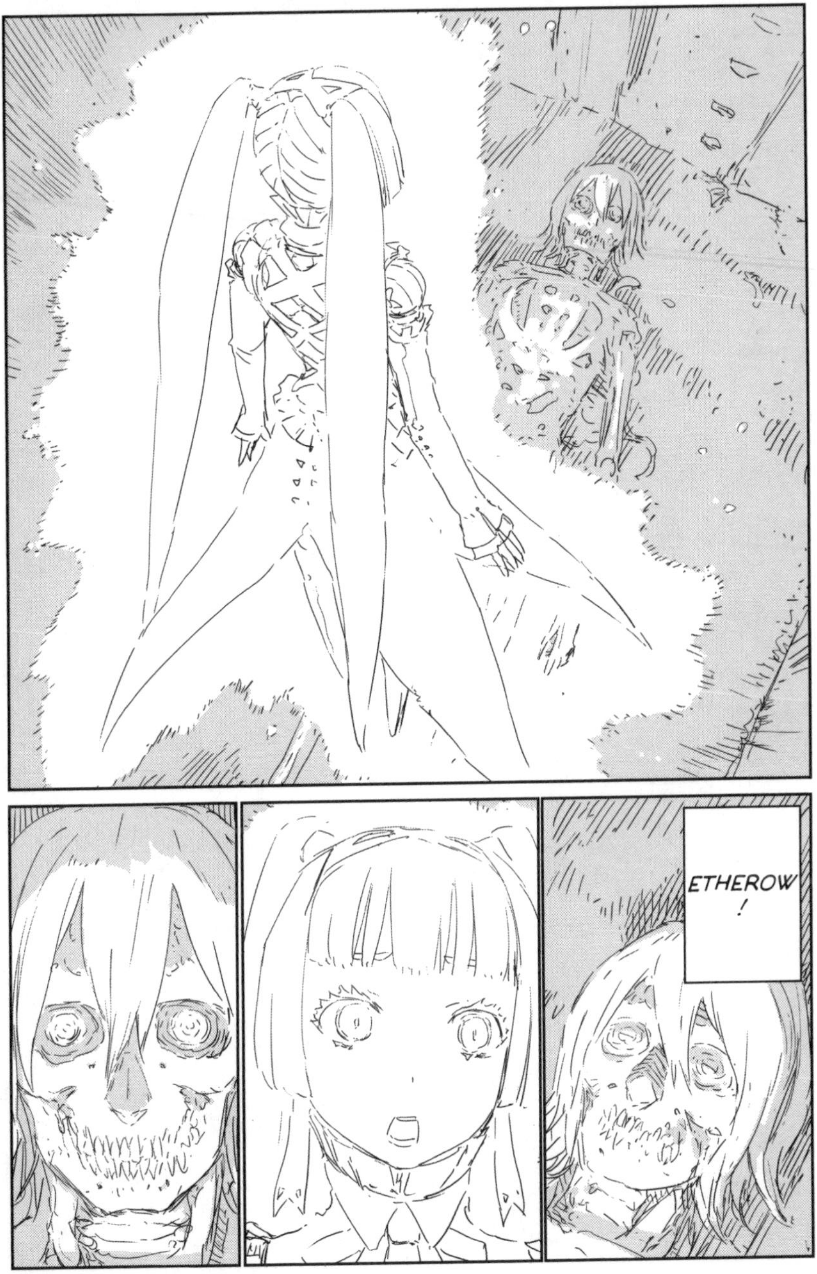
ETHEROW
!

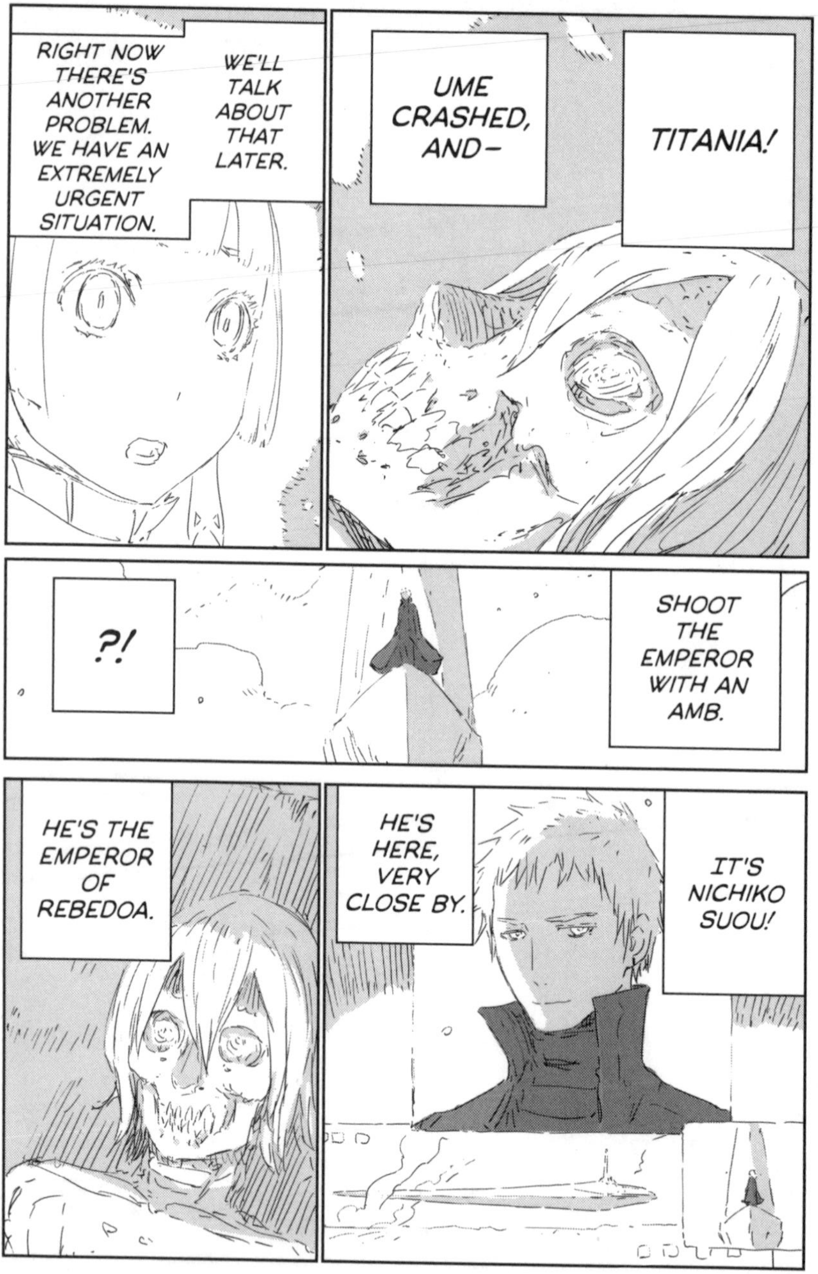
TITANIA!
UME CRASHED, AND–
WE'LL TALK ABOUT THAT LATER.
RIGHT NOW THERE'S ANOTHER PROBLEM. WE HAVE AN EXTREMELY URGENT SITUATION.
SHOOT THE EMPEROR WITH AN AMB.
?!
IT'S NICHIKO SUOU!
HE'S HERE, VERY CLOSE BY.
HE'S THE EMPEROR OF REBEDOA.

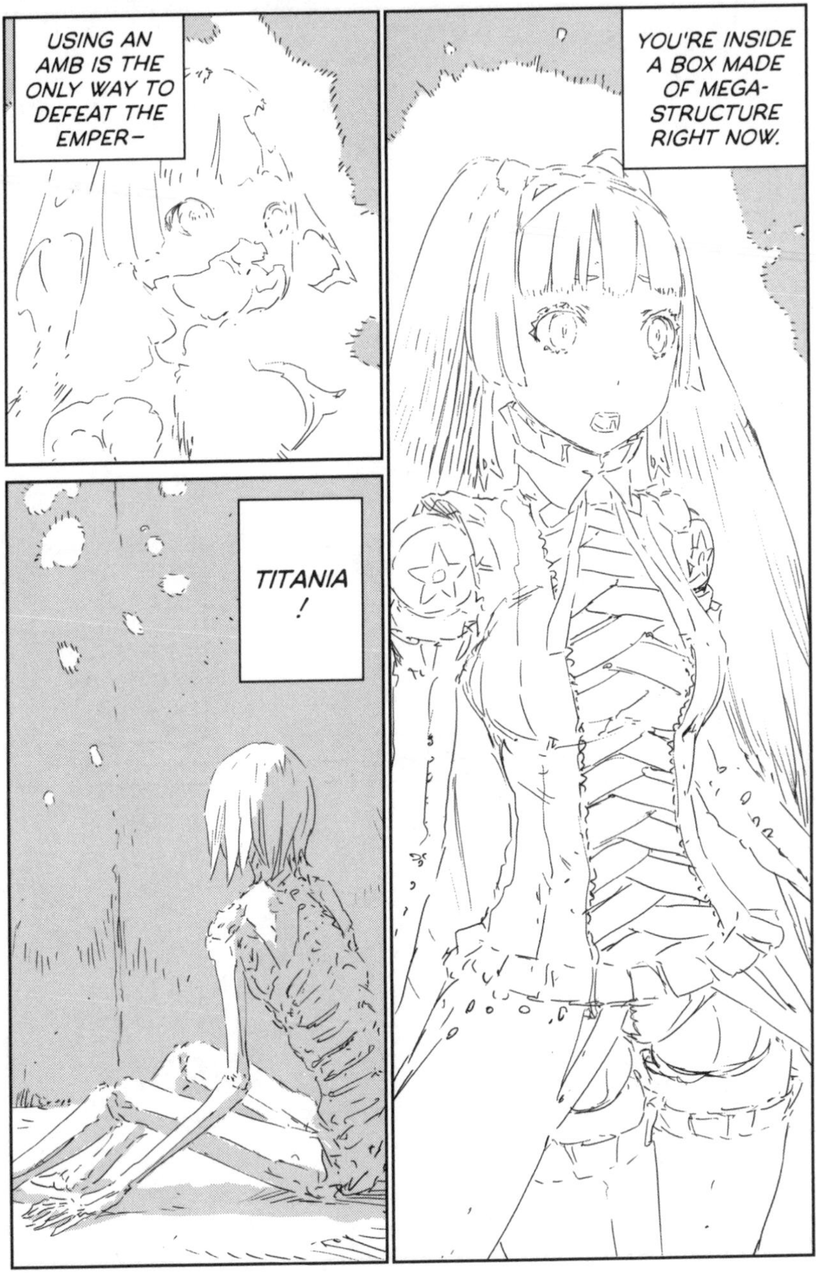
YOU'RE INSIDE A BOX MADE OF MEGA-STRUCTURE RIGHT NOW.
USING AN AMB IS THE ONLY WAY TO DEFEAT THE EMPER—
TITANIA !

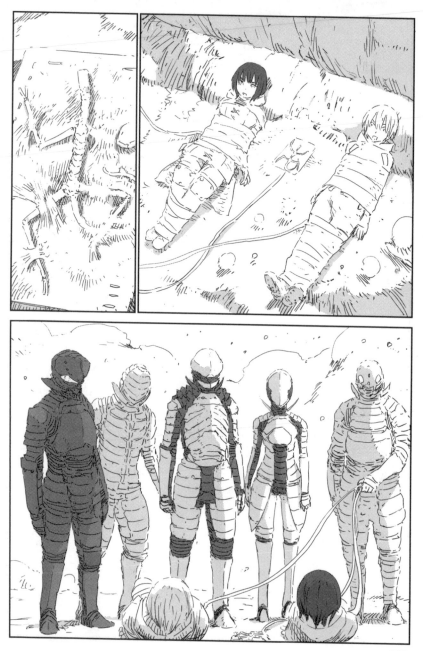

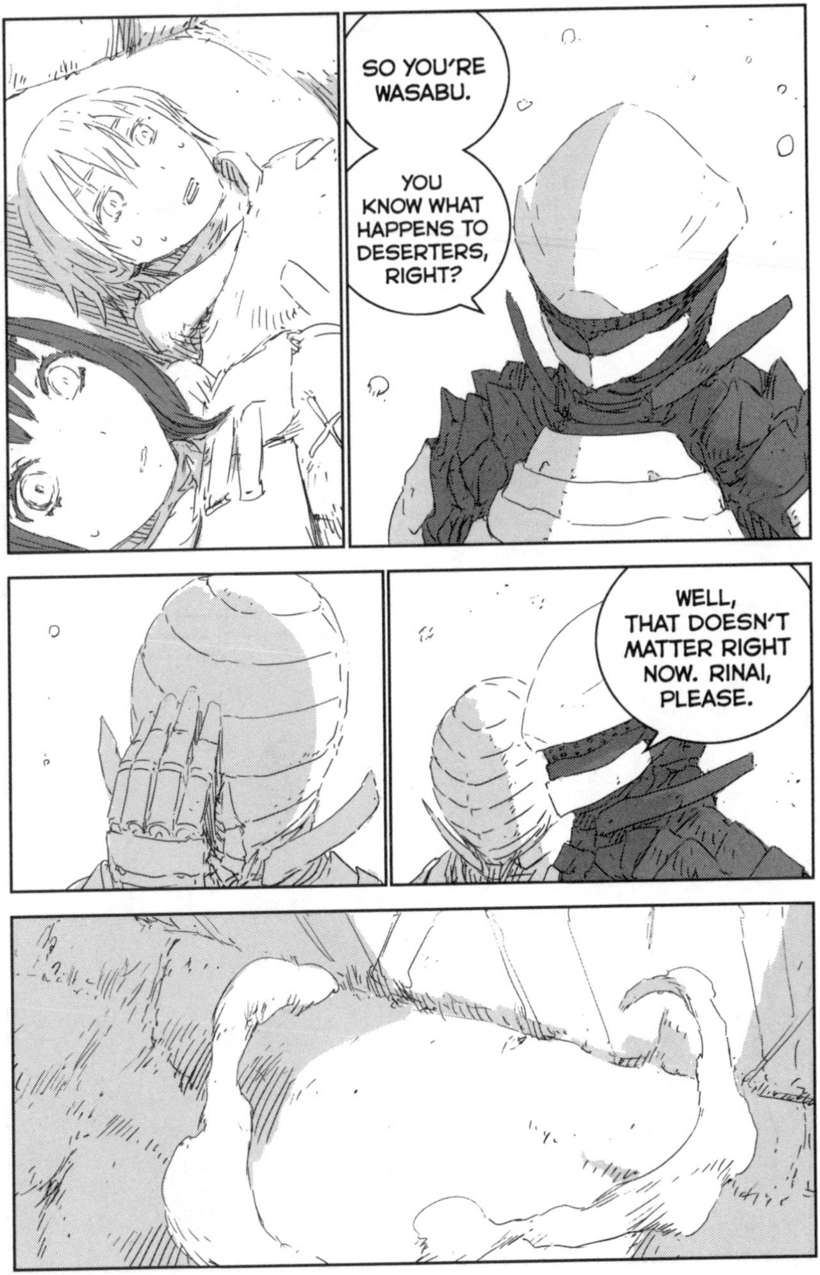
SO YOU'RE WASABU.
YOU KNOW WHAT HAPPENS TO DESERTERS, RIGHT?
WELL, THAT DOESN'T MATTER RIGHT NOW. RINAI, PLEASE.

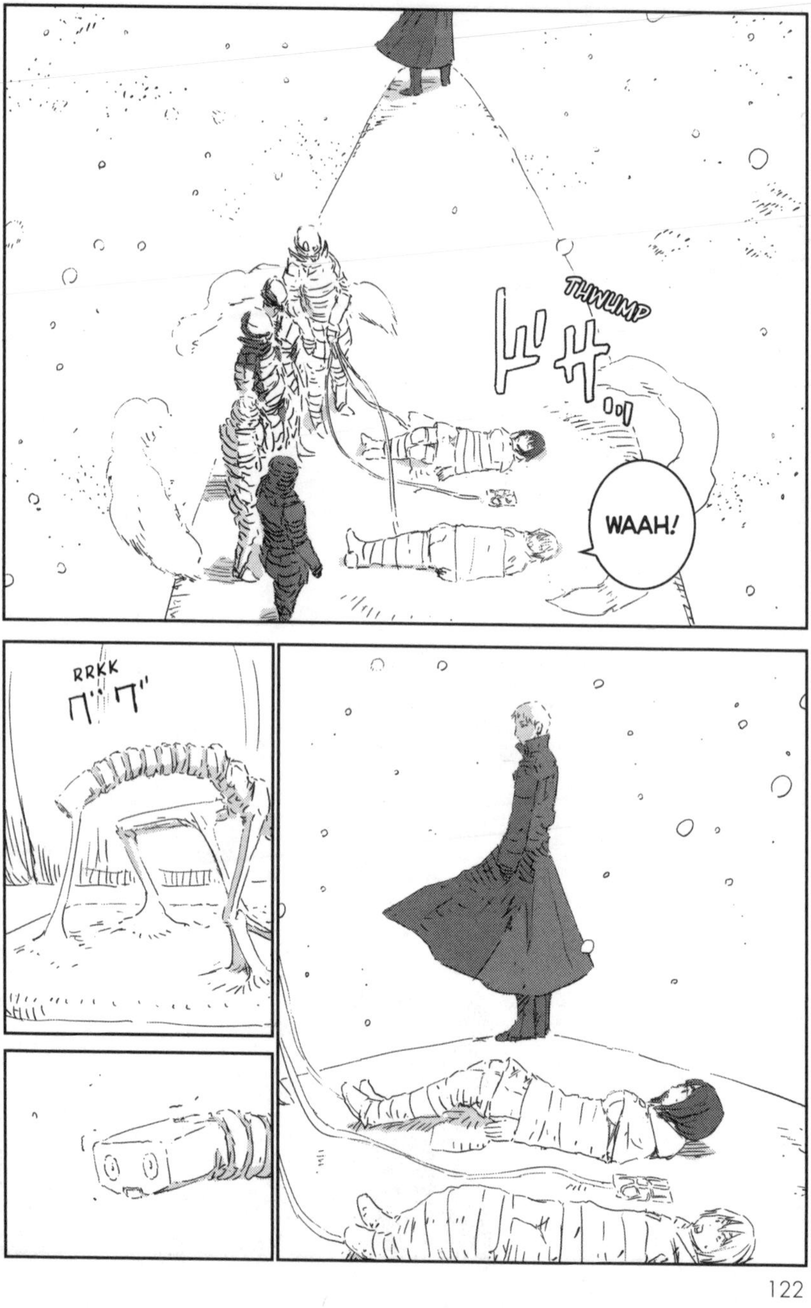
THWUMP
ドサッ
WAAH!
RRKK

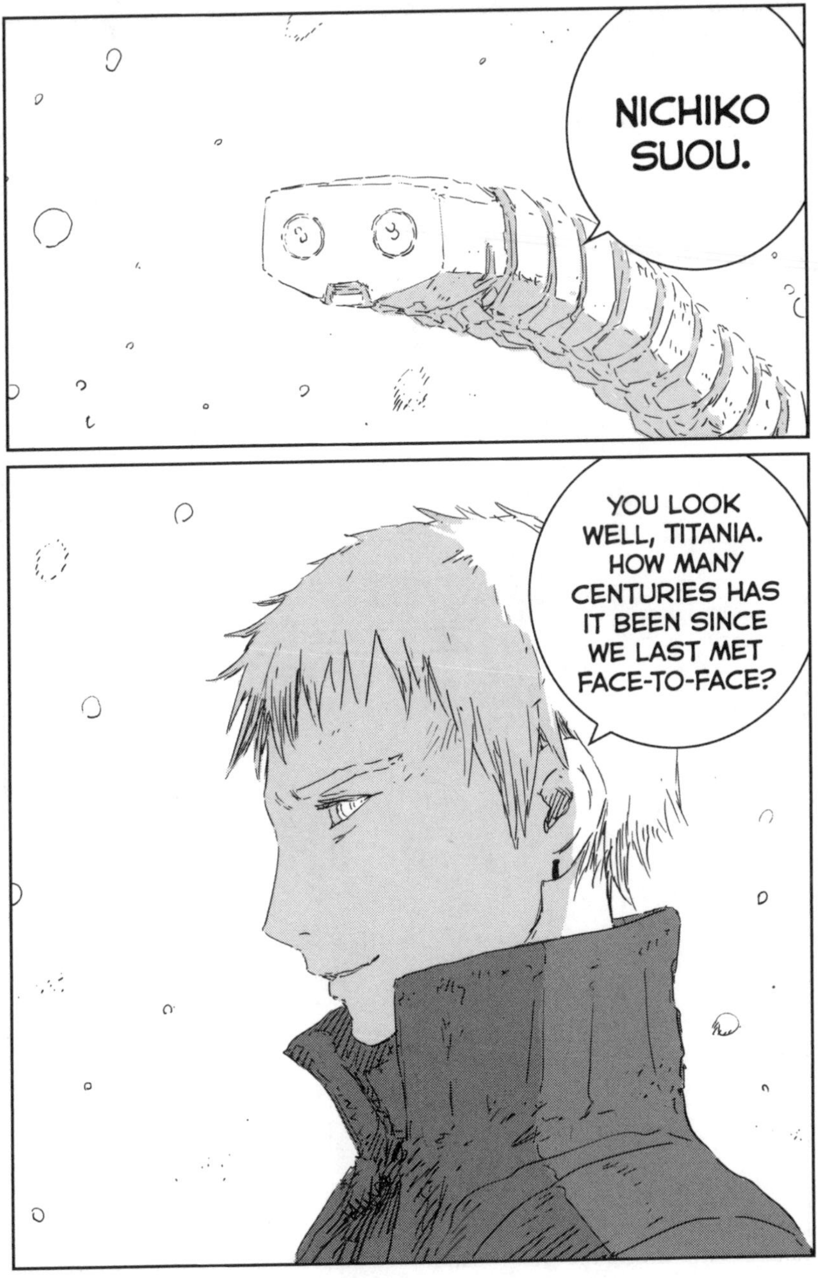
NICHIKO SUOU.
YOU LOOK WELL, TITANIA. HOW MANY CENTURIES HAS IT BEEN SINCE WE LAST MET FACE-TO-FACE?

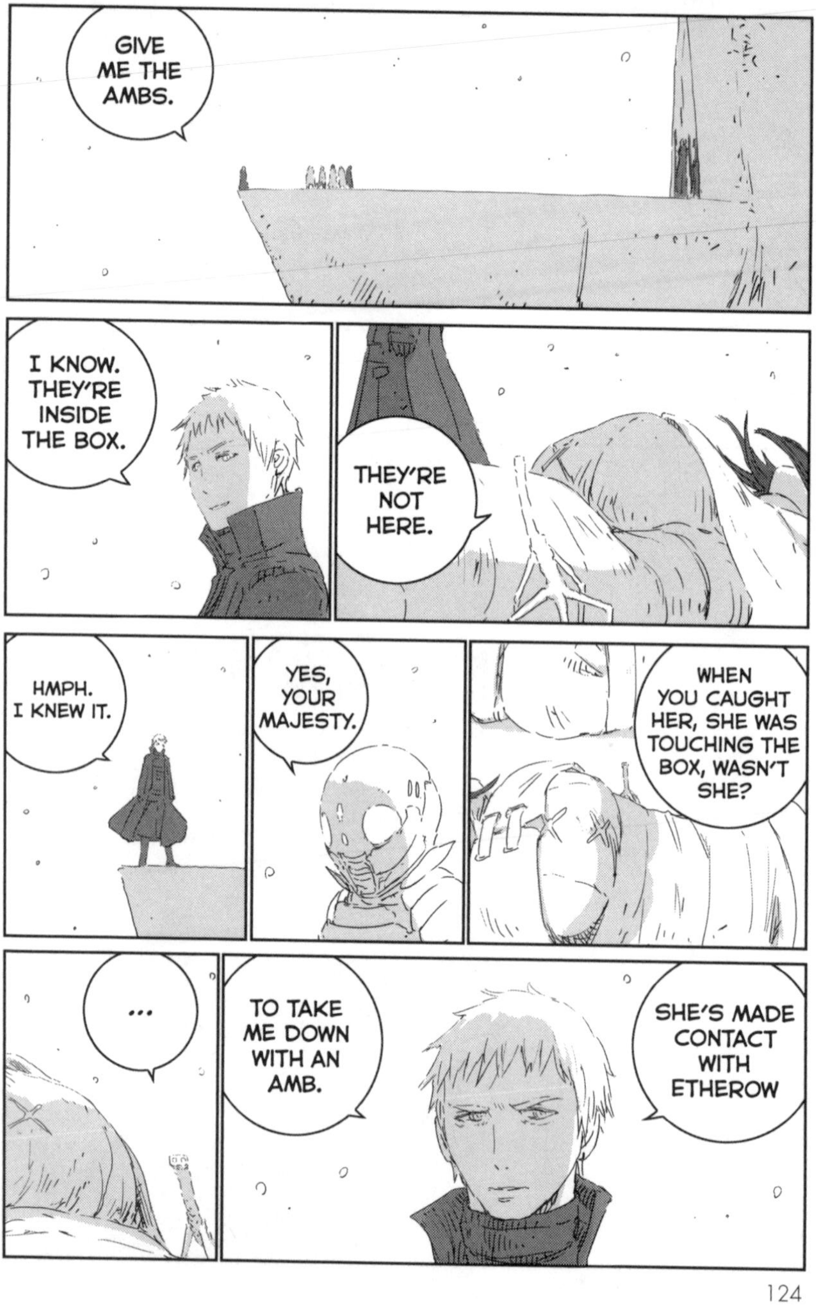
GIVE ME THE AMBS.
THEY'RE NOT HERE.
I KNOW. THEY'RE INSIDE THE BOX.
WHEN YOU CAUGHT HER, SHE WAS TOUCHING THE BOX, WASN'T SHE?
YES, YOUR MAJESTY.
HMPH. I KNEW IT.
SHE'S MADE CONTACT WITH ETHEROW
TO TAKE ME DOWN WITH AN AMB.
...

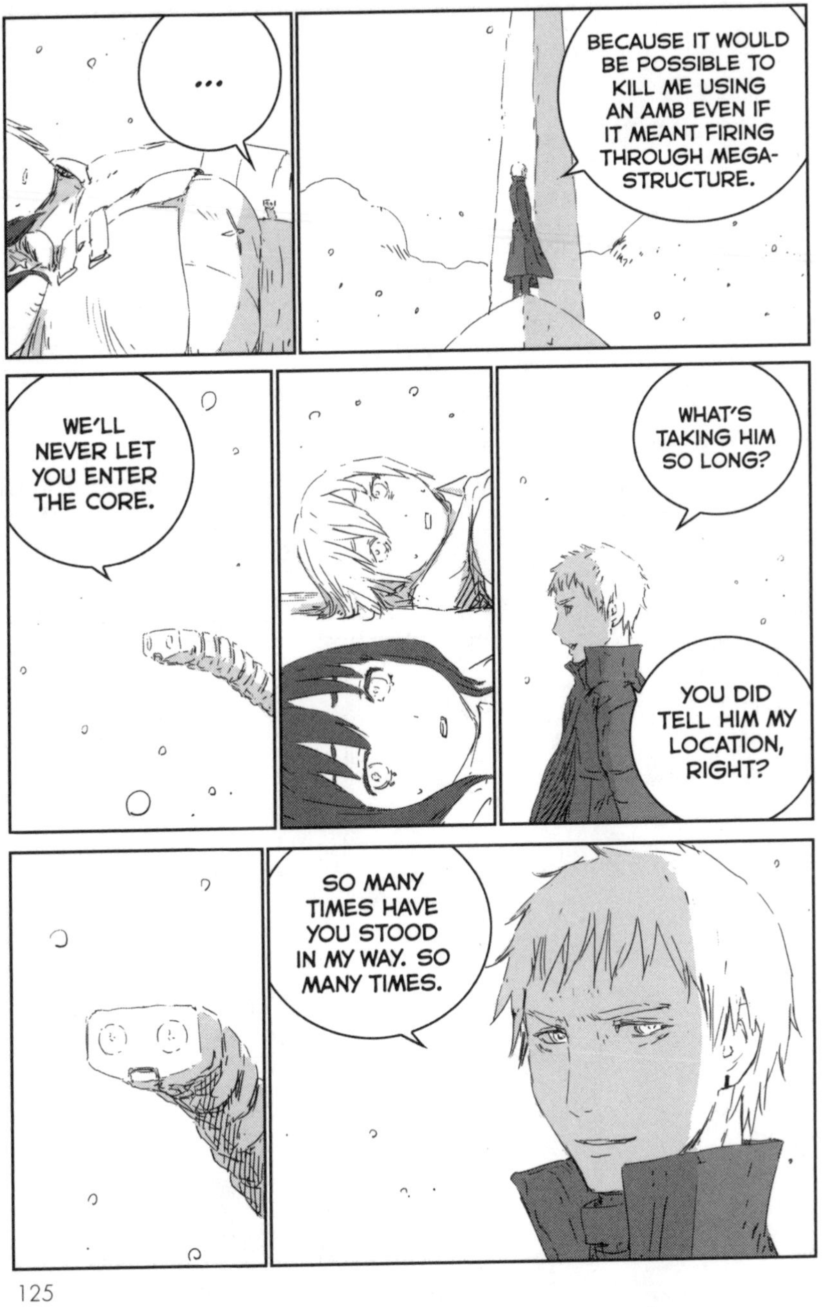
BECAUSE IT WOULD BE POSSIBLE TO KILL ME USING AN AMB EVEN IF IT MEANT FIRING THROUGH MEGA-STRUCTURE.
...
WHAT'S TAKING HIM SO LONG?
YOU DID TELL HIM MY LOCATION, RIGHT?
WE'LL NEVER LET YOU ENTER THE CORE.
SO MANY TIMES HAVE YOU STOOD IN MY WAY. SO MANY TIMES.

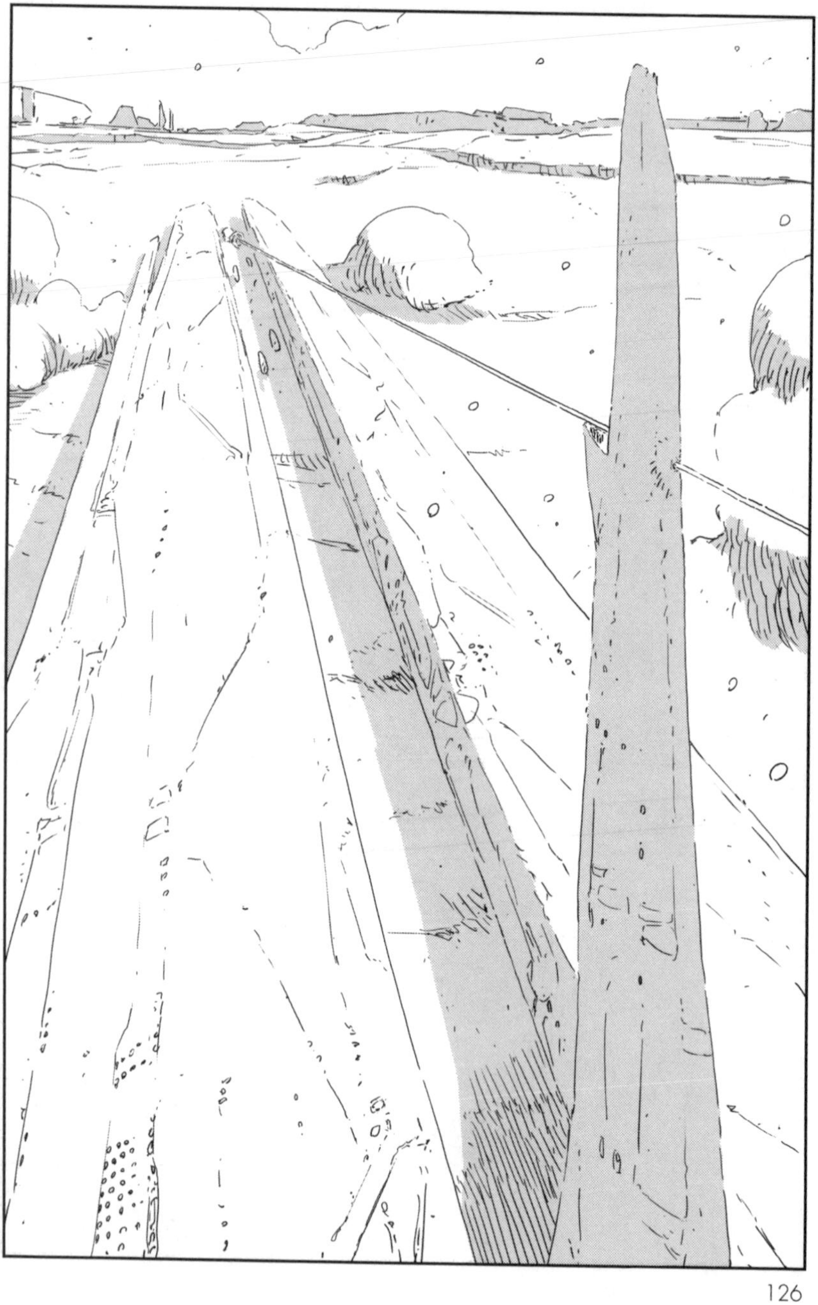

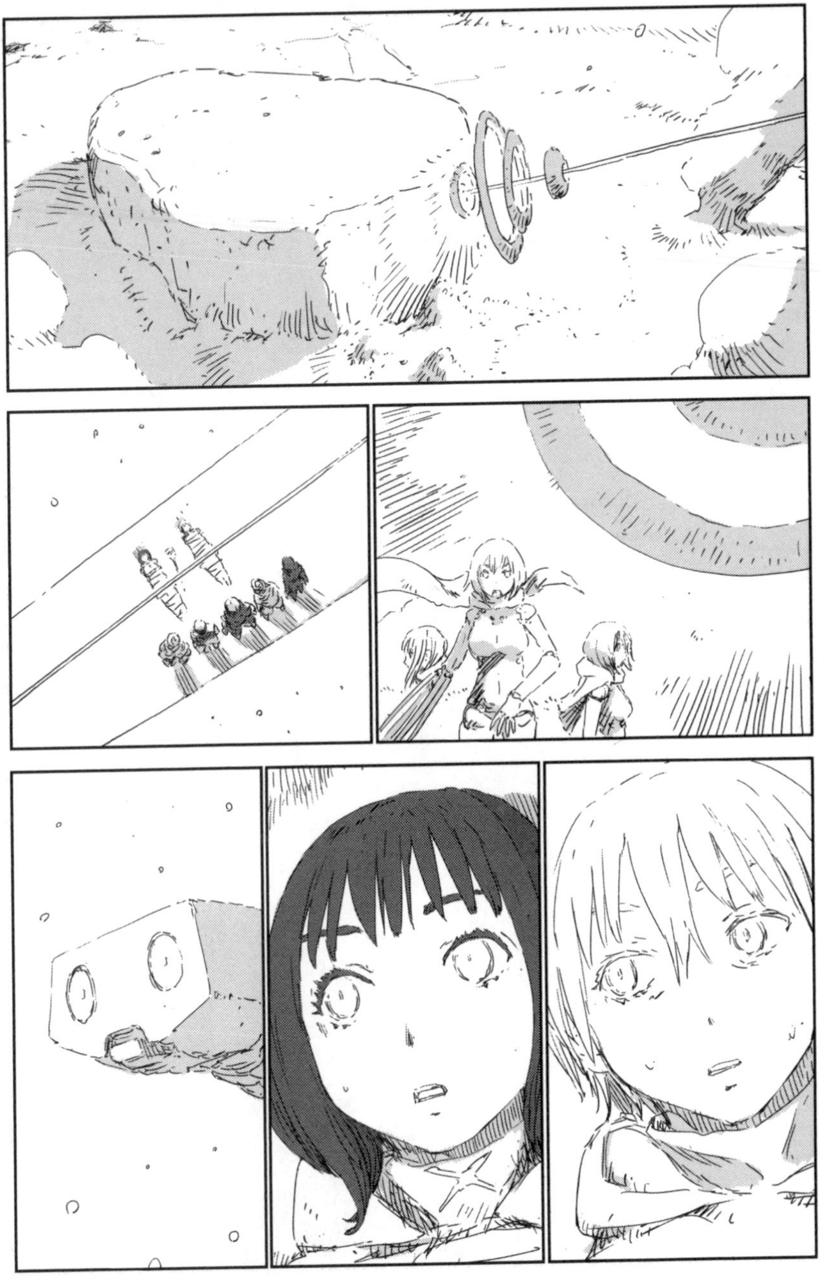

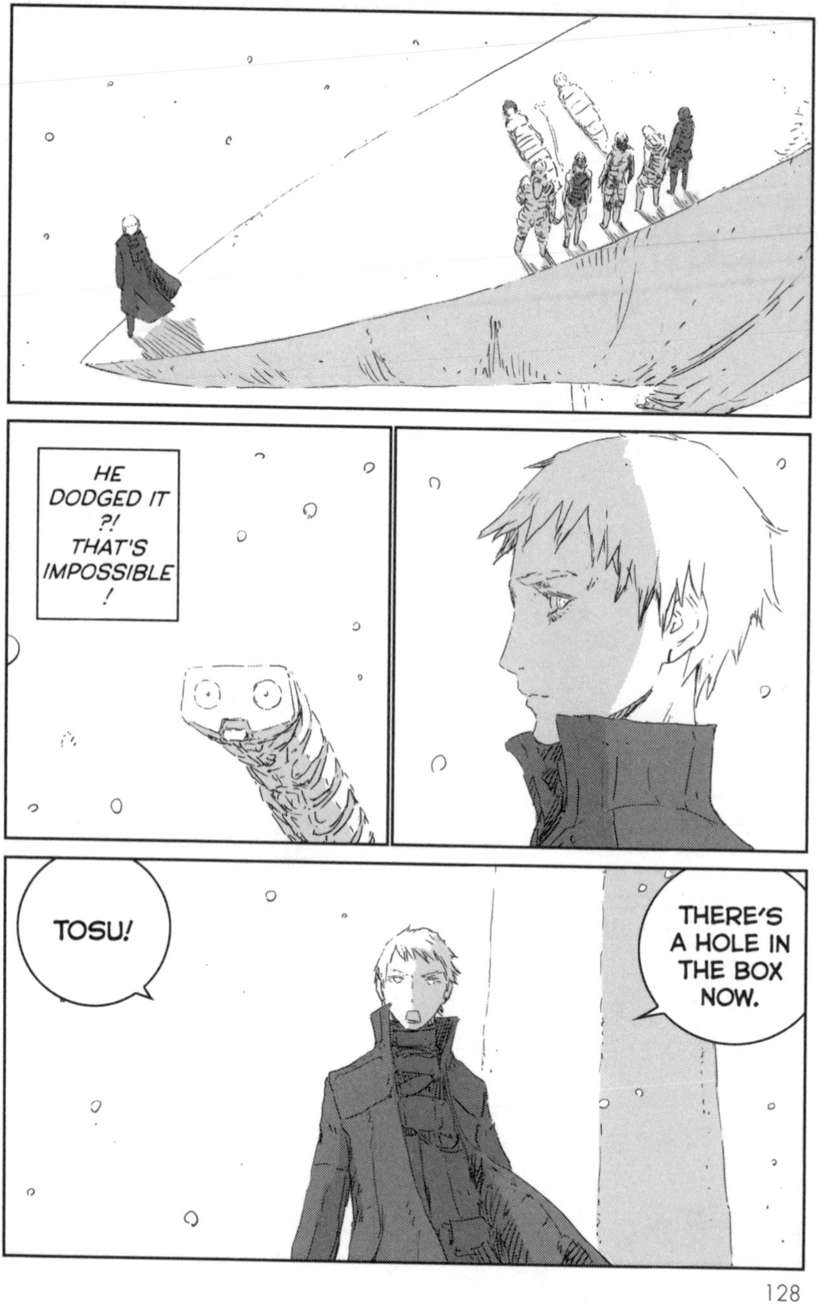
HE DODGED IT ?! THAT'S IMPOSSIBLE !
THERE'S A HOLE IN THE BOX NOW.
TOSU!

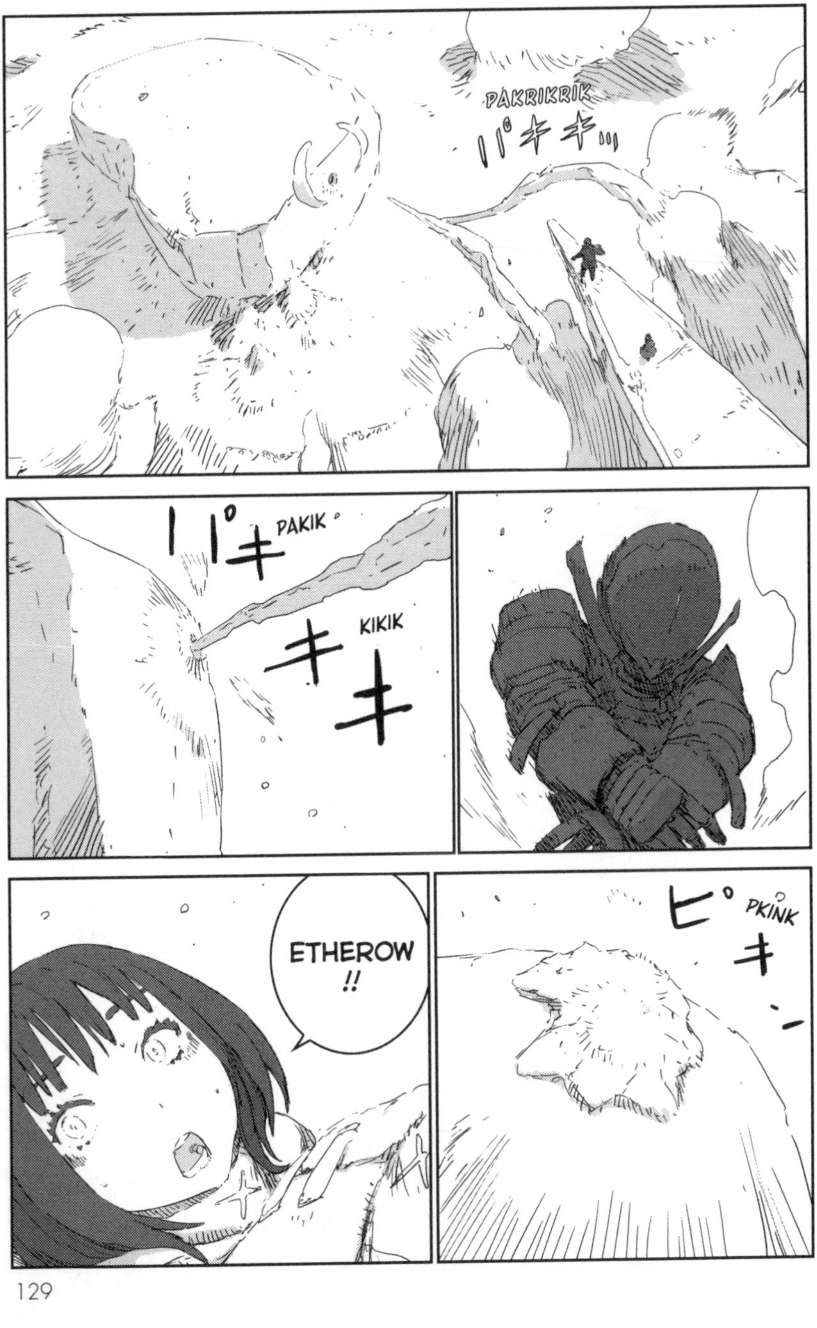
PAKRIKRIK
パキキッ
パキ
PAKIK
KIKIK
キキ
ピキ
PKINK
ETHEROW !!

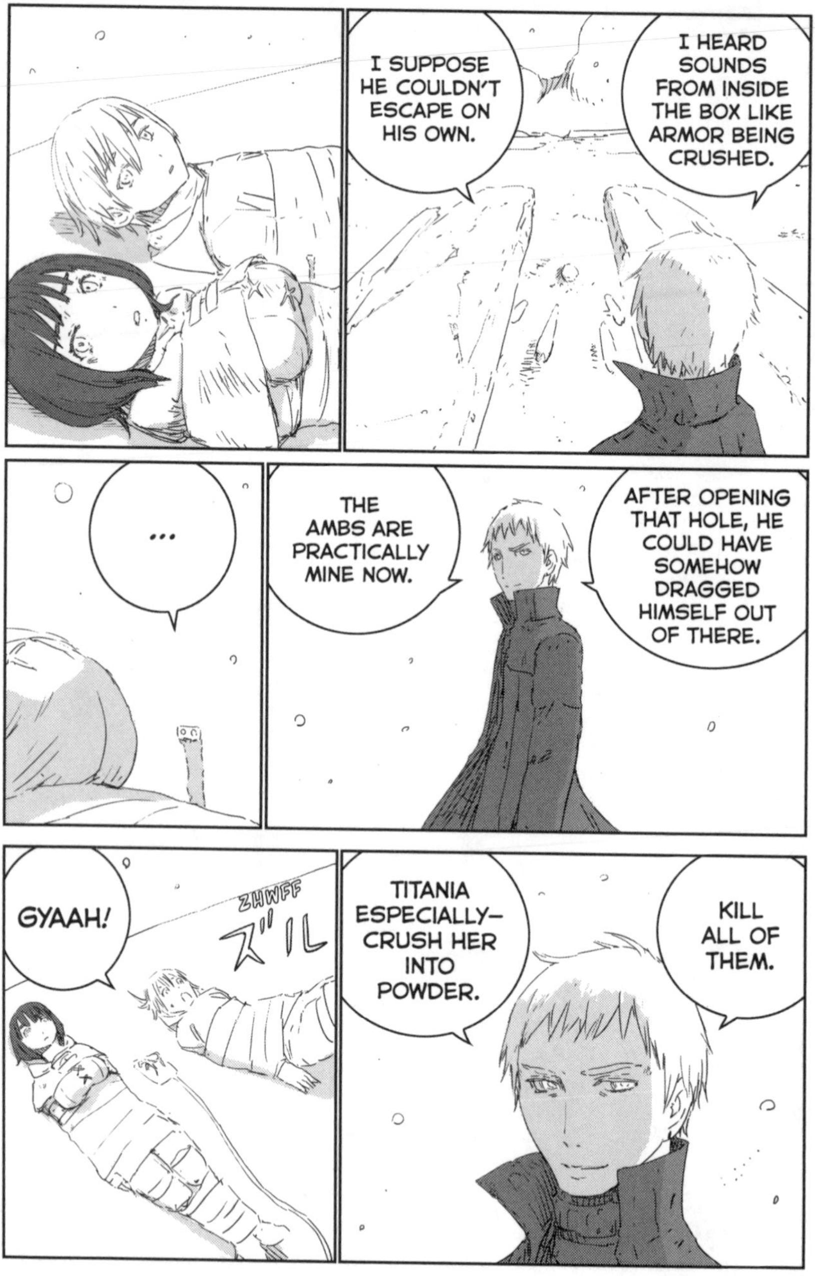
I HEARD SOUNDS FROM INSIDE THE BOX LIKE ARMOR BEING CRUSHED.
I SUPPOSE HE COULDN'T ESCAPE ON HIS OWN.
AFTER OPENING THAT HOLE, HE COULD HAVE SOMEHOW DRAGGED HIMSELF OUT OF THERE.
THE AMBS ARE PRACTICALLY MINE NOW.
...
KILL ALL OF THEM.
TITANIA ESPECIALLY— CRUSH HER INTO POWDER.
ZHWFF
ズル
GYAAH!

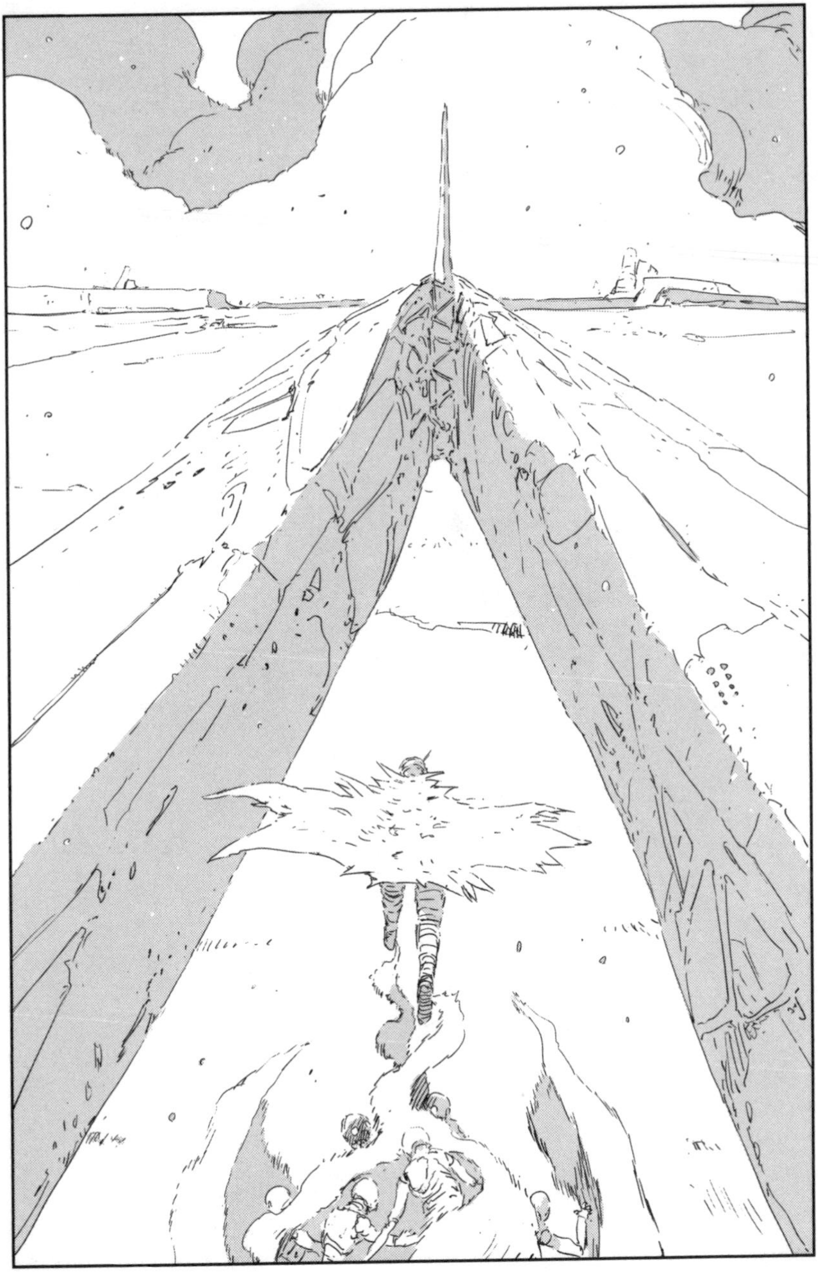

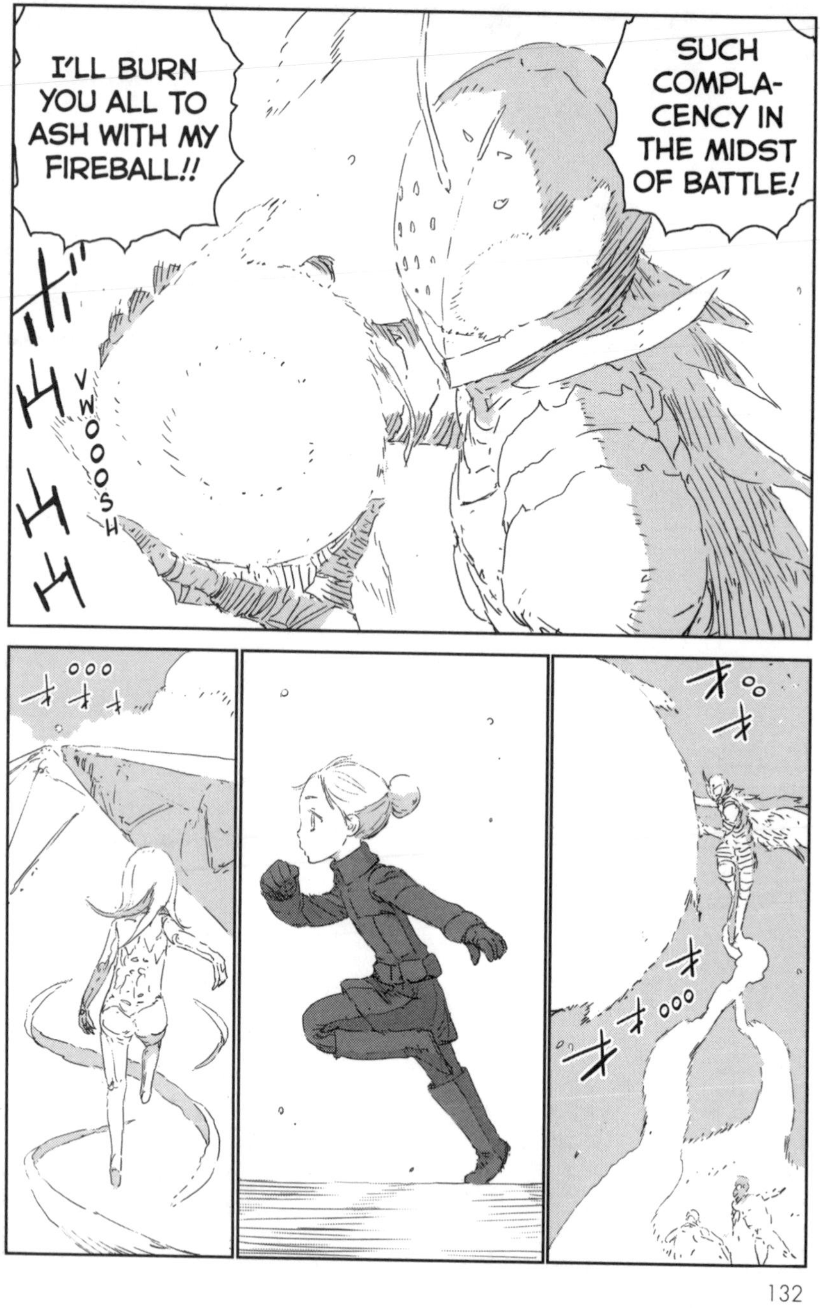
SUCH COMPLACENCY IN THE MIDST OF BATTLE!
I'LL BURN YOU ALL TO ASH WITH MY FIREBALL!!
VWOOOSH

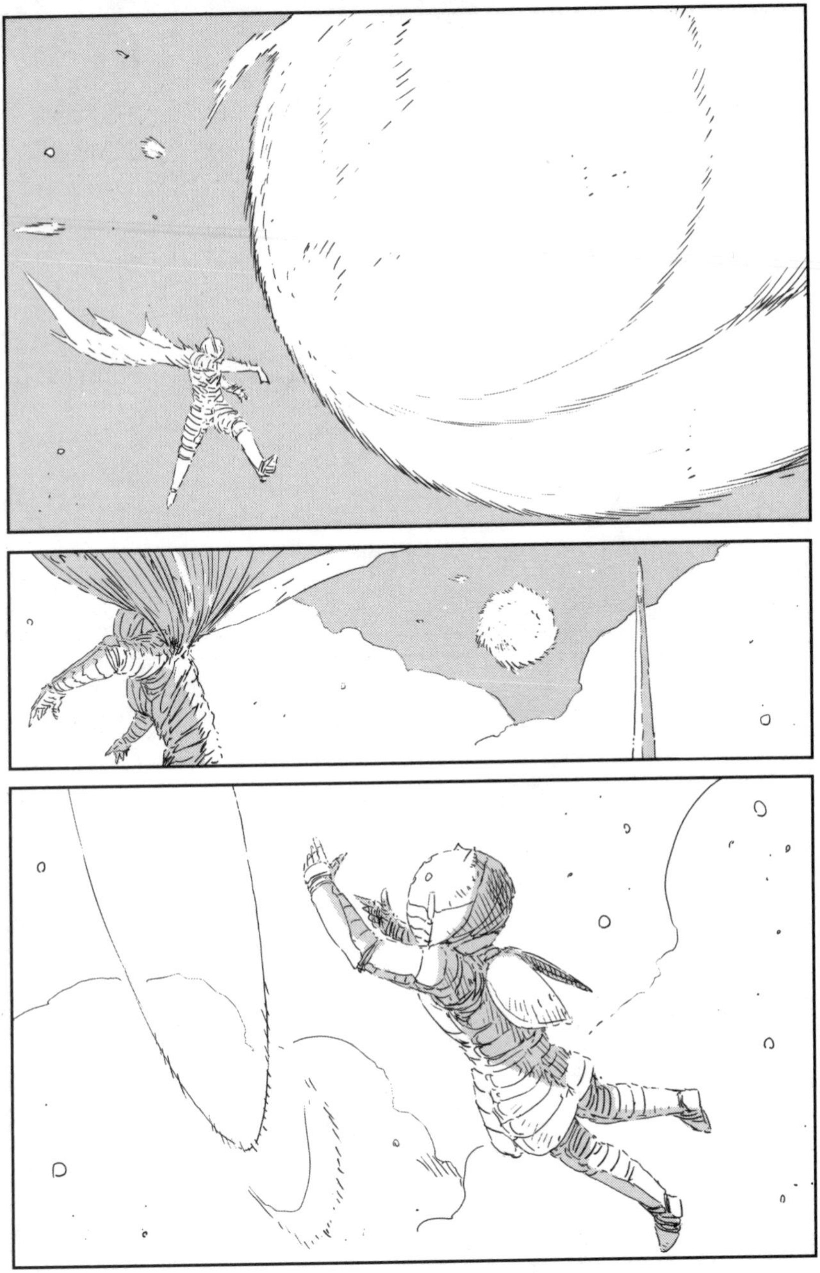

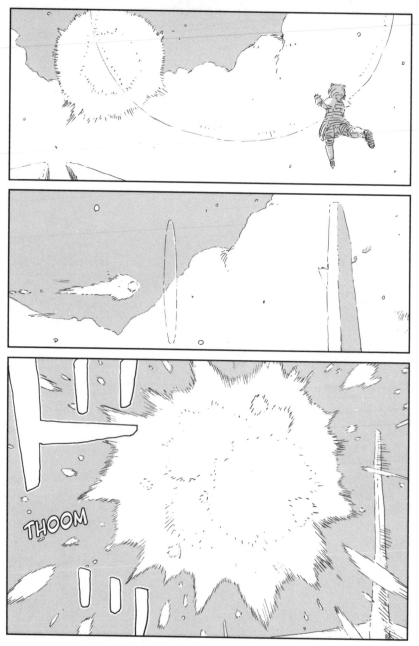

THOOM

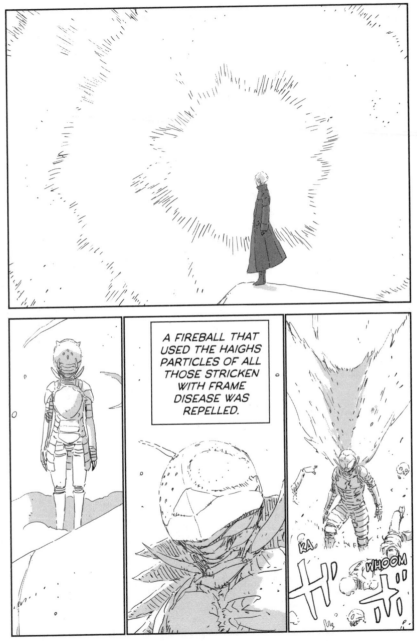

A FIREBALL THAT USED THE HAIGHS PARTICLES OF ALL THOSE STRICKEN WITH FRAME DISEASE WAS REPELLED.

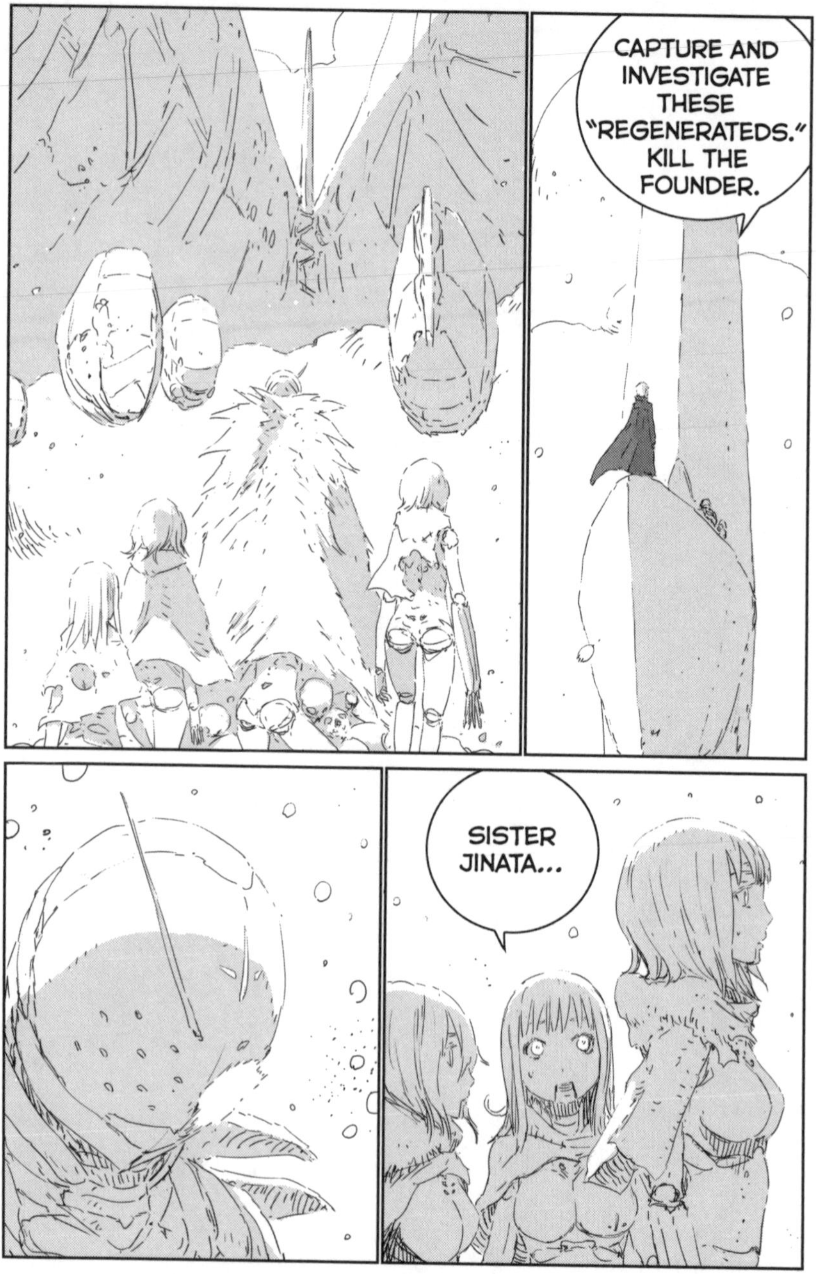
CAPTURE AND INVESTIGATE THESE "REGENERATEDS." KILL THE FOUNDER.
SISTER JINATA...

CHAPTER 35 END

APOSIMZ

X

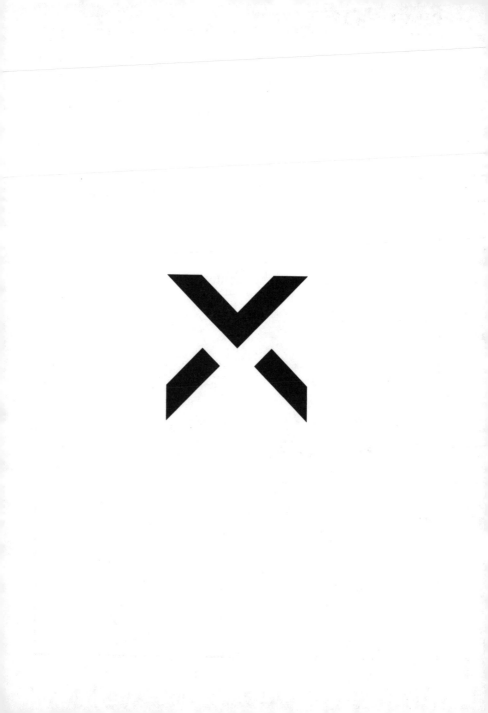

CHAPTER 36

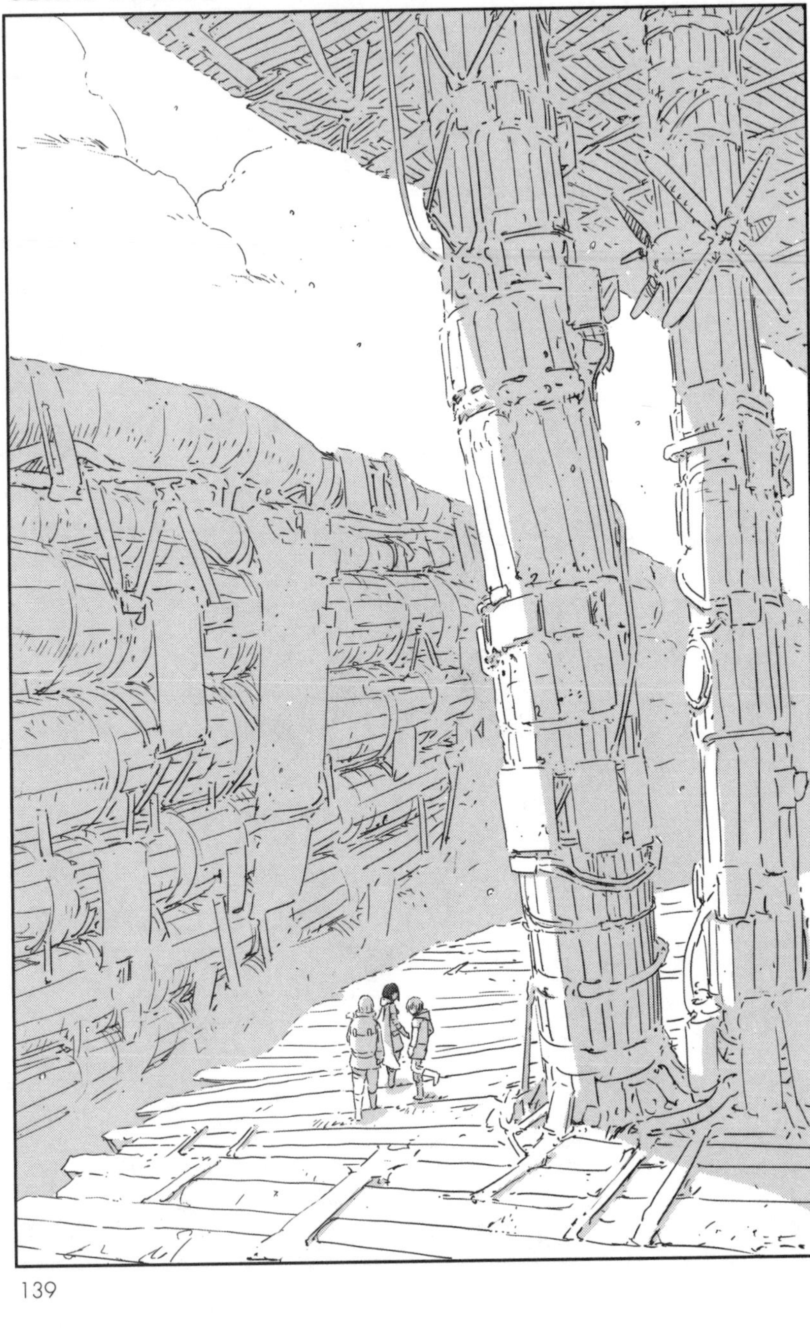

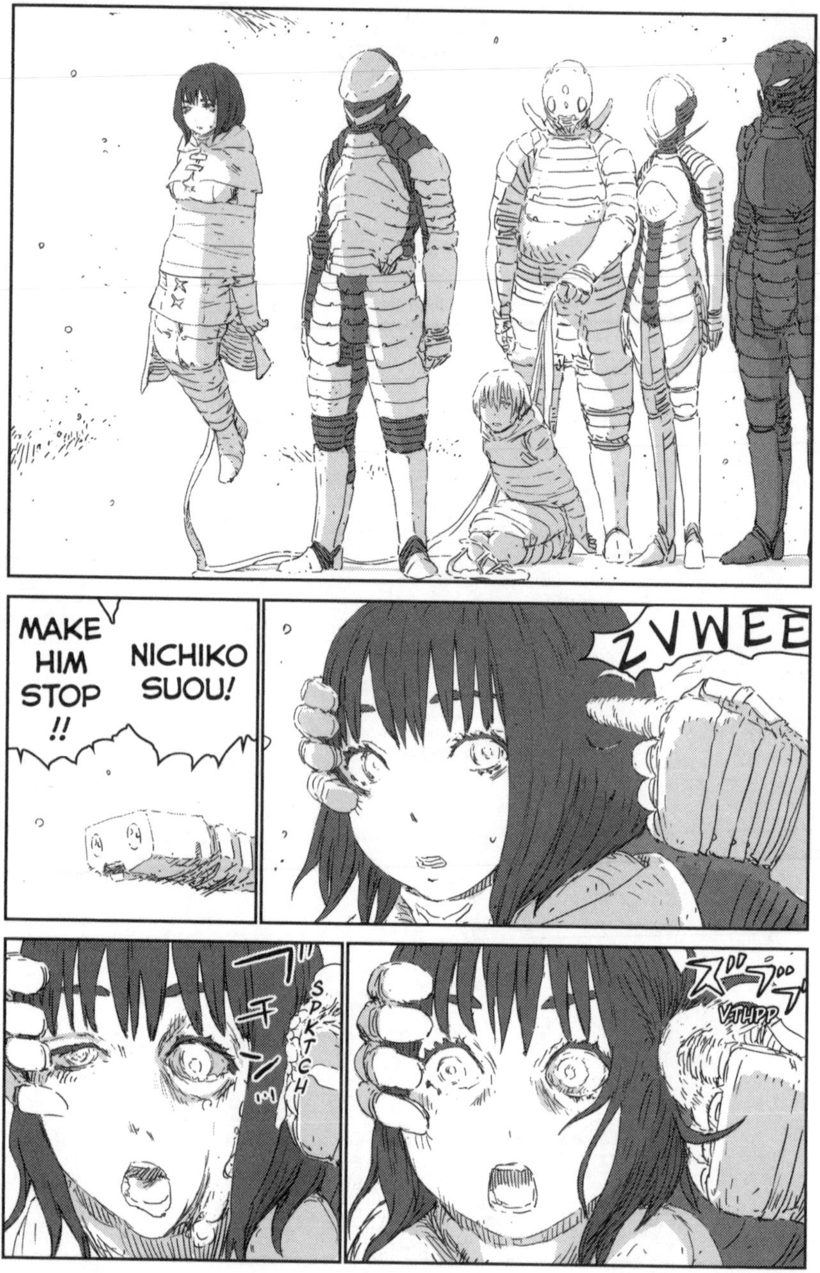
ZVWEE
NICHIKO SUOU!
MAKE HIM STOP !!
VTHPP
SPKTCH

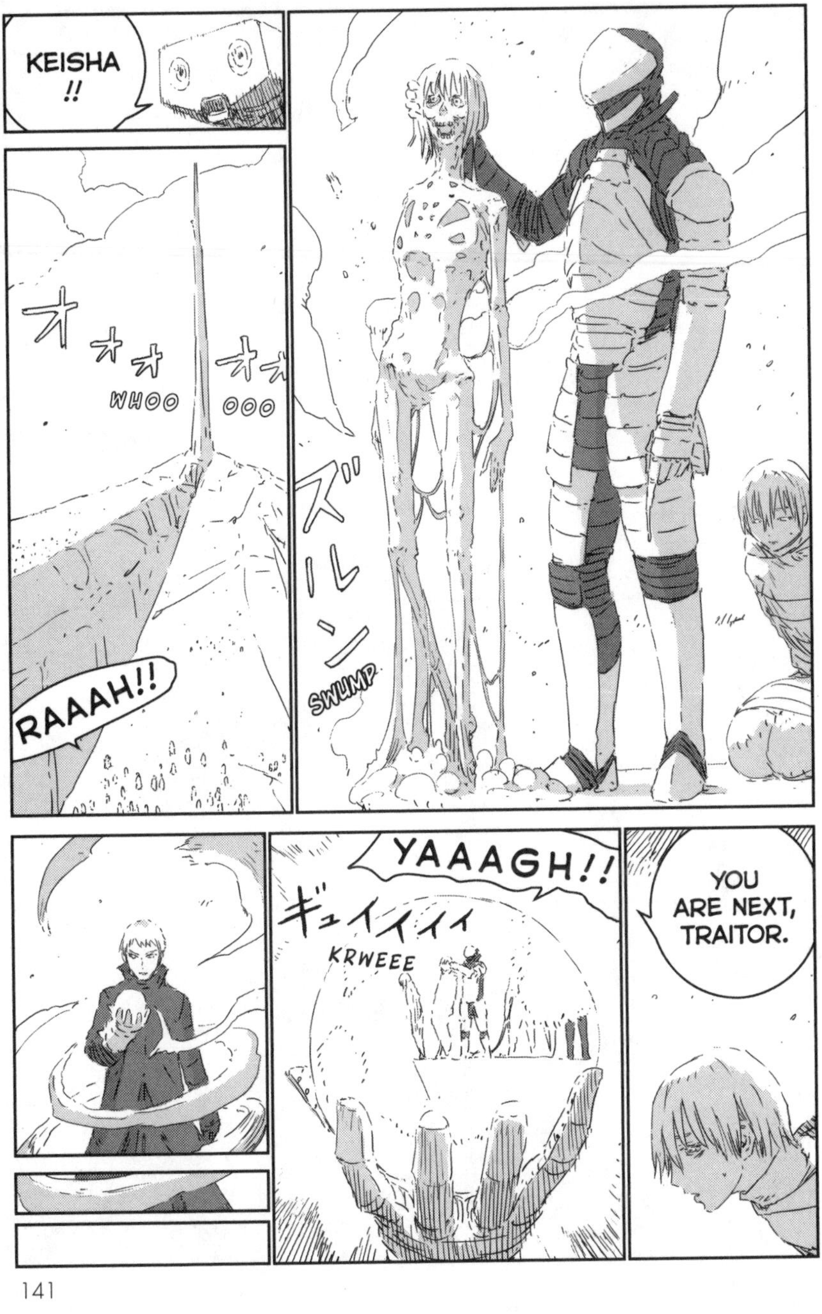
ズルン
SWUMP
KEISHA!!
オォォォオォ
WHOO OOO
RAAAH!!
YOU ARE NEXT, TRAITOR.
YAAAGH!!
ギュイイイイ
KRWEEE

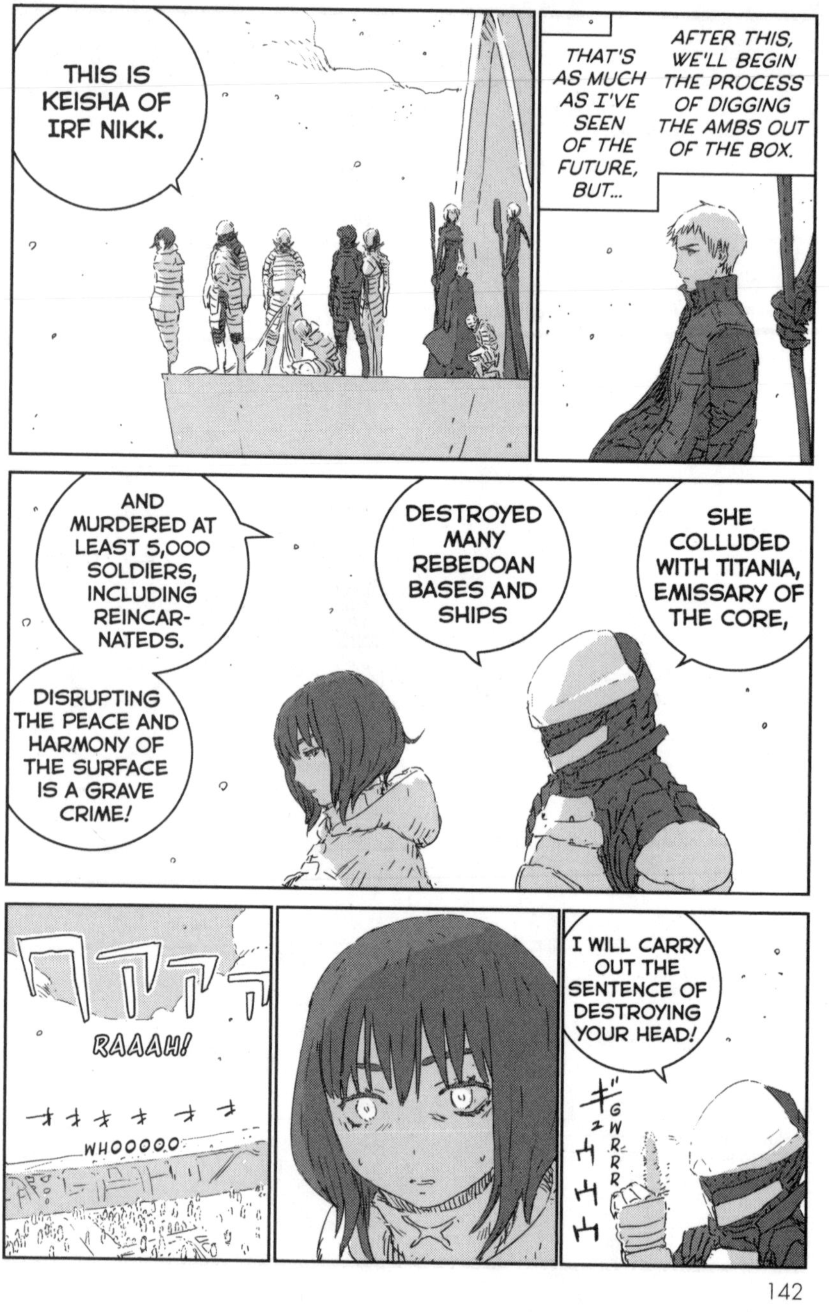
THAT'S AS MUCH AS I'VE SEEN OF THE FUTURE, BUT...
AFTER THIS, WE'LL BEGIN THE PROCESS OF DIGGING THE AMBS OUT OF THE BOX.
THIS IS KEISHA OF IRF NIKK.
SHE COLLUDED WITH TITANIA, EMISSARY OF THE CORE,
DESTROYED MANY REBEDOAN BASES AND SHIPS
AND MURDERED AT LEAST 5,000 SOLDIERS, INCLUDING REINCAR-NATEDS.
DISRUPTING THE PEACE AND HARMONY OF THE SURFACE IS A GRAVE CRIME!
I WILL CARRY OUT THE SENTENCE OF DESTROYING YOUR HEAD!
GWRRR
RAAAH!
WHOOOOO

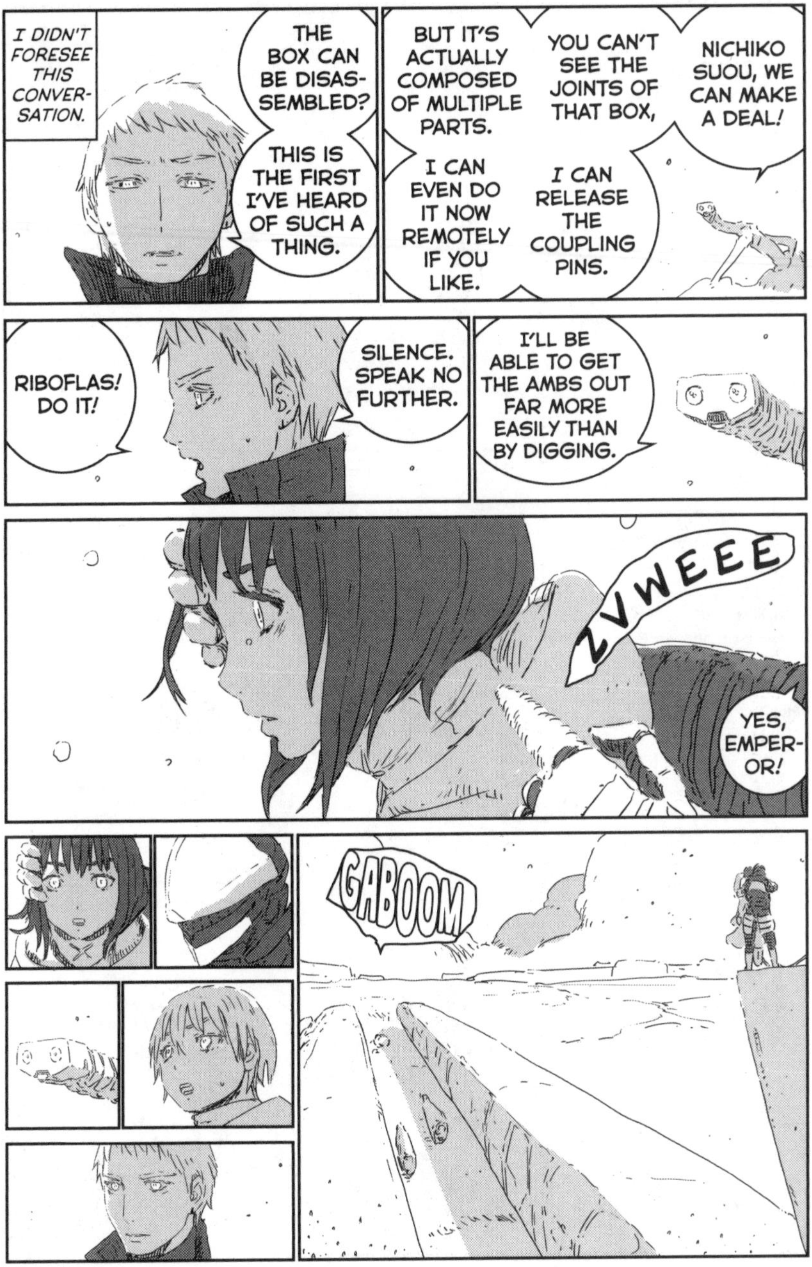
NICHIKO SUOU, WE CAN MAKE A DEAL!
YOU CAN'T SEE THE JOINTS OF THAT BOX,
BUT IT'S ACTUALLY COMPOSED OF MULTIPLE PARTS.
I CAN RELEASE THE COUPLING PINS.
I CAN EVEN DO IT NOW REMOTELY IF YOU LIKE.
THE BOX CAN BE DISAS-SEMBLED?
I DIDN'T FORESEE THIS CONVER-SATION.
THIS IS THE FIRST I'VE HEARD OF SUCH A THING.
I'LL BE ABLE TO GET THE AMBS OUT FAR MORE EASILY THAN BY DIGGING.
SILENCE. SPEAK NO FURTHER.
RIBOFLAS! DO IT!
ZVWEEE
YES, EMPER-OR!
GABOOM

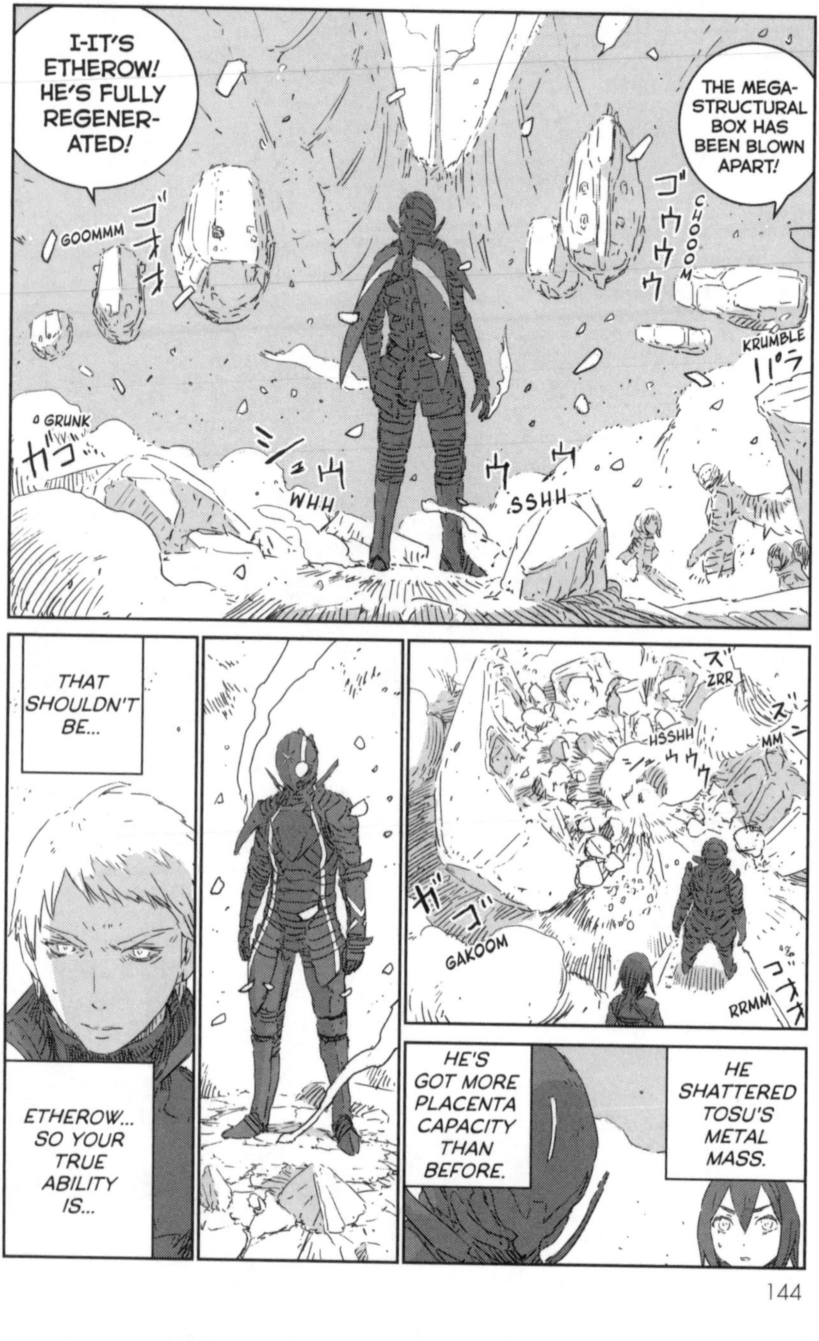
THE MEGA-STRUCTURAL BOX HAS BEEN BLOWN APART!
CHOOOM
I-IT'S ETHEROW! HE'S FULLY REGENER-ATED!
GOOMMM
KRUMBLE
SSHH
WHH
GRUNK
ZRR
MM
HSSHH
GAKOOM
RRMM
HE SHATTERED TOSU'S METAL MASS.
HE'S GOT MORE PLACENTA CAPACITY THAN BEFORE.
THAT SHOULDN'T BE...
ETHEROW... SO YOUR TRUE ABILITY IS...

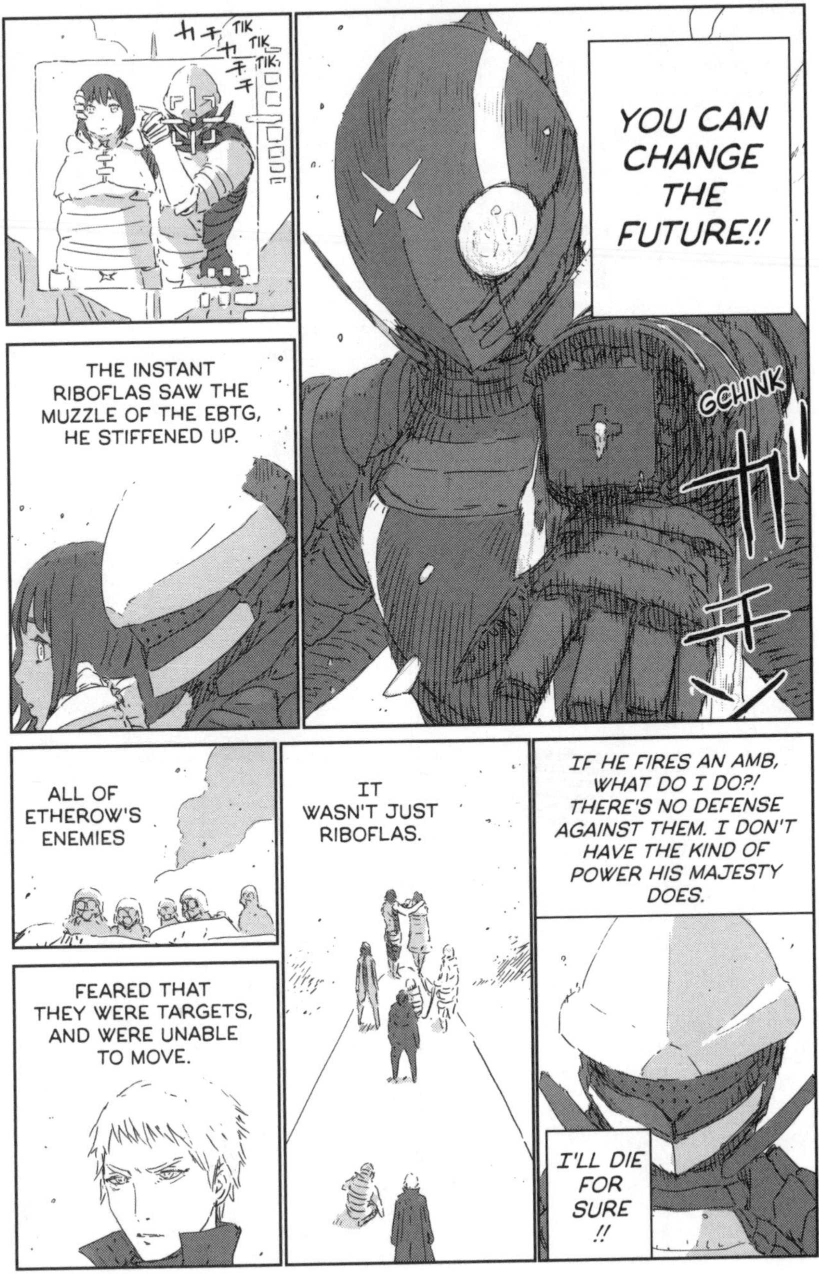
YOU CAN CHANGE THE FUTURE!!
GCHINK
TIK TIK TIK
THE INSTANT RIBOFLAS SAW THE MUZZLE OF THE EBTG, HE STIFFENED UP.
IF HE FIRES AN AMB, WHAT DO I DO?! THERE'S NO DEFENSE AGAINST THEM. I DON'T HAVE THE KIND OF POWER HIS MAJESTY DOES.
I'LL DIE FOR SURE !!
IT WASN'T JUST RIBOFLAS.
ALL OF ETHEROW'S ENEMIES
FEARED THAT THEY WERE TARGETS, AND WERE UNABLE TO MOVE.

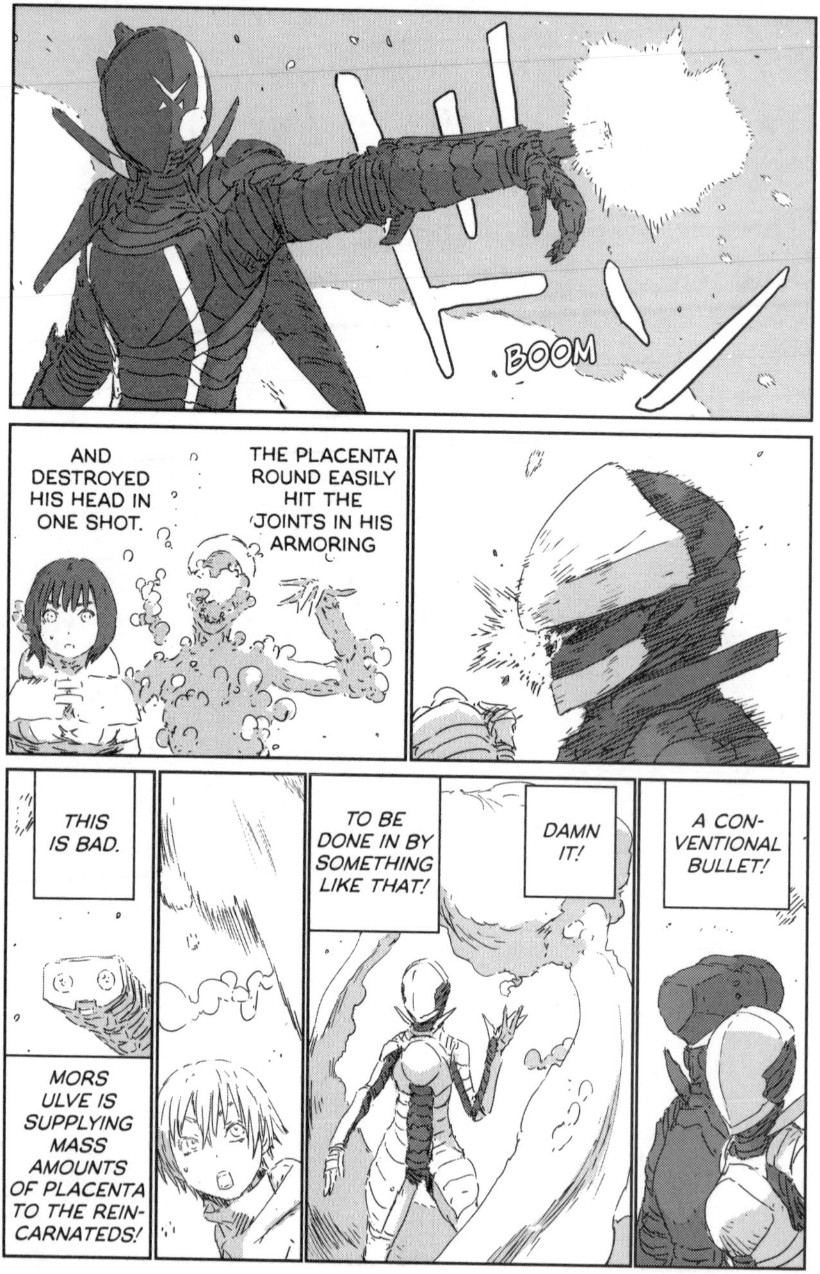
BOOM
THE PLACENTA ROUND EASILY HIT THE JOINTS IN HIS ARMORING
AND DESTROYED HIS HEAD IN ONE SHOT.
A CON-VENTIONAL BULLET!
DAMN IT!
TO BE DONE IN BY SOMETHING LIKE THAT!
THIS IS BAD.
MORS ULVE IS SUPPLYING MASS AMOUNTS OF PLACENTA TO THE REIN-CARNATEDS!

IN A FRENZY, ALHEKINO FORMED A MASSIVE ARROW OF PLACENTA WHICH SHE FIRED AT ETHEROW.
AT ALMOST THE SAME TIME, OOA FIRED HIS CAPTURE CORD WITH FULL FORCE.
IT WAS AN IMPOSSIBLE FAILURE.
THEY COLLIDED FAR BEFORE REACHING ETHEROW, AND THERE WAS A FEROCIOUS REACTION.
ボーン
BOOMM
VISIBILITY ON THE BRIDGE WAS REDUCED TO ZERO.

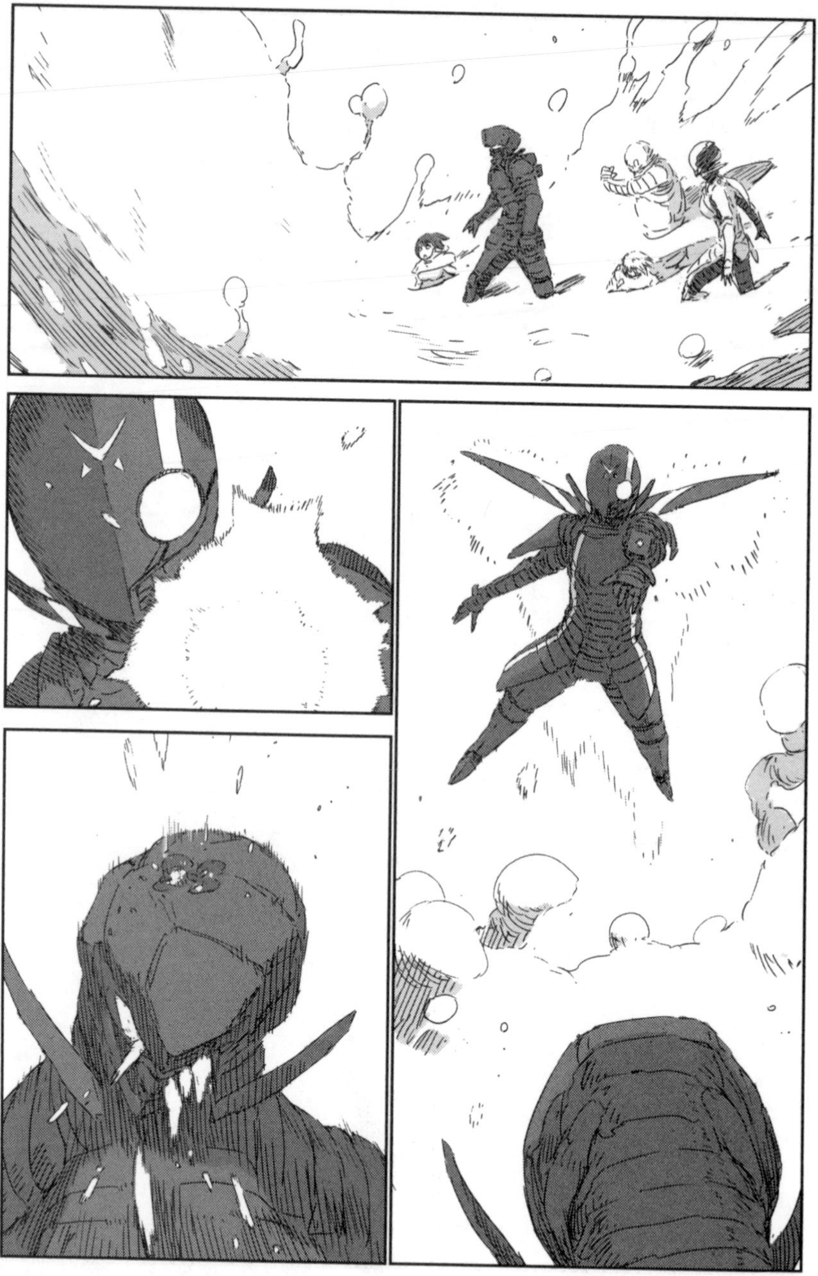

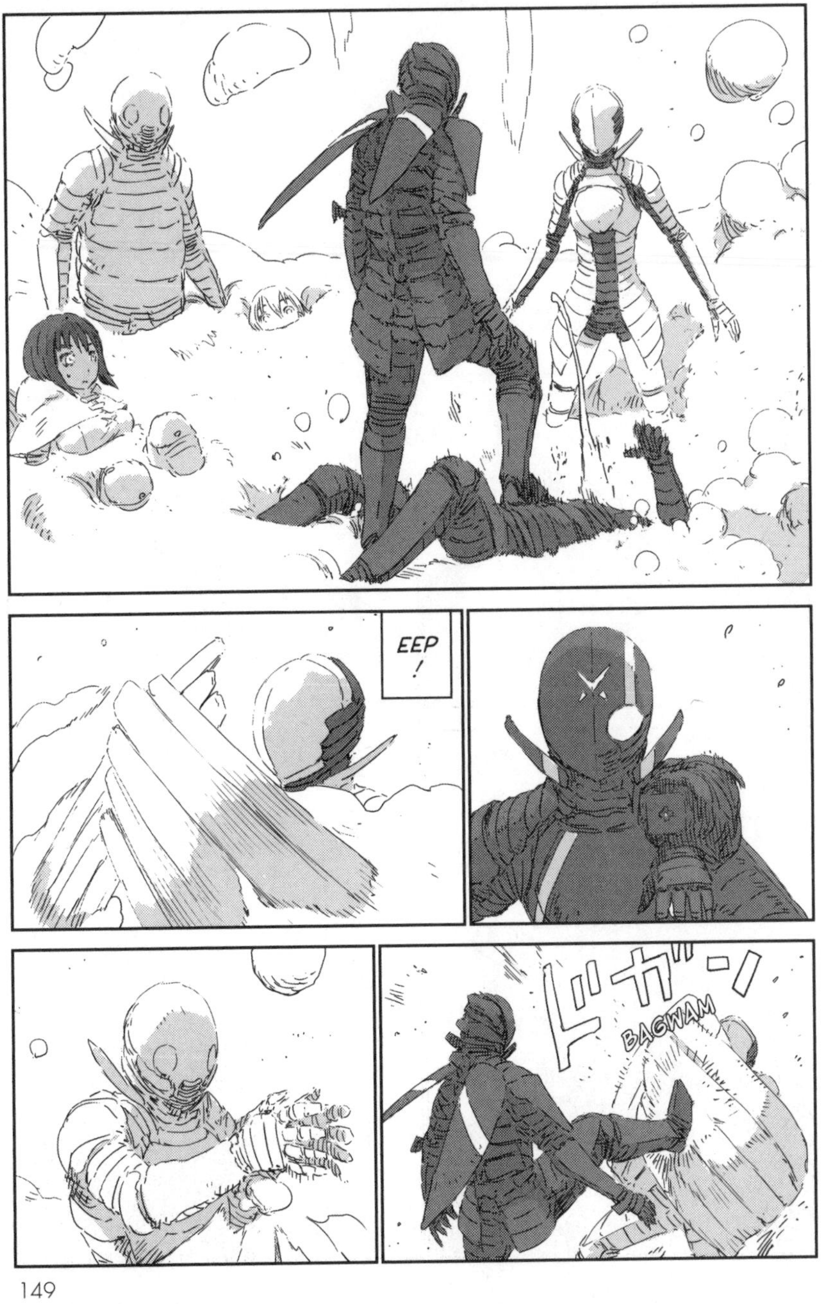
EEP !
ドガーン
BAGWAM

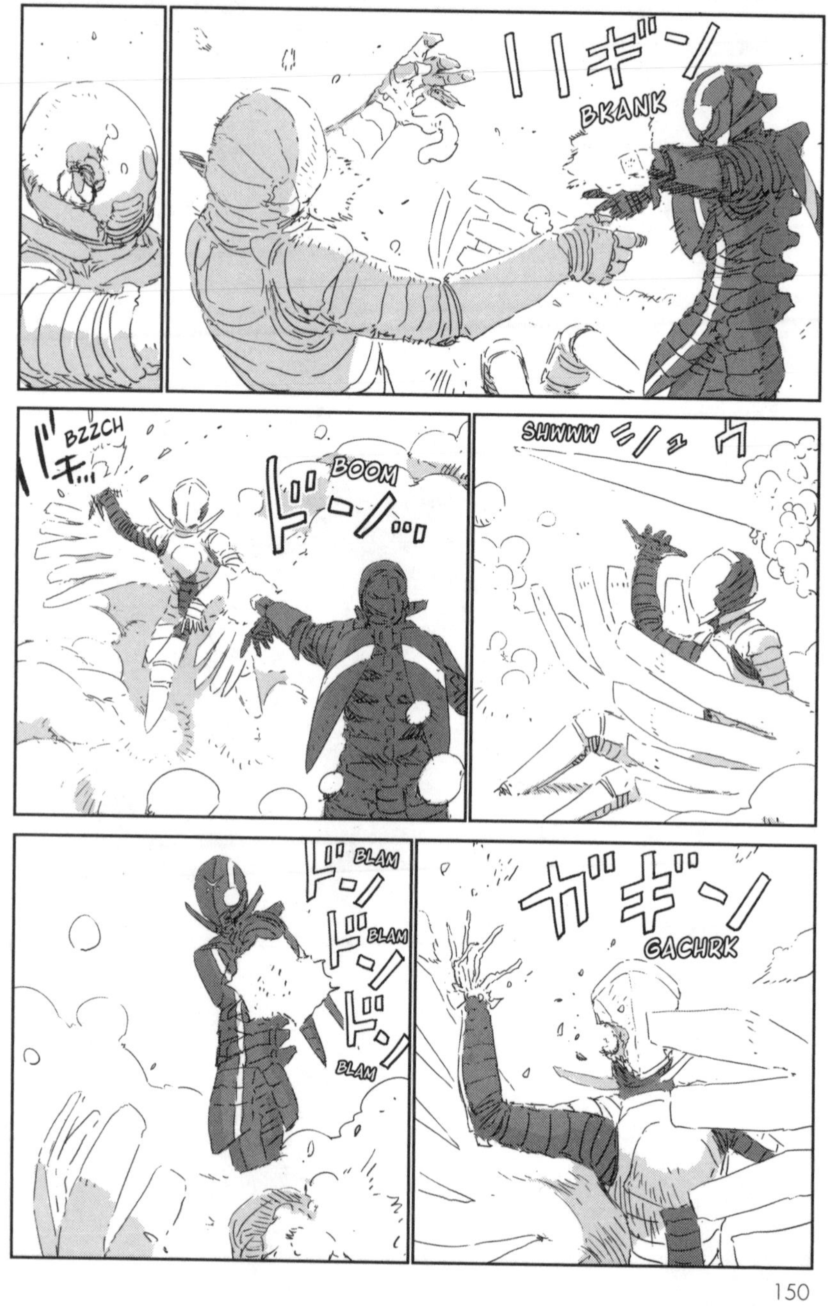
ハギーン
BKANK
SHWWW シュゥ
バチ...
BZZCH
ドーン...
BOOM
ガギーン
GACHRK
ドーン
BLAM
ドーン
BLAM
ドーン
BLAM

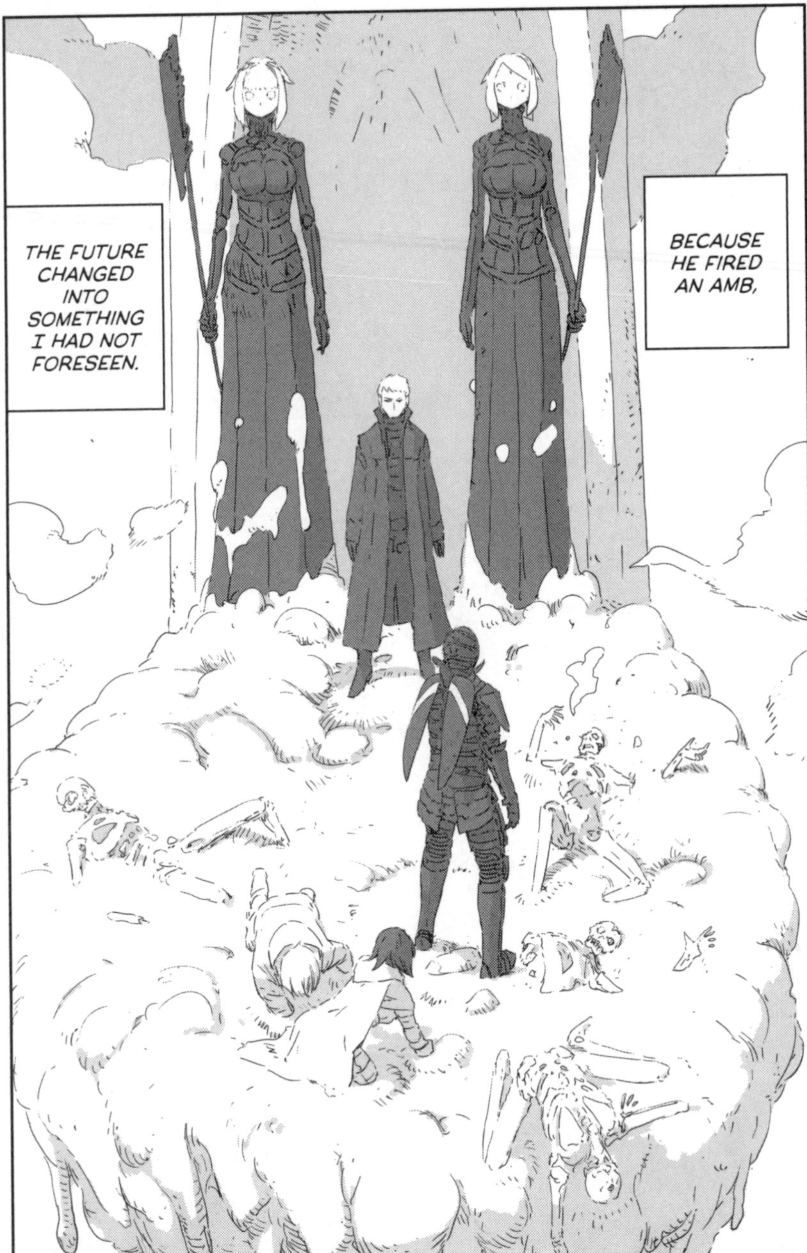
BECAUSE HE FIRED AN AMB,
THE FUTURE CHANGED INTO SOMETHING I HAD NOT FORESEEN.

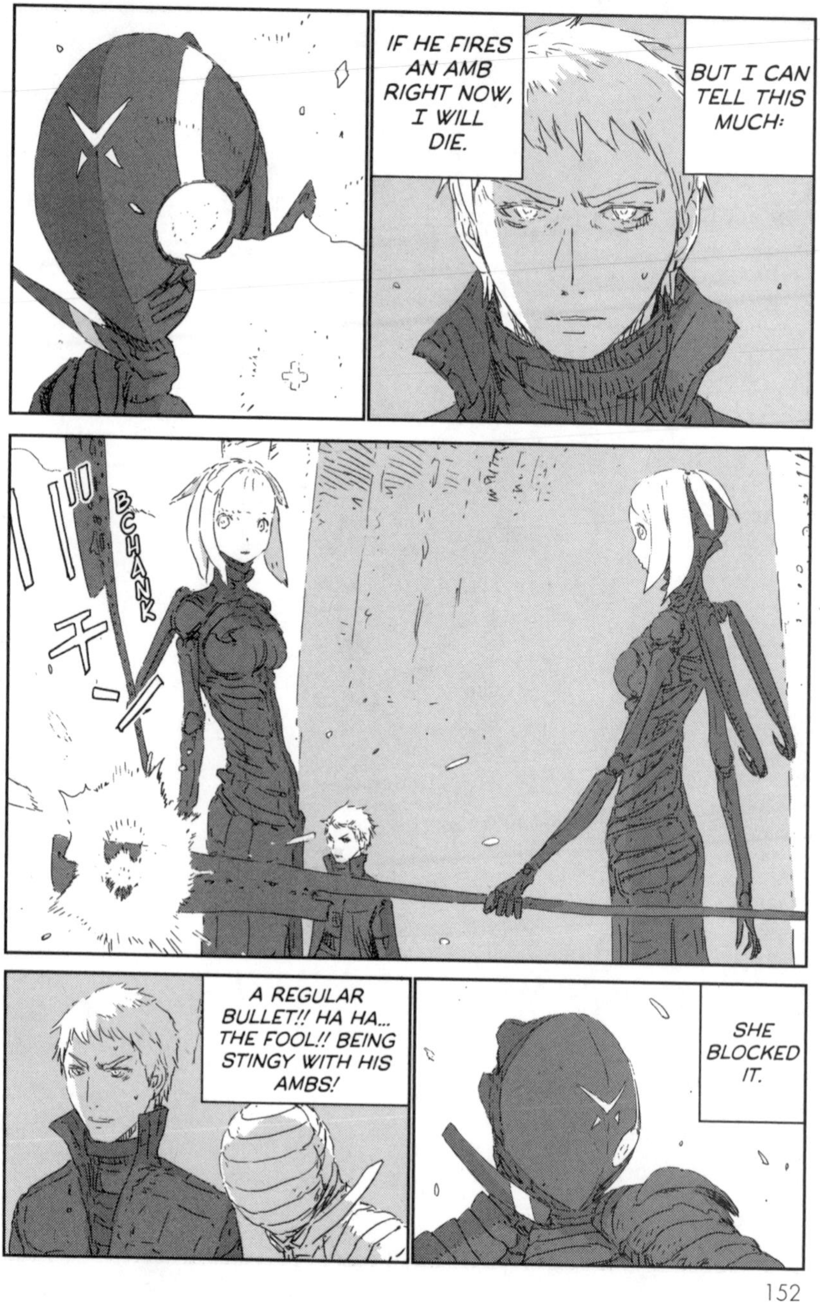
IF HE FIRES AN AMB RIGHT NOW, I WILL DIE.
BUT I CAN TELL THIS MUCH:
BCHANK
SHE BLOCKED IT.
A REGULAR BULLET!! HA HA... THE FOOL!! BEING STINGY WITH HIS AMBS!

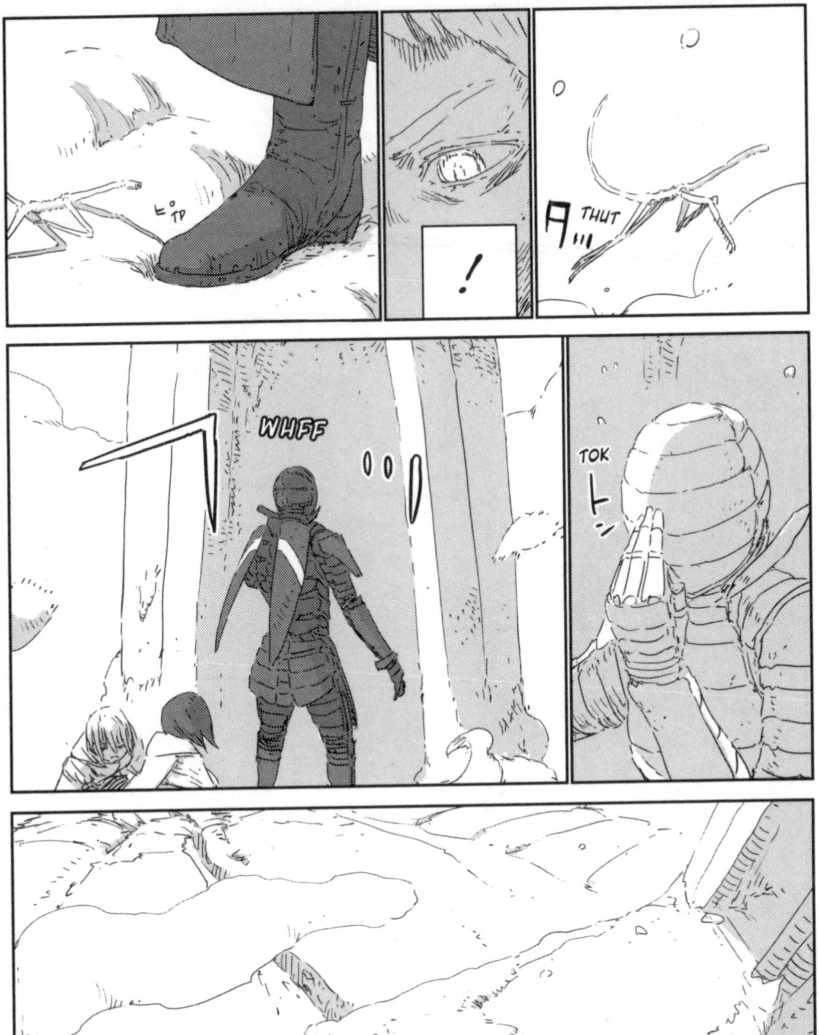
THUT
タッ
!
TP
ピ
TOK
トン
WHFF

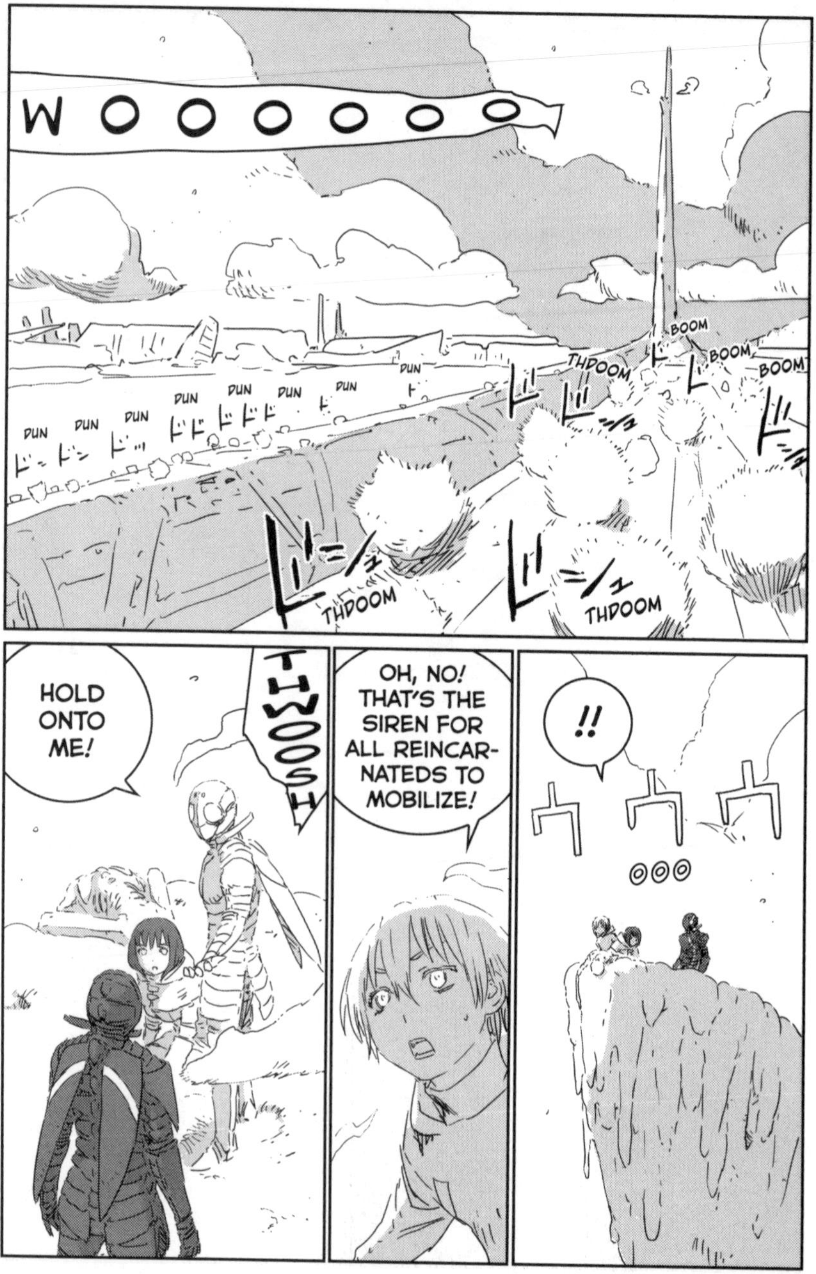
WOOOOOO
BOOM
BOOM
BOOM
THDOOM
DUN DUN DUN DUN DUN DUN DUN DUN
THDOOM
THDOOM
!!
OH, NO! THAT'S THE SIREN FOR ALL REINCAR-NATEDS TO MOBILIZE!
THWOOSH
HOLD ONTO ME!

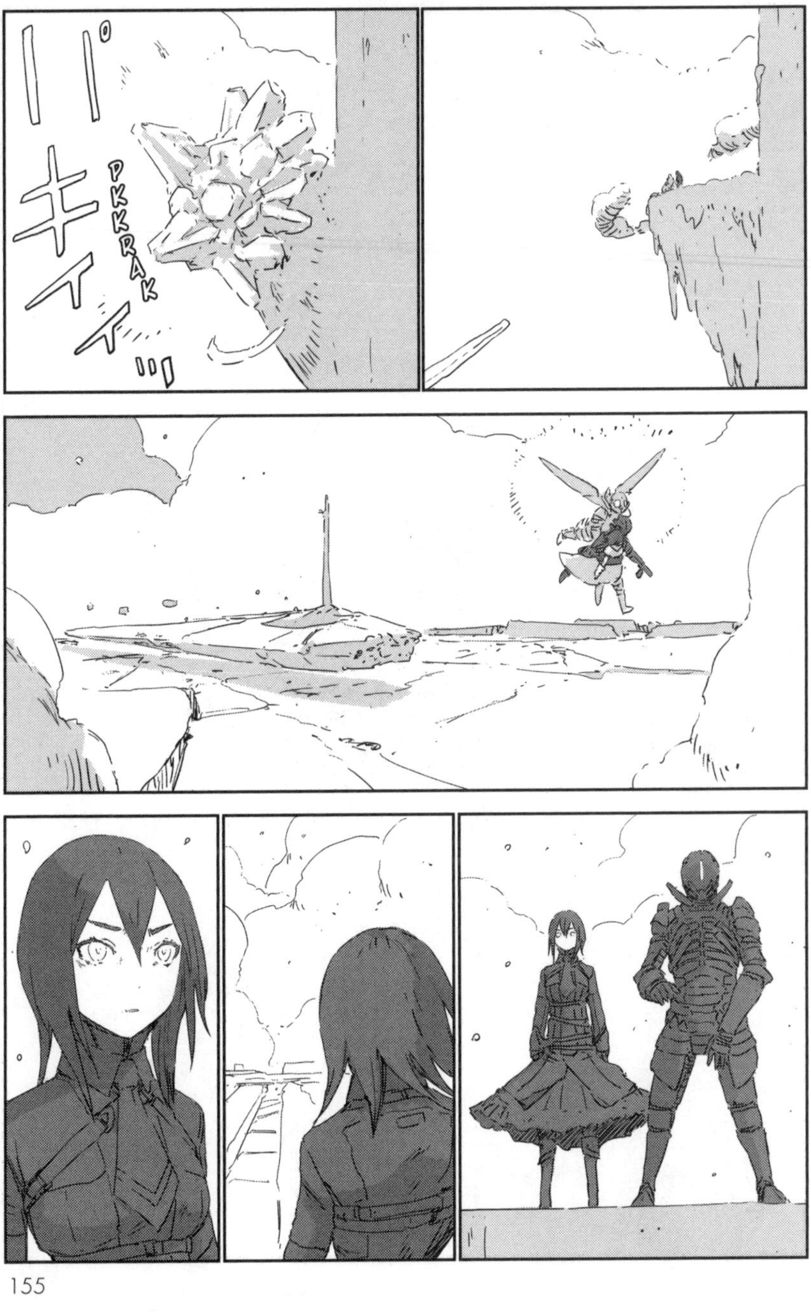
パキイイッ
PKKRAK

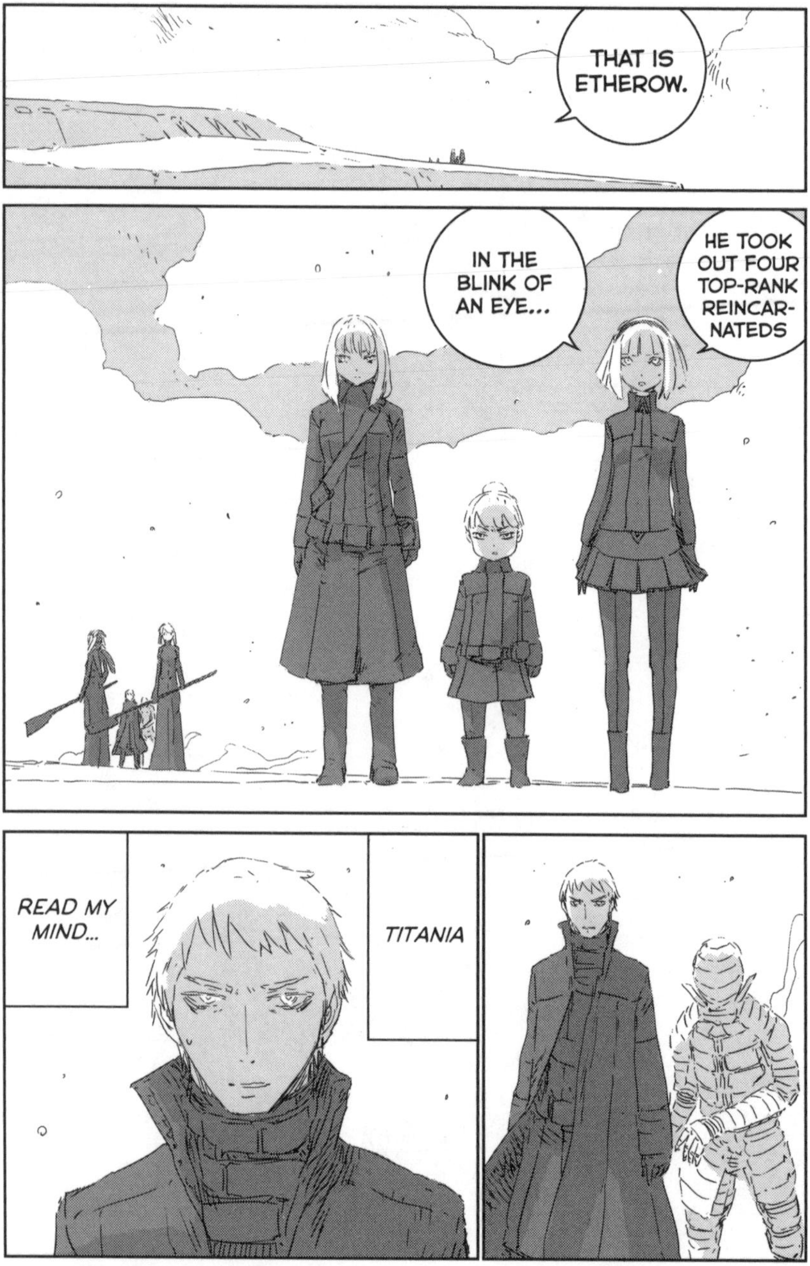
THAT IS ETHEROW.
HE TOOK OUT FOUR TOP-RANK REINCAR-NATEDS
IN THE BLINK OF AN EYE...
TITANIA
READ MY MIND...

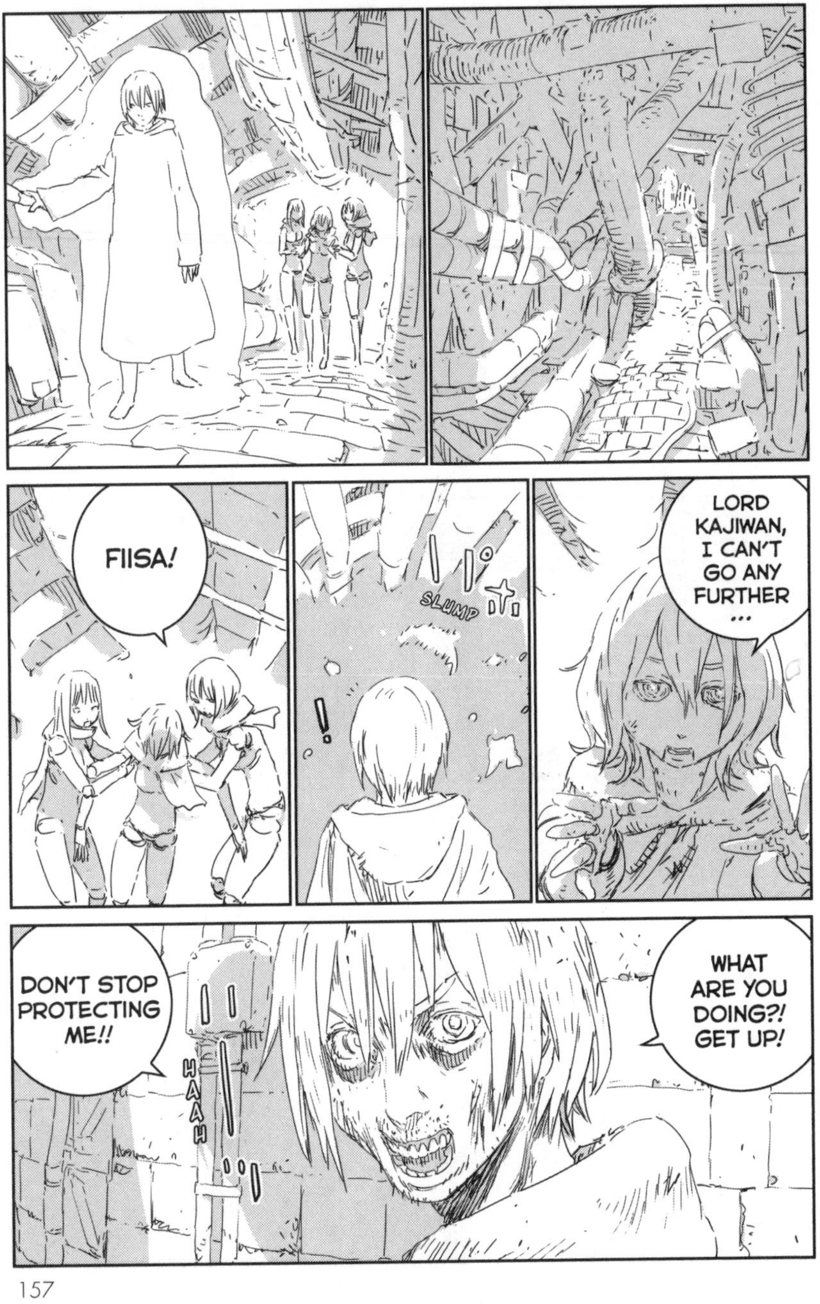
LORD KAJIWAN, I CAN'T GO ANY FURTHER ...
SLUMP
FIISA!
WHAT ARE YOU DOING?! GET UP!
DON'T STOP PROTECTING ME!!
HAAAH

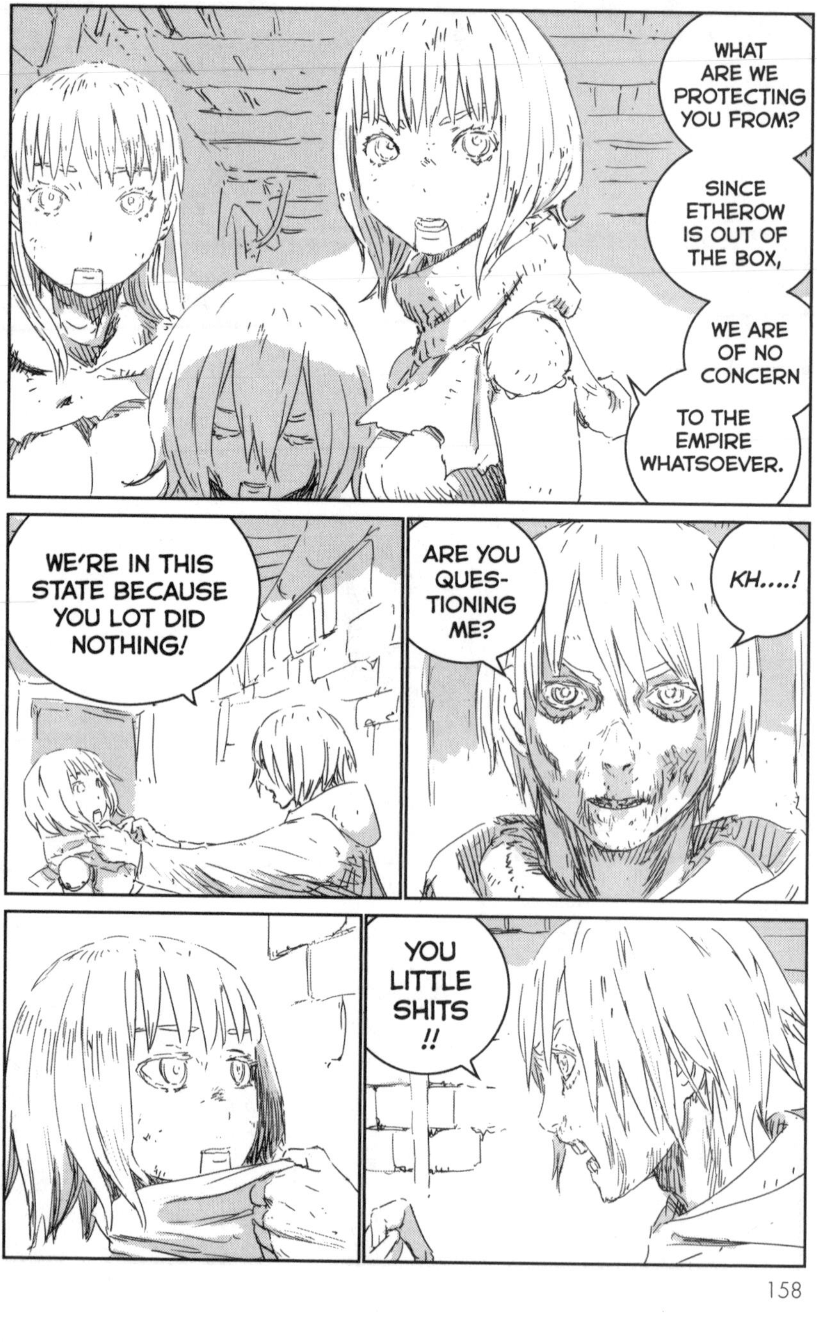
WHAT ARE WE PROTECTING YOU FROM?
SINCE ETHEROW IS OUT OF THE BOX,
WE ARE OF NO CONCERN
TO THE EMPIRE WHATSOEVER.
KH....!
ARE YOU QUES-TIONING ME?
WE'RE IN THIS STATE BECAUSE YOU LOT DID NOTHING!
YOU LITTLE SHITS !!

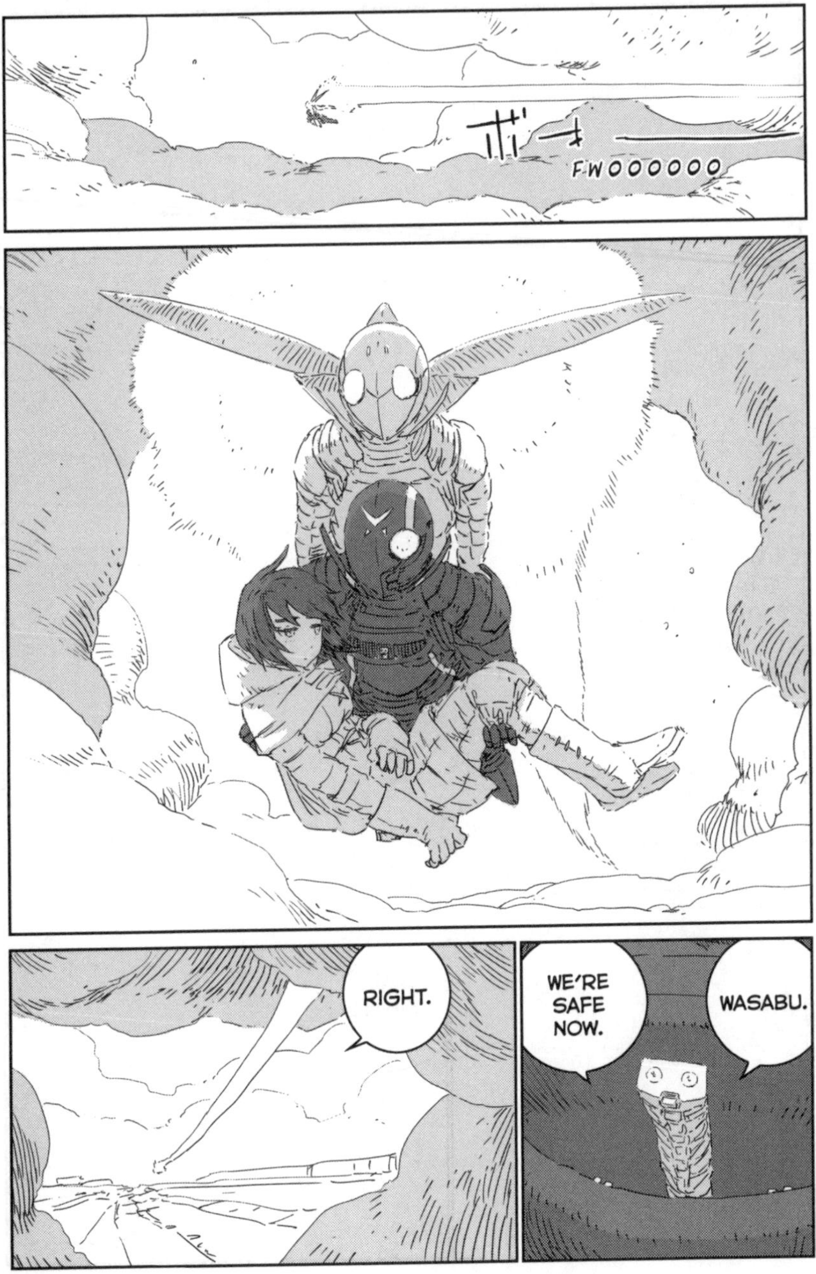
FWOOOOOO
WASABU.
WE'RE SAFE NOW.
RIGHT.

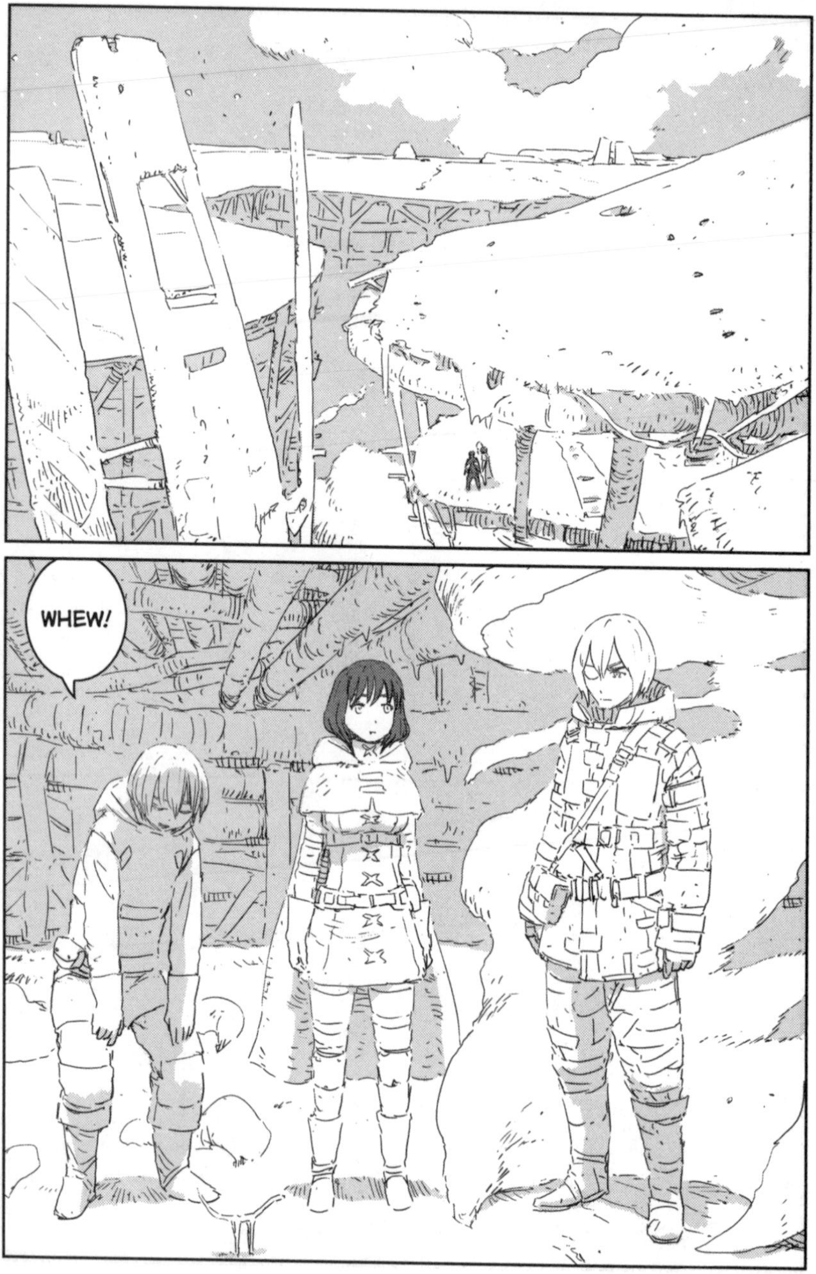
WHEW!

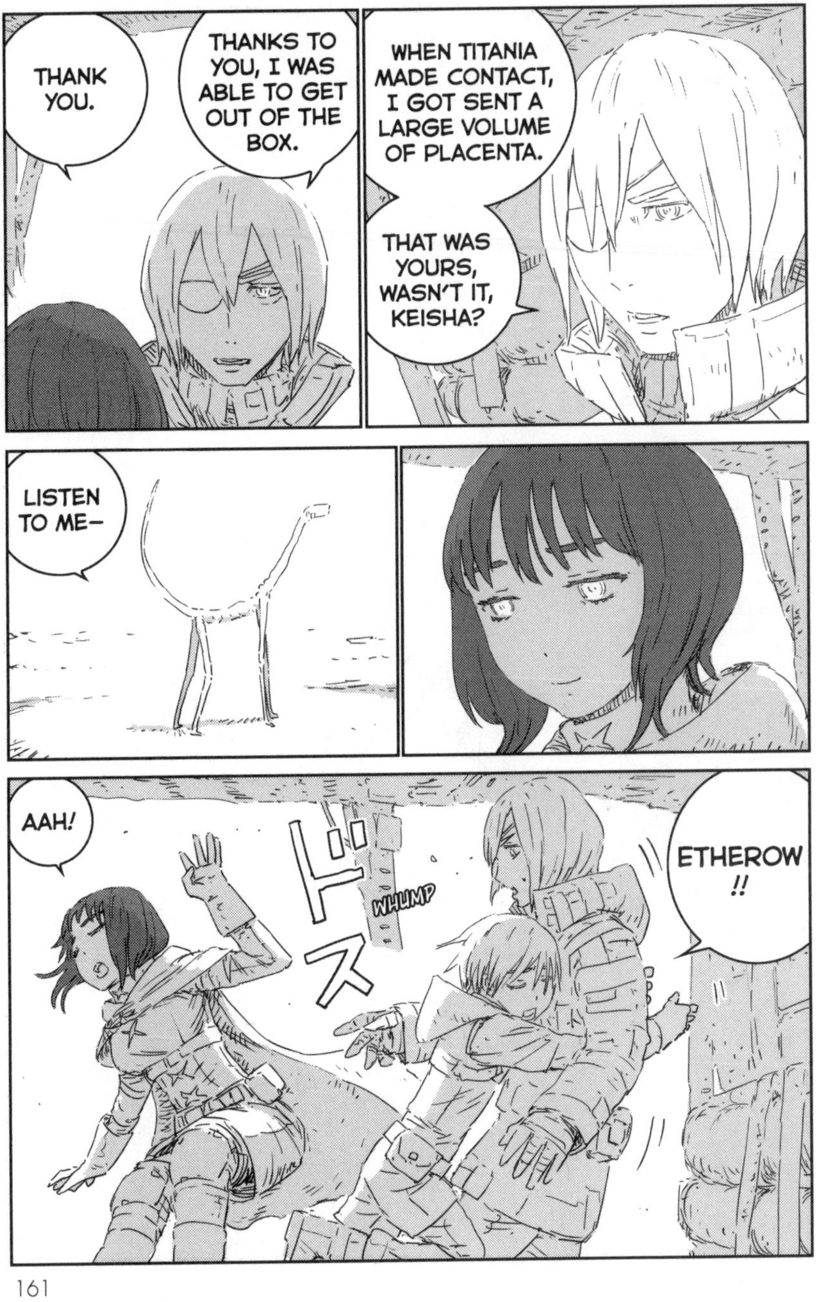
WHEN TITANIA MADE CONTACT, I GOT SENT A LARGE VOLUME OF PLACENTA.
THAT WAS YOURS, WASN'T IT, KEISHA?
THANKS TO YOU, I WAS ABLE TO GET OUT OF THE BOX.
THANK YOU.
LISTEN TO ME—
ETHEROW !!
ドス
WHUMP
AAH!

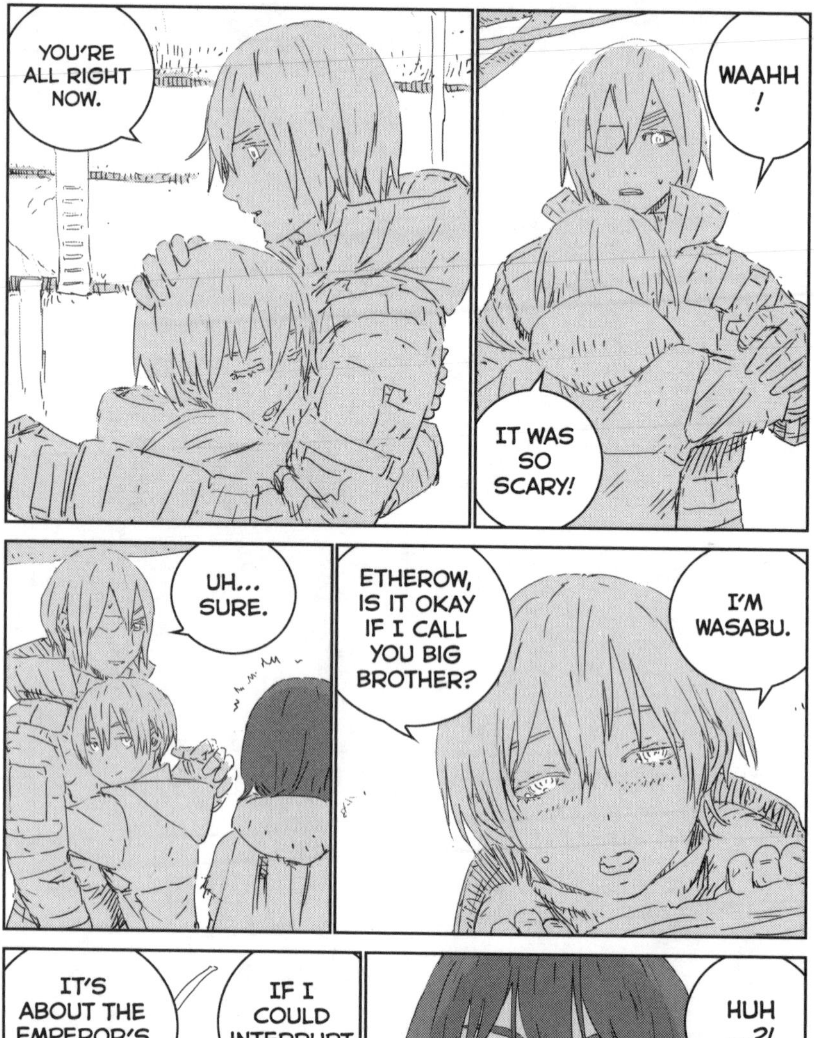
WAAHH!
IT WAS SO SCARY!
YOU'RE ALL RIGHT NOW.
I'M WASABU.
ETHEROW, IS IT OKAY IF I CALL YOU BIG BROTHER?
UH... SURE.
HUH ...?!
IF I COULD INTERRUPT ...
IT'S ABOUT THE EMPEROR'S ABILITIES...

CHAPTER 36 END

CONTINUED IN VOLUME 7

APOSIMZ volume 6

A Vertical Comics Edition

Translation: Kumar Sivasubramanian
Production: Grace Lu
            Darren Smith

Copyright © 2020 Tsutomu Nihei. All rights reserved.
First published in Japan in 2020 by Kodansha, Ltd., Tokyo
Publication for this English edition arranged through Kodansha, Ltd., Tokyo
English language version produced by Vertical Comics,
an imprint of Kodansha USA Publishing, LLC

Translation provided by Vertical Comics, 2021
Published by Kodansha USA Publishing, LLC, New York

Originally published in Japanese as *APOSIMZ 6* by Kodansha, Ltd.
APOSIMZ first serialized in *Monthly Shonen Sirius*, Kodansha, Ltd., 2017-

This is a work of fiction.

ISBN: 978-1-949980-66-0

Manufactured in Canada

First Edition

Kodansha USA Publishing, LLC
451 Park Avenue South
7th Floor
New York, NY 10016
www.readvertical.com

Vertical books are distributed through Penguin-Random House Publisher Services.